'*Co-Creating Brands* provides the next genera
necessary knowledge and skills to work with the complex subject of
branding in a fast-changing and networked world.'

*Charles Trevail, CEO, Interbrand Group*

'For too long, brand management books have remained stuck with an
old way of thinking based on the omniscient, omnipotent organisation's
perspective and relying on outdated concepts. In this fascinating book,
Ind and Schmidt and their co-creators offer the brand management
student a contemporary way of thinking. Their examples from all
over the world show that brand co-creation is not only theoretically
convincing, but also clearly helps brands to succeed in the marketplace.'

*Jörg Henseler, Professor and Chair
of Product-Market Relations, University of Twente*

'Ind and Schmidt pull together cutting-edge thoughts on how brands
may come to be created through a co-created process in which
varying constituents all play a part in the brand's construction and
maintenance. The book contains contributions from an impressive
group of prestigious figures, as it takes theory and shows how it can
be turned into practice. Everyone with an interest in modern brand
management will benefit from *Co-Creating Brands*.'

*Barry J. Babin, Morris Lewis Professor
of Marketing and Chair, University of Mississippi*

'Co-creation has become the only way to think about brands. In
*Co-creating Brands*, Ind and Schmidt bring this reality to life by showing
how the power of consumers to influence brands provides tremendous
opportunities for those organisations that adopt an open attitude and
are willing to learn with others.'

*Salima Douven, Director Digital Strategy &
Operations at Henkel*

'Brands are a lighthouse in an ineluctably changing world. But many consumers want to be more than shoppers, they want a sense of partnership. That's where wise managers can leverage this clear-cut and thorough book which encourages you to explore collaborative creativity and brand management further. Professors Ind and Schmidt provide you with a step-by-step guide to setting up, and managing a co-creative brand management system, that will sustain your brand in this era of upheaval and transformation.'

*Nicolas Bry, Founder, Orange Intrapreneurs Studio*

NICHOLAS IND &
HOLGER J. SCHMIDT

# co-creating
# brands

## Brand Management
## from a Co-Creative Perspective

BLOOMSBURY BUSINESS
LONDON · OXFORD · NEW YORK · NEW DELHI · SYDNEY

BLOOMSBURY BUSINESS
Bloomsbury Publishing Plc
50 Bedford Square, London, WC1B 3DP, UK

BLOOMSBURY, BLOOMSBURY BUSINESS and the Diana logo are
trademarks of Bloomsbury Publishing Plc

First published in Great Britain 2019

A catalogue record for this book is available from the British Library

Library of Congress Cataloguing-in-Publication data has been applied for

ISBN: 978-1-4729-6226-3; eBook: 978-1-4729-6225-6

2 4 6 8 10 9 7 5 3 1

Typeset by Deanta Global Publishing Services, Chennai, India
Printed and bound in Great Britain by CPI Group (UK) Ltd, Croydon CR0 4YY

To find out more about our authors and books visit www.bloomsbury.com
and sign up for our newsletters

In fond memory of Walter Schmidt (1937–2019)
and Greta Ind (1931–2019)

# Contents

# Contents

# List of Co-Creators

*Dr. Carsten Baumgarth* is Professor of Brand Management at the Berlin School of Economics and Law (Germany).

*Rinske Brand* is a place branding strategist and founder of BRAND The Urban Agency, a boutique agency focussed on making cities greener, smarter, more innovative and dynamic.

*Dr. Nick Coates* is Global Creative Consulting Director at C Space. The focus of his PhD was on French Caribbean literature.

*Dr. Francisco Guzmán* is Professor of Marketing and Distinguished Teaching Professor for the Department of Marketing, Logistics, and Operations Management in the G. Brint Ryan College of Business at the University of North Texas.

*Christin Franzel* was CMO of Ottobock from 2012 to 2018, where she oversaw Global Marketing Communications. She was responsible for the rebranding process, Global Brand Management as well as Sport Marketing & Sponsorship and Digital Transformation.

*Fabian Gärtner*, at the time of editing this book, was a Master Student at Koblenz University of Applied Sciences. He studied Business Management with a focus on International Business and Marketing.

*Dr. Lucy Gill-Simmen* is a Lecturer in Marketing at Royal Holloway, University of London.

*Dr. Richard Gyrd-Jones* is Professor (MSO) at Copenhagen Business School and Docent at Oulu Business School, Finland. His research focusses on challenges to managing brands in the context of multiple stakeholder eco-systems with a particular emphasis on brand identity co-creation and issues around the implementation of branding strategies at a managerial level in large organisations, SMEs and start-ups.

*Ranim Helwani* is a MSc Candidate in Economics and Business Administration at Copenhagen Business School.

*Oliver Hirschfelder* studied business administration at the HTWG Konstanz, before joining Siemens in the areas of strategy, business development and R&D management. His current responsibilities at Siemens Gas & Power include the identification and evaluation of new business areas in combination with the concrete implementation of corresponding business models.

*Dr. Oriol Iglesias* is an Associate Professor and Head of the Marketing Management Department at ESADE Business School.

*Dr. Eric L. Kennedy* is an Assistant Professor of Marketing at Grand Valley State University in Grand Rapids, Michigan.

*Dr. Anna Karina Kjeldsen* focusses on corporate communication and branding in public sector organizations in her research. She holds a PhD in strategic communication and is Associate Professor at Business Academy Aarhus, Denmark.

*Dr. Robert Kozinets* is Professor of Journalism at the University of Southern California. His research focus in on the social and economic impacts of new digital communication systems. He invented the method of netnography.

*Dr. Samuel Kristal* has a PhD from the University of Twente and the Berlin School of Economics and Law. His thesis focussed on brand co-creation.

*Matthias Lorenz* is Senior Director A1 Telekom in Vienna. In the role of a Partner, he worked for the consultancies Oliver Wymann and Roland Berger. He was a Trainee at Preussag and studied Business in Kiel.

*Peter G.C. Lux* is Managing Partner of Lux MarkenPartner in Zurich. The group's specialists enable companies to develop and manage comprehensive brand systems based on the systemic brand approach.

*Dr. Stefan Markovic* is Associate Professor in Marketing and holds the Chair of the Marketing Ethics Research Cluster, Department of Marketing, at Copenhagen Business School.

*Dr. Judith Meyer* is Senior Brand Consultant at Brand Trust GmbH in Nuremberg. The fashion and lifestyle specialist advises companies, SMEs and start-ups. Core to her work is the development of promising brands and their implementation in enterprises.

*Dr. Line Schmeltz* holds a PhD in strategic CSR communication and is Associate Professor at Aalborg University, Denmark. Her research focusses on CSR communication, corporate branding and strategic communication.

*Dr. Gerhard Schwarz* is a philosopher and works as an organizational consultant with a focus on ethics, value-orientation, identity, cultural and brand development (www.gerhardschwarz.berlin). He runs the Brand Ethics Research Office in Berlin (www.brandethics.org).

*Dr. Pieter Steenkamp* is a Lecturer in the marketing department of the Cape Peninsula University of Technology in Cape Town. His research focusses on brand management.

# Foreword
# by Venkat Ramaswamy

At the turn of the millennium, the late C. K. Prahalad and I put forth the idea in our book, *The Future of Competition* (2004), of 'co-creating unique value with customers'. We described the next practices of value creation – one based on *experiences* of individuals in an interconnected world of *de-centered* and *democratised* value creation through *networked interactions*. Fast forward to today and every enterprise must create experience-based value through networked interactions of customers (employees, partners, and stakeholders) and smart, connected offerings. Networked interactions, propelled by the Internet and the forces of digitalisation, ubiquitous connectivity, globalisation, and social media, have become the new locus in creating value and accelerating the de-centering of value creation toward the experiences of individuals. Customers want to define choices in a manner that reflects their view of value and expressions of personalisation by interacting and transacting in their preferred language and style across multiple channels. Customer experience has become central to enterprise value creation, innovation, strategy, and executive leadership.

At the same time, networked interactions have also accelerated the democratisation of value creation and the engagement of individuals in the value creation process. Networked individuals around the globe are no longer passive and docile recipients of what is on offer. Rather, they expect to be active participants and collaborators in the value creation process, bringing to bear their own creativity in the design and development of offerings. Progressive enterprises have extended their resource base through practices such as crowdsourcing, open innovation, and mass collaboration, and by tapping into user communities and social networking among customers and stakeholders. In the book *The Power of Co-Creation* (2010), Francis Gouillart and I, looked at over forty cases in more than twenty sectors (including automotive, consumer durables, capital intensive equipment, industrial goods and services, fast moving consumer goods, retail, entertainment, media, travel services, and business technology and professional services). We found enterprises were 'connecting, listening and participating' with individuals in the *co-creation* of value based on their lived and desired experiences and were capitalising on new information and communications technology platforms designed to deliver more effective engagement with individuals. As we noted, 'the activity chain of the enterprise no longer solely creates value, nor is its value proposition unilaterally defined by the organisation'.

It has now become evident that the future of value creation lies in a new paradigm of co-creation, one where value is interactively created based on the lived experiences of individuals, through purpose-built platforms of engagement and increasingly through 'emergent' experiences spurred by new cloud-enabled mobile applications of augmented/virtual reality (AR/VR), artificial intelligence (AI), and the Internet of Things (IoT) in an 'interaction-first' world. As Kerimcan Ozcan and I argue in *The Co-Creation Paradigm* (2014), a 'co-creative perspective' is now the *default* in the management of organisations and offerings. However, embracing the co-creation paradigm requires considerable organisational transformation in 'letting go' of traditional unilateral control over the management process and instead shifting to the intersection of stakeholding individuals and organisations, and designing and developing new organisational management systems around it.

This brings me to the book *Co-Creating Brands,* an impressive, accessible, essential guide to navigating the landscape of *brand* management of organisations and offerings. Nicholas Ind is no stranger to the phenomenon of co-creation, having immersed himself in a parallel journey for the past two decades, by diving deep into the lived experiences of brands and brand value co-creation and authoring such books (among others) as *Living the Brand* (2001) and *Beyond Branding* (2004) – both of which I devoured after discovering them a bit too late. More recently he produced, with Clare Fuller and Charles Trevail, *Brand Together* (2013) – a remarkable and inspiring book on how to involve all stakeholders, in co-creating brands, and developing more effective brand strategies in the new interconnected world of customer engagement and participation.

What makes *Co-Creating Brands*, co-authored with brand management expert Holger J. Schmidt, unique is that it pulls together and effectively captures the essence of the *why and what* of brand co-creation. It shows how enterprises have caught up with the sea change in the de-centering and democratisation of value creation – where every business is becoming a *digitalised* business – and the shift in the locus of brand management and innovation to the intersection between organisational enterprises and stakeholding individuals.

But it does more than that. It also discusses in detail the *how* of brand co-creation, providing a valuable and practical guide to setting up and managing a co-creative brand management system that combines generating and understanding brand-related insights, designing and adjusting brand strategy, and creating brand equity together with stakeholding individuals. What's more, a variety of carefully chosen global examples, spanning different kinds of brands, and cutting across the private, public, and plural sectors, are not only conceptually revealing but illustrate the enormous promise of brand value co-creation in practice. At the same time, the book balances the importance of managers thinking not only about the benefits, but also the risks of co-creation – and how to mitigate the latter. Moreover, a major strength of the book is the way in which the authors have engaged with the voices and collaborative contributions of researchers, managers, and consultants, which are carefully woven into the context of each chapter, while showcasing the very power of a co-creative approach in enlivening the value of the book to readers.

As brand experiences become the very basis of brand value co-creation, this book also raises several new important questions and food for thought, from dealing with the loss of control over brand evolution, power struggles, finding the middle ground between polyphony and cacophony, balancing heterogeneous matters of concern, positive and negative freedom, and perhaps most important, cultivating *trust* in an era of discontent with traditional institutions and their relationship with society. How brands connect with desirable values in a digitalised society and nurture a sense of meaningful (public) purpose is becoming one of the defining challenges for their organisational stewards. Technological advances, for instance in machine learning and artificial intelligence, raise important questions of inclusiveness, privacy, and brand ethics. It also opens up new areas of inquiry into the role of digitalised non-human actors in platforms of brand engagement.

Finally, while the emphasis of the co-creation discourse in brand building has been largely anchored in an enterprise perspective, with attendant concerns about being potentially exploitative, in the concluding chapter, Ind and Schmidt discuss the need to explore brand value co-creation as much from the perspective of individuals, who by interacting through platforms of engagement emancipate themselves and create meaningful emergent experiences and enhance well-being.

Best wishes to all in nurturing the mindset that this book inspires to co-create not just a brand, but a brand-new world of participatory engagement.

Prof. Venkat Ramaswamy
www.venkatramaswamy.com

# Introduction

This is a textbook. Sort of. The word 'textbook' probably conjures up an image of a door-stop – something that you *have* to read rather than want to. So, when we set out to write this book, we wanted to do something different: to create a book that you can read end-to-end or dip in and out of. A book that encourages you to explore further the subject of collaborative creativity and brand management. Our goal has been to write something that is substantial yet accessible; connected to the past but forward-looking; challenging and credible. We want to give you insight into a new way of thinking about brands, based around the idea of involving customers in what a brand is and does. This represents a change from the view that brands are fixed entities and regards them instead as phenomena that are fluid and adaptive. The implication is that customers (and indeed other stakeholders) are no longer passive recipients of a brand's message, but are actively involved in moulding its meaning and shaping its future. This raises some interesting issues about control, influence and openness and what will be required of managers in the way they build brands in a participative world.

To present our approach, we have drawn on studies into the flourishing field of co-creation. Alongside this research, we have used relevant theories rooted in a human-centric brand philosophy and insights based on interviews and case studies. Each chapter features a set of learning objectives, examples, suggested further reading and reflections/questions to stimulate thinking and discussion. And true to the co-creation theme, the book contains a variety of voices. When we started writing, we thought it was important to incorporate the latest thinking within the field. So we invited researchers, managers and consultants from around the world to share their work and experiences. Our co-creators have enlivened the book and brought a fascinating diversity of ideas for you to investigate – everything from describing a workshop with the wealthy elite in Los Angeles to using online ethnographic research into coffee culture, to understanding the diversity that defines an art museum brand.

The narrative of the book flows in a structured way – but with some interesting digressions and examples. To provide readers with a common starting point, in Chapter 1 we set out a simplified history of brand management. In Chapters 2, 3 and 4, we explore some of the core issues related to co-creative brand management. Chapter 2 shows how the traditional view of brand management has been subverted through the participation of stakeholders, with the effect that managers can no longer control but only influence brands. In Chapter 3 we use our research, and that of other authors, to look at the motivations of organisations to co-create and also why customers give up their time to take part in online communities and co-creation events. Along the way we take a journey to Los Angeles to hear about the practice of co-creation for a hospitality brand called Hakkasan. Chapter 4 looks at the ways in which organisations set up and manage the process of co-creating. The next cluster of chapters (5, 6, 7 and 8) are about a co-creative brand management system. In Chapter 5 we build on earlier models of brand management to outline the emergence of the co-creation system itself and its three inter-connected elements, which we then explore and illustrate with examples in the three subsequent chapters: generating and understanding brand-related insights, adjusting brand strategy and co-creating brand equity. In Chapter 9, we show how co-creating brands works in different contexts. In addition to the consumer examples given earlier in the book, such as those concerning LEGO, IKEA and adidas, this chapter shows how co-creation can be used in such diverse areas as healthcare, city branding and business-to-business branding. Finally, in Chapter 10, we discuss the strengths and the opportunities of co-creating brands, and also its limitations.

To help guide you through the text, at the beginning of each section you will find a mind-map illustration.

To check what we have written makes sense, we invited two academic readers and a student to read the text and to challenge our ideas. This certainly helped us to revisit some things we had taken for granted and to enhance the logic of the text. We hope the result is a usable book that can benefit students and managers.

Our thanks to our co-creators: Rinske Brand, Carsten Baumgarth, Nick Coates, Christin Franzel, Lucy Gill-Simmen, Francisco Guzman, Richard Gyrd-Jones, Ranim Helwani, Oliver Hirschberger, Oriol Iglesias, Eric Kennedy, Anna Karina Kjeldsen, Robert Kozinets, Samuel Kristal, Matthias Lorenz, Peter Lux, Stefan Markovic, Judith Meyer, Line Schmeltz, Gerhard Schwarz and Pieter Steenkamp.

And thanks also to our designer Patrick Ind, illustrator Eirunn Kvalnes and our 'test readers': Carsten Baumgarth, Fabian Gärtner and Oriol Iglesias. Finally, a special thanks to Venkat Ramaswamy for his insightful and generous foreword.

For additional content and support material visit www. cocreatingbrands.org

'A MIND IS LIKE A PARACHUTE. IT DOESN'T WORK IF IT IS NOT OPEN.'

– Frank Zappa

'MAN IS A NETWORK OF RELATIONSHIPS, AND THESE ALONE MATTER TO HIM.'

– Antoine de Saint-Exupéry

MoMA

MEISSEN

Levi's

ANCIENT
GREECE
1ST CENTURY
BRANDING

BECKHAM
7

KATAXI

THIS IS A BRAND

THIS IS
ALSO A BRAND

THIS IS
ALSO A BRAND

Ford

SCHOOLS OF
BRAND
MANAGEMENT

JANUS

IMAGE SCHOOL

IDENTITY SCHOOL

BRAND
IMAGE

CREATE
AN IMAGE
OF THE
BRAND

CUSTOMER

ADVERTISEMENT
is KEY

BRAND
IDENTITY

BRAND
MEANING
IN NETWORKS
OF
INTERACTION

INTERNAL
STAKEHOLDERS

EXTERNAL
STAKEHOLDERS

IDENTIFYING
THE CORE

CO-CREATIVE SCHOOL

# CHAPTER ONE

# A short history of brands and their management

In this chapter ...

Nowadays brands are everywhere: services are brands, art museums are brands, as are places and people. When brands are all around us, it's easy to believe that we know exactly what a brand is. Yet in practice, people rarely agree on a definition of the concept: it's a promise, it's an offer, it's the glue that holds an organisation together, it's a portfolio of meanings. In fact, it's all these things and more, which might make it seem a rather fuzzy concept – especially as over time the way people see brands has evolved. To help you through this maze, in this chapter we will briefly describe how brands emerged, the value that they can add in our lives and how the thinking about them has developed in tune with changing media habits and patterns of consumption. We won't weigh you down here with too much detail, but we'll provide just enough background to give you a sense of the ever-developing world of branding and to give us a good starting point for the rest of the book. We'll finish this chapter by looking at five different schools of thought that have contributed to the development of brand management. In reality there are more than five, but these are the most significant. We will zoom in on three schools in particular (image, identity, co-creation) as a prelude to the theme of this book: co-creating brands.

## Learning Objectives

After reading this chapter you should:

- have an understanding of what a brand is and know the definitions of the most important brand management terms (e.g., brand image, brand identity, brand meaning);
- have an understanding of how brands have been managed in the past and how people's thoughts about brands and branding have changed dramatically over time;
- know the essence of the three core schools of brand management and be able to explain them.

## A branded world

Few topics have been so extensively discussed in management science and practice in recent years as brand management. Whether in the context of consumer, industrial or service markets, commercial or not-for-profit-companies, global enterprises or small businesses, strong brands are in demand wherever intense competition prevails. And this is not only true for the business world. The word 'brand' is used with abandon to describe everything from David Beckham to the Roman Catholic Church to the Museum of Modern Art (MoMA). Not all organisations and people like the word 'brand', both because it has strong commercial associations and because, as Naomi Klein pointed out in her influential 1999 book *No Logo: Taking Aim at the Brand Bullies*, it is also associated with manipulation. But 'brand' is here to stay.[1] This raises the thorny issue of what a brand actually is.

A classic and widely used definition comes from The American Marketing Association, which begins: 'A brand is a name, term, design, symbol, or any other feature that identifies one seller's good or service as distinct from those of other sellers.'[2] Other commentators echo these words by giving emphasis to the things that managers do to a product or service that make it different from rival offers, while adding a proviso that the enhancements they make must meet the perceived needs of consumers.[3] The researchers Cleopatra Veloutsou and Elena Delgado-Ballester turn the definition around by leading with the idea that a brand exists in the minds of stakeholders as 'an evolving mental collection of actual (offer related) and emotional (human-like) characteristics and associations which convey benefits of an offer identified through a symbol, or a collection of symbols, and differentiates this offer from the rest of the marketplace.'[4] This definition focusses on the potential benefits (broadly: functional performance, emotional associations and self-expression) that a brand offers.[5] We buy brands such as Apple, BMW, HP, Siemens or British Airways because we believe they will deliver on what the brands claim. We choose them because they reduce some of the risk usually associated with the purchase of a product or service. It's almost like an insurance policy – which can help reassure us, especially when we buy something for long-term use or where the initial investment is quite high or where the performance of the offering cannot be tested beforehand. Other brands help us make choices in confusing or complex situations. Brands such as Amazon and Google help us to process information more quickly and to do our shopping without too much deliberation. They just make it easy for us. Interestingly, this works also in contexts not associated with deep emotions, such as academia and, more specifically, physics. Consider the following quote from a blog by Philip Moriarty, a professor, physicist and tutor for the School of Physics and Astronomy at the University of Nottingham, which highlights the power of brands and also their potential dark side:[6]

> In academia, journal brand is everything. I have sat in many committees, read many CVs, and participated in many discussions where candidates for a postdoctoral position, a fellowship, or other roles at various rungs of the academic career ladder have been compared. And very often, the committee members will say something along the lines of "Well, Candidate X has got much better publications than Candidate Y" …

without ever having read the papers of either candidate. The judgment of quality is lazily "outsourced" to the brand-name of the journal. If it's in a *Nature* journal, it's obviously of higher quality than something published in one of those, ahem, "lesser" journals.

Brands can also be deeply emotional, especially when they trigger strong memories connected to loved ones or childhood. It's why some people feel a love for brands such as Kinderschokolade (Ferrero's famous brand of children's chocolate), Oreo and Disney. When it comes to self-expression, some brands open up another world. If we own a grill made by Weber or a luxury wine fridge made by Liebherr, it tells others something about us. When we wear a Rolex or drive a Tesla, we express what is important to us and what we stand for.

For the organisation, recognising the desire that consumers feel for certain brands can help achieve economic goals. Intangible assets, such as a skilled workforce, patents, know-how – and brands – generate most of corporate growth and shareholder value, with one study suggesting that intangible assets account for over half the market capitalisation of public companies.[7] Highly desirable brands are both good at creating awareness and building a customer-centric perspective through the performance of their products and services, and adept at developing the ability to empathise with target audiences, differentiate themselves from competitors and create emotional relationships. This in turn builds attitudinal loyalty and stronger repurchase and recommendation rates.[8] Additionally, we can see that companies with strong brands are able to charge more for a comparable product made by the competition, are more resilient in times of crisis or economic recession, employ more motivated employees and find it easier to attract the best talent. This indicates the power of brands, and illustrates how and why they are able to help secure future cash flows and have a positive impact on sales and profits.[9]

All in all, brands can be understood as mediators between companies and consumers. De Chernatony and Riley, in a classic article from 1998, 'propose a concept of the brand as a multidimensional construct, matching a firm's functional and emotional values with the performance and psychosocial needs of consumers.'[10] While such research argues for the power of brands, we can also see that a lot of hype around brands can feed into the phenomenon of anti-brand activism.[11] To better understand where we are now, it is worthwhile taking a brief journey into the past to better appreciate the positives and negatives of brands.

## Early evidence of branding

While the American Marketing Association definition of a brand is quite recent, brands have served as signs of ownership long before modern brands appeared. Inscriptions and paintings on ancient Egyptian gravestones show that signs were used nearly 4,000 years ago to mark cattle.[12] Roman glassmakers also successfully used trademarks (as early as the first century) to reassure customers about the high quality of their wares. Someone buying a vitreous vettel in a local market could rely on the producer's promise, especially if the vettel was from the glassworker Ennion. How do we know? Some of the glassware survived, bearing the Greek inscription 'made by Ennion'.[13] The first trademark register in the Western world, which dates from 1537, also demonstrates the importance of a sign to denote a brand. In this instance the catalyst was the explorer Hernan Cortes' use of three crosses in conquered Mexico as a sign to mark his herd. This prompted the Spanish Crown to found an organisation in New Spain whose members – all of them cattle breeders – had to use different brands, which were then registered in a book.[14]

In the eighteenth and nineteenth centuries, brands became more and more popular. Faster and more secure transport routes made it possible to ship goods over longer distances. People at places far away from the location where a specific good was produced needed to be reassured about the product's quality, and the producers realised that a good reputation could help them to stand out against competitors with similar but inferior products and, ultimately, to outstrip their rivals' sales. The German brand Meissner Porzellan was founded at the beginning of the eighteenth century in Saxonia and has used the logo of crossed swords since 1722. It is an early example of a brand that understood the power of branding many years before industrialisation really took off.[15] Other 'old' brands include Bass (1777), Schweppes (1783) and Jim Beam (1795).

## The era of brands

Even though we can track these early examples of brands and brand management, the concept of brands only really starts to come to the fore in the second part of the nineteenth century (when industrialisation brought changes that made it possible to manage brands systematically). Improved infrastructure, new communications capabilities, production methods and packaging technologies, along with the emergence of larger retailers and changes in consumer culture led to the increasing popularity of consistent-quality consumer products that were marketed through large-scale advertising – branded products, in other words.[16] Examples of this phase in branding include American Express, founded in the 1850s as an express mail service company, Colgate toothpaste and Levi jeans (from 1873), Listerine (originally a germicide invented in 1879) and Coca-Cola (from 1886). The enduring success of these brands set in train the basic principles of brand management that are still around today: quality, broad availability, well-designed packaging, continuity of price policy and thoughtful communications. Brands brought something back that consumers had lost in the industrial revolution: the personal connection between the seller and the buyer. Even though with mass production the consumer and the producer were alienated from each other in a way that they had never been before, brands created a sense of connectivity: the feeling there was a real person who stood behind the brand and lent it their endorsement. This is why many early brands – Ford, Harley-Davidson and Heinz – often used personal names and symbols.

In the exciting early years of brand management, advertising was considered to be the key success factor in brand building. From 1918 to 1920, revenues of the advertising industry doubled in just two years, and by 1930, that spending had increased by a factor of 10.[17] Advertisers were confident enough to 'dictate the food that the baby shall eat, the clothes the mother shall wear, the way in which the home shall be furnished'.[18] Huge advertising agencies like BBDO, J. Walter Thompson and McCann Erickson opened their doors and grew prosperous creating newspaper ads and billboards, followed by radio spots, followed, from the 1950s, by television spots. Based on theories of scientific advertising, advertising men convinced their clients that the right functional or emotional conditioning would make the consumer react in the desired way. In a second step, they also sought to create loyalty to a brand 'by creating the impression, valid or not, that something truly set it apart from others like it'.[19]

Procter & Gamble, a company today known for famous brands like Oral B, Wella, Pampers, Fairy, Old Spice and Gillette, was one of the pacemakers of brand building. Initially, the responsibility for single brands was placed in different hands in different functional areas, such as sales, marketing, research & development. Yet as this system reached its limits (due to unclear responsibilities and high bureaucratic requirements), Procter & Gamble changed track. In a 1931 memo by a manager (Neil McElroy) to his bosses at the company, the idea of brand management as a practice involving 'brand men', analysing, defining and then managing brands, was established and then adopted.[20] McElroy's brand men set about controlling the delivery of the different brands that the company produced. The brand managers had the task of coordinating the contributions of the individual departments, as well as those of external service providers to the brand (such as advertising agencies) and optimally positioning 'their' brand in the market. This was highly effective because it enabled the company to put competing products onto the market, but ignored the possibility of synergies between the brands. The Procter & Gamble company was behind the scenes – not at the front of the stage. This more prominent and interactive approach is what Aaker and Joachimsthaler call a house of brands strategy, with independent, unconnected brands each maximising its impact in a market.[21]

As the Procter & Gamble approach became widely adopted, a growing understanding of the brand as 'a consumer's idea of a product' developed.[22] The idea of a brand as a picture in the consumer's mind centred on the notion that brand management could position the brand by building a positive, consistent, clear and differentiated picture of it.[23] This picture was defined by the marketing department and market research managers (using the latest consumer insights) to create a Unique Selling Proposition (USP) that could then be communicated by highly researched advertising executions.[24]

This brand building approach endured for a long time, but changes such as globalisation, ever more intense competition, shortened product life cycles, more demanding and knowledgeable consumers, the growing importance of intangible assets and a high number of mergers and acquisitions led to a recognition that the house-of-brands strategies had weaknesses. The alternative was the idea of a branded house strategy whereby a company's reputation was more important, synergies could be better exploited and the organisation behind the brands more easily explained. Whereas a house of brands contains independent, unconnected brands, a branded house such as Caterpillar, Virgin or Sony 'uses a single master brand...to span a set of offerings that operate with only descriptive subbrands'.[25] Learning from the fast-growing service sector that (as in the case of airlines, hotels or consultancies) was typified by the branded house model and well-established brands such as automotive manufacturers Mercedes and BMW,[26] corporate branding developed as a model[27] and in the 1980s and 1990s came to enjoy far more attention.[28] This resulted in a switch from the old marketing approach, which had been more or less exclusively focussed on consumers, to a new philosophy that recognised the increasing financial value of a brand, and the importance of multiple stakeholders in the brand management process. As corporate brands usually have a much wider scope and impact than product brands, the focus expanded from consumers to include all stakeholders, including employees, job candidates, potential investors, local communities, suppliers and the general public.

With a stakeholder perspective, a broadening and deepening of the brand management discipline occurred. Broadening is the idea that the practice of brand management could now be applied to new fields such as services, business-to-business industries and public sector organisations. Deepening involved brand managers leaving behind their earlier focus on communications and embracing a new strategy that tried to integrate the marketing approach in a way that would provide people with a consistent experience of the brand's promise at all brand touch points. This in turn led to the development of the concept of internal branding, which held that employees needed to live the brand as a means to enhance the customer's brand experience through their interactions. Internal branding recognised that a brand's image was not only formed through marketing communications, but also through the way employees thought and behaved. A further aspect of the stakeholder perspective was the growth in Corporate Social Responsibility (CSR). The economist Milton Friedman argued in a 1970 article that companies only owed a responsibility to their shareholders, but he also recognised that CSR could be good for building a company's reputation. Contra Friedman, a stakeholder perspective emerged which said that companies had a broader responsibility to all their audiences and to society.

The next step in the coming-of-age of brand management was soon evident. Early in the twenty-first century, at the same time as the emergence of digitalisation and the Internet, an influential 2004 article by two academic researchers, Vargo and Lusch, created a new brand management perspective.[29] Vargo and Lusch argued that the value of consumption lay not in the product itself but in the service it delivered. According to their Service-Dominant Logic argument, value is derived and determined in-use rather than in-exchange. A car in itself does not deliver value standing outside your house (except perhaps for you and the neighbours to admire) but rather when you experience driving it somewhere. Thus, value is co-created between what is provided by the company and the act of consumption. At the same time that Vargo and Lusch were talking about the co-creation of value, two other writers, Prahalad and Ramaswamy, observed that consumers were no longer simply passive recipients of whatever organisations chose to offer, rather that they had expertise, skills and knowledge that could be co-opted to help co-create and develop new and relevant ideas.[30] The emergence of the Internet in particular meant that more and more people could engage directly with brands via social media and exchange ideas in brand communities. As you will see in the chapters that follow, this change has had important consequences for brand managers, because brands are no longer solely under their control.

## Schools of brand management

This *tour d'horizon* through the history of brands and their management was designed to get us to a common starting point.[31] Here, you should note that the developments described above didn't occur in a strictly linear way and that the approaches to deal with the different challenges that emerged had large overlaps. Nevertheless, it is clear that brand management had progressed from a focus on the single product to a focus on value creation; from a focus on advertising to a focus on brand touch points; from a focus on outputs to a focus on processes (brands as 'relationship partners'[32]); from a focus on brand image (via a focus on identity) to a focus on co-creation. These different focal points in the history of brand management have also been called schools – of which there are at least five.[33]

1) The image school concentrates on establishing a clear and attractive positioning for the brand
2) The behavioural school focusses on influencing consumers' brand knowledge via various marketing instruments

3) The identity school focusses on living a precise and transparent brand identity

4) The strategic school links business strategy with the brand's financial performance

5) The co-creative school argues that brand management can provide direction, but is no longer in control of the brand meaning, which is co-created together with consumers.

Let's look at the three that are most relevant for this book's storyline: the image school, the identity school and the co-creative school.

**The image school** focusses on the views external stakeholders have of the brand. Brand image can be defined as 'the perception formed to the mind of a member of the external audience about the brand after one real or mental encounter with the brand'.[34] Hence, brand management focusses on image building activities and the central idea is that a brand is something that can be managed by creating an idea about the product or service in the consumer's mind. Therefore, the first step in building a brand is to identify strong functional or emotional customer needs. Then, in the second step, and more or less regardless of the nature of the offering, the brand should be – maybe even artificially – designed in order to be attractive to consumers and to meet their expectations. This is an outside-in-approach to brand management. According to the image school, in order to build the desired brand image, brand managers should rely primarily on advertising. Advertising is designed 'to inform consumers of the functional capabilities of the brand while simultaneously imbuing the brand with symbolic values and meanings relevant to the consumer'.[35] Simultaneously, advertising is necessary to differentiate the brand's product from similar offers.

Contrary to the image school, which has been traditionally more associated with product brands, **the identity school** focusses on the internal audiences for the brand and sees the brand's identity as the starting point for all brand management activities. The identity perspective emerged when the focus of brand management research moved to the corporate brand. Brand identity can be defined as 'the symbols and the set of the brand associations that represent the core character of the brand that the team supporting the brand aspire to create or maintain as identifiers of the brand to other people'.[36] This implies that a brand is far more than its name, logo or visual code,[37] and also more than a product of good advertising. It is a promise made to people. And since promises must be kept, brand management is about highlighting and developing the most valuable and valued strengths of a company, a product or a service.[38] According to this school, and unlike the image school, brand managers must start the brand management process by identifying the core competencies and distinctive features of the brand itself.[39] Then, in the second step, the brand must be expressed in a consistent, engaging and enduring way. This is an inside-out approach to brand management.

This insider emphasis means managers need to have a deep understanding of the unique attributes of the brand.[40] Hence, those that subscribe to identity-based approaches stress brand identity design as a key objective and argue that external image emerges indirectly over time, based on customers' previous and holistic experiences with the brand.[41] In a nutshell, the identity school focusses on a brand's values and on ways to make the value proposition come alive for customers and employees.[42] It includes not only traditional marketing activities such as external and internal communications, but also a broad range of human resources and change management instruments, such as brand-related training of employees, incentives for brand-related behaviours and brand workshops.[43] Consequently, the marketing department has to co-work with other corporate functions to achieve its goal of creating and sustaining an identity.[44]

**The co-creative school** incorporates ideas from the image and identity school and focusses on how brand meaning evolves. Brand meaning can be defined as a reflection of 'internal and external stakeholders' mindset about a brand'.[45] In the co-creative school, brand management is no longer simply an internal activity solely initiated by the branded company,[46] nor are brands solely a product of advertising. Due to the rise of interactivity facilitated by social media,[47] and the corresponding social effects such as the rise of (online) communities,[48] the increasing demand for customised products,[49] and the emergence of platform businesses that are interconnected networks of stakeholders who together co-create value for the final user,[50] brand managers can still provide direction, but they no longer control the brand.[51] Managers can load the brand with messages and intended associations designed inside the organisation. However, the reception of those messages is variable and meaning will be created 'by consumers who create relations, emotions and communities around brands' independent of the organisation'.[52] This puts pressure back on on managers to adapt to the always-evolving meaning of the brand. The co-creative school, which will be described in more detail in the following chapters, is like the Roman god Janus, who looks two ways at the same time. Here, the brand looks inwards and outwards as it tries to balance the company and stakeholders' views of the brand.[53]

We close this chapter with some interesting thoughts about the history and future of the brand management discipline, provided by a long-time expert in this field.

## Looking back and forward

*INTERVIEW WITH PETER G.C. Lux*

**Mr Lux, for decades you have observed how companies build and communicate relationships with their customers. What has remained the same, what has changed?**

Right at the start one of the famous million-dollar questions! Do we have two days for my answer? But seriously, I would like to say in advance that what was still normal 50 years ago will hopefully not become a special experience in the course of digitisation: that is, personal contact and the exchange of ideas between company representatives and customers. Despite CRM, big data, digitisation, all the marketing finesse and virtualisation efforts, direct personal relationships were, and will be, the river 'in which the brand floats' to modify Mao's much-quoted statement. The growth and long-term survival of businesses will ultimately depend on it.

But back to your initial question. A basic current behind all the changes over the past decades has been the change from a seller's to a buyer's market. Typical for the seller's market was that demand exceeded scarce offers and a multitude of unmet needs motivated manufacturers to innovate quickly. The asymmetry for the customer in product knowledge motivated him to contact the salesperson, the customer service department and the company's service technician on his own initiative. His relationships with companies were more open and more attuned to his basic needs to create a more pleasant life for himself. Companies were able to communicate with customers and build lasting relationships with comparatively little effort, compared to today. This market-structural background placed brands such as Bosch, Miele, Nivea and Siemens at the top of the rankings.

The situation is different in a buyer's market that has already entered the stage of hyper-competition. The supply of products, goods and services in many segments exceeds demand. For the critical, price-conscious buyer, decisions have become either costly, such as for special technical products or mobile phone contracts, or hardly necessary in terms of product benefits. This is because the competitor has equally good products. You can easily see this in the context of consumer goods.

It was the Internet and social media that liberated customers from this feeling of powerlessness. This even gave customers double power. They have the money the company wants. And they now have a much greater freedom of choice. Purchasing platforms, product and performance assessments, price comparisons or even influencers are all factors that make things easier for the company, but make it more difficult for it to retain customers. The reason being that a better offer is only a click away. To counteract this, more and more companies are using innovative methods such as re-targeting or programmatic advertising. In the best case, they increase sales. But do they also promote resilient customer relationships? According to GfK's findings (2019), the migration of existing customers in the FMCG segment, which accounts for almost 70 per cent of sales, averages 30 per cent per year. After two years, a brand has on average only half of its existing customers!

The conclusion is: customer behaviour has changed dramatically and customer relationships with companies, especially in FMCG markets, have become more volatile, non-binding and superficial. Consumers are more critical of corporate communications. Knowledge of the manipulability of technically conveyed communication content and the tsunami of communication stimuli to which buyers and consumers are exposed on a daily basis strengthens their ability to ignore corporate messages. These are just some of the reasons why budgets for influencer marketing, sponsorship and digital marketing are currently being increased in many places.

**How has the communications industry changed?**
For marketing consultancies and advertising agencies, you can see there is increasing specialisation and networking, while globalisation and digitisation is challenging the ability of these advisors to retain clients. As a counter: management consultancies, design, advertising, PR, Media and digital agencies have been moving from national to international networks. With regard to customer relations and market communications, complex, differentiated and cross-media forms have developed. Large corporations and the larger medium-sized companies have the resources and know-how for this. But many smaller SMEs have challenges as well. The enormous pace of innovation in the IT sector in recent years will continue. Marketing and brand managers will be called upon to find meaningful applications for AR, VR and AI that allow customers and interested parties to deal 'naturally' with the artificial realities of marketing.

As brand management consultants, it has been interesting to observe that companies are increasingly expressing a need for generalists to support employees and decision-makers in planning and controlling the use of their communication technologies as an overall system and in making sensible use of the swelling feedback that this triggers. In my opinion, keeping an eye on the entire network of effects of customer communication will be the be-all and end-all of future corporate communication.

In the general focus on external marketing communication, an important consequence of globalisation and outsourcing is easily overlooked. Many companies have long since ceased to be self-contained entities and have become semi-open organisations. They are networks that allow suppliers and customer companies to exchange information, knowledge and experience in real time. Customers in the B2B market can contact the supplier's individual specialist directly without the need for a sales representative. Machines are monitored by the manufacturer via remote control and customer employees are instructed on the screen in the event of malfunctions. In the industrial market in particular, a field is developing of new communication methods that are particularly suitable for personal relationships and open up new dimensions in brand building. However, external service providers will have to be familiar with the rules, laws and conditions in other markets and cultures.

And the development of corporate design must also not go unmentioned. 'You never get a second chance to make a first impression,' we used to say to our customers in London. Why? Relationships between companies and customers succeed much more easily and quickly if the unknown counterpart, i.e. the company, seems to be assessable for the customer in his reactions and behaviour patterns at the first encounter – as long as there are no disappointments. Corporate design makes a major contribution to this. Companies have to start with this if they want to build lasting relationships with their customers. The fact that rationalisation effects can also be achieved through stringent design has greatly accelerated the spread of Corporate Design.

This was one of the reasons why in 1962 Lufthansa commissioned Otl Aicher and his group 'E5' at the Ulm College of Design to develop a 'corporate design', as it was then called. Following the ideology 'Form Follows Function', a prototype was created that set standards for many other companies and design agencies. The fact that this programme also had such a signal effect in other industries and markets was due to the rules of the seller's market, which shaped the economic upswing until the 1980s. That is why Lufthansa was not primarily interested in winning new customers, but in self-promotion and customer confidence. Lufthansa had to make itself known as safe, organised, reliable and enterprising to its passengers – most of whom were unfamiliar with airlines – what a surprising idea!

Today, corporate design is one of the basic behaviours of a company that seriously strives for long-term relationships with its customers and wants to remain recognisable in the visual noise of the market. A coherent visual framework that seems appropriate to all stakeholders and is not to be confused with competitors is now one of the standards of a company that wants to present itself to its stakeholders in a credible and contemporary manner. However, 'Form Follows Function' has lost some of its commitment when you think of some of the recently revised trademarks.

**You are regarded as a pioneer of the corporate identity idea, founded the first corporate identity agency in 1978 in Switzerland and advised clients such as BMW, Continental, Lindt and Deutsche Telekom, to name just a few major brands. Did they have a different understanding of brands in the seventies than people do today?**
Oh yes, at that time brand thinking was still very much influenced by the manufacturer's point of view instead of the customer's point of view, as it is today. Trademarks, product or company image and corporate design were not yet understood as a whole. A trademark had to receive an 'update' or 'upgrade', depending on whether the logo still showed the style characteristics of a past epoch or whether the client had decided to address a more demanding clientele with his offer and thus exploit a higher price segment. Upgrading then often resulted in an image campaign which, however, was not yet geared to a brand core but to the results of an image survey. These usually mirrored a comparison with competitors or their products using standard batteries of items. And the simple goal

was not to build up an unmistakable image, which would have required a strategic brand core or at least a core performance idea of the brand, but to compensate for image weaknesses vis-à-vis the competition. To date, some insurance companies and financial service providers have not yet been able to free themselves from this pattern. The corporate design had to create the link between the tradition-signalling trademarks and the image campaigns seeking customer proximity. Whether the one fit with the other was the result of a plausible argumentation by consultants and creative people, but not of a systematic and tested derivation from a brand core, as is practiced today by professional brand management.

The understanding of trademarks was a legal one at the time. The brand had to clearly refer to the manufacturer. Distinctiveness was thus to be provided solely by the trademark. It had to assure the customer that he was buying an original product. That was it, essentially. All other communicative measures and media, including corporate design, served to sell the product in terms of content and design. The brand ideas that developed in people's minds were shaped by the product and/or the history of the manufacturer. For the first time, our programme for BMW aligned all manifestations, contents and many processes of the brand to a strategic, differentiating brand core for a broad public.

**It is often said that brand managers are losing control over their brands and that the networked consumer has gained more power through digitalisation and social media. Is it still possible to systematically build up brands under these conditions?**
If by 'systematically building up' you mean a controllable process from A to Z, the answer is clear: 'no'. And not because companies and their brand-related activities have been exposed to critical resonance since the rise of the Internet and the spread of the social media. This often forces companies to make costly corrections in order to retain the favour of buyers and interested parties. We now have a rich and differentiated pool of knowledge from the research and findings of critical brand practitioners of the last two decades as to how and by

what means brands form and change in the minds of their relationship groups. We know that the quintessence of every brand is a relatively robust web of meaning in episodic memory, which is confirmed or modified by the combination of many observed details, the comparison of repetitive brand experiences with one's own life experience and ultimately in social and societal discourses. This is an endless chain of only partially consciously perceived impressions and feedback. In this process unpredictable emergence intervenes again and again. To speak of 'systematic construction' has always been and remains an illusion.

Incidentally, 'steering' and its counterpart ('controlling') are concepts that have been misappropriated for social purposes from the technical field. The phases that are decisive for brand building take place in everyday social communication and interaction. Here, the control of communication – of opinions, behaviour, feelings – from the position of the company never worked.

## What does this mean for the management of brands in the present and future?

Digitalisation of customer relations will prevail in all industries and companies. All participants must learn to think ahead, try out and understand how networking and digitalisation can change existing business processes. It will take courage to make communication between companies, brand stakeholders, competitors and society not only faster, more accurate and more flexible, but also more personal. The danger is already looming that digitalisation will lead to the dissemination of increasingly similar stories and activities, which can be consumed everywhere at any time from any source. Ultimately, this leads to a perceived levelling and communicative 'overfeeding', from which relationship groups would then distance themselves.

In companies, there will be a change in the role of brand management. On the basis of comprehensive corporate governance, a distinction will finally be made between strategic responsibility and responsibility for implementation. The central strategic responsibility for the brand will be assumed at board level because it is becoming increasingly important that internal processes that contribute to the external impact of the brand also run according to the specifications of the strategic brand core and must lead to corresponding results. For many processes in areas such as R&D, sales and logistics, service, but also human resources, there will be opportunities to become more efficient. By focussing specifically on the brand, employees will also rediscover what makes sense in their day-to-day work.

Marketing and corporate communication will retain the implementation competence for brand content at all external touch-points. They will be judged by their ability to ensure that the brand specifications have been incorporated into the activities and measures in a stringent and convincing manner. This will require intelligent concepts for hybrid communication, for which the strengths of analogue and digital channels and media can be played out and combined.

Finally, an established brand organisation will emerge that networks all those internally and externally responsible for brand work. The digitalisation of communication, data and work processes has already led to an increase in the number of technology specialists and other specialists within the company and at external service providers. This group must be managed. This will take place in the circle of an extended brand management group, to which internal specialists and external specialists belong. The aim of this internal brand institution will be to gain a common understanding of the brand, to discuss developments with customers, competitors and society and to decide on reactions and tactical changes.

**And another very personal question: which brand is your favourite brand and why?**
I don't have a favourite brand. But I have great respect for BMW's brand management, how it transforms the brand into e-mobility. I admire Patek Philippe's brand management, which for decades has managed to vary the core idea of the brand in illustrated stories without becoming boring and while keeping the brand image and customer relationships

congruent and consistent. The managing partner of Werner & Mertz GmbH, Reinhard Schneider, and his brand management have achieved an exemplary performance. They have consistently aligned their Frosch brand to the 'Cradle to Cradle' principle, which is still a rarity in the international brand landscape.

(Note from the authors: In Germany, Frosch is a well-known brand. The brand has been offering eco-friendly cleaners and other household products since 1986 and has a reputation as a pioneer in sustainability. The 'cradle-to-cradle' principle describes the idea of a sustainable circular economy where all resources will be recycled after use.)

## Summary

In the world of business and beyond, brands have become powerful and influential. Among the drivers of the changing world of brands are mega-trends such as globalisation and digitalisation. These have led to an increase in the variety of offers and the intensity of competition in many markets, while at the same time multiplying the possible communication channels and creating an environment in which strong brands have grown. Accordingly, Chapter 1 was designed to introduce you to some of the major developments in the history of brand management and to outline the important viewpoints on brands and the ways they are managed. The implication of this chapter is that we live in a time when brand managers have far less control over brands than they used to. This opens up interesting challenges and opportunities for brand management.

## Reflections/questions

1) Wherever you happen to be when reading this book, look around. How many different brands are visible to you?

2) Think about your latest shopping experience. Which brands did you buy, and what was the reason for choosing them compared to other similar ones?

3) What is your favourite brand? What comes to mind and how do you feel when you think about it? Now think about a brand you would never buy. What comes to mind now and how do you feel about the brand you dislike?

4) Think about a TV advertisement that you enjoyed watching. How did the brand in this advertisement present itself? What do you think? How do you think the brand owner was trying to position the brand?

5) Do you think a brand can stay successful if it doesn't deliver what it promises?

6) What is the difference between brand identity, brand image and brand meaning?

7) Which companies, besides the ones mentioned in this text, follow a branded house strategy? Which follow a house-of-brands strategy?

## We recommend the following reading to expand your learning experience:

Aaker, D.A. & Joachimsthaler, E. (2000). 'The brand relationship spectrum: The key to the brand architecture challenge', *California Management Review, 42*(4), 8–23.

De Chernatony, L. & Dall'Olmo Riley, F. (1998). 'Defining a "brand": Beyond the literature with experts' interpretations', *Journal of Marketing Management, 14*(5), 417–443.

Merz, M.A., He, Y. & Vargo, S.L. (2009). 'The evolving brand logic: a service-dominant logic perspective', *Journal of the Academy of Marketing Science, 37*(3), 328–344.

Schmidt, H.J. & Redler, J. (2018): 'How diverse is corporate brand management research? Comparing schools of corporate brand management with approaches to corporate strategy', *Journal of Product & Brand Management*, 27(2), 185–202.

Urde, M., Baumgarth, C. & Merrilees, B. (2013). 'Brand orientation and market orientation – From alternatives to synergy', *Journal of Business Research, 66*(1), 13–20.

Veloutsou, C. & Delgado-Ballester, E. (2018). Guest editorial. *Spanish Journal of Marketing – ESIC, 22*(3), 255–272.

BUYER
SUPPLIER
CUSTOMER
INFLUENCER
BRANDS ARE BUILT TOGETHER

## THE FOUR PRINCIPLES OF CO-CREATION

FOCUS ON PEOPLE

BUILDING TRUST

BEING OPEN

BEING HUMBLE

BRANDS ARE FLUID

LEGO

## THE GIFT OF CO-CREATION

NETWORKS OF INTEREST

BRAND TRANSPARENCY

LISTEN & LEARN
ORGANIZATION
INFLUENCE
INDIVIDUALS

CREATORS
COMMUNITIES
adidas
PARTNERS
CUSTOMERS

# CHAPTER TWO

# The era of co-creation

## In this chapter ...

In this chapter, we set the scene for the development of a co-creative approach to brand management. However, before we can establish the principles that underpin co-creation, we need to understand the context. Like many in the field of marketing and brand management, we were brought up on a diet of management control and marketing communications, typical of the image and identity schools that you read about in Chapter 1. As we have practised and then taught brand management, it seemed that there was something not quite right about this way of thinking. Were marketing communications always vital in building brands? And could managers really control their brands in a participative world dominated by the Internet? This questioning set us on a path that led us to believe that brands are co-created by an organisation and all its stakeholders.

Here, we briefly describe the way brands have been managed and the changes that have taken place that have undermined the control-based approach. Then we set out a new model for brand management and four principles that define a co-creation mindset. Illustrating the various arguments in this chapter is the example of the Danish toy brand, LEGO. It has been much written about as a case, but that is because it shows what an open, co-creative philosophy can achieve for a company.

# Learning Objectives

After reading this chapter you should

- understand that brands are built together with stakeholders, such as customers, suppliers, buyers and other influencers;
- appreciate that organisations need to have a human-centric philosophy that encourages openness and the processes to support it;
- realise that managers can no longer control brands but that they can still have influence if they share knowledge and encourage dialogue.

# Conventional Wisdom about Brand Management

Conventional wisdom suggests that brands are owned and controlled by organisations: market researchers provide insights into market opportunities, brand managers develop and implement plans, and communication professionals produce campaigns that tap into the needs and desires of consumers. Not surprisingly, definitions of brand often reflect this orientation. Yet, as we shall see in this book, the role of the all-powerful 'brand man' is changing and what has been learned has to be adapted to a different context that requires new attributes.

# Challenging Conventional Wisdom

The **first** challenge to conventional wisdom emerges from an obvious place – the Internet. Go back to the mid-1990s, to a pre-Google/Facebook world. Brand management was concerned with how to build a brand by using the tenets of the identity school (with some links to the image school). Products and services were developed based on the brand identity and informed by what was learned from market research. Communications were then created that would tell people about the brand's benefits. It was a linear model that read from the organisation outwards to stakeholders – although it is important to remember that there were some feedback loops, as market research was absorbed back into some parts of the business. It was a tidy model, because it saw things from the perspective of the organisation.

What the Internet changed was the model's direction and complexity. Rather than one-way communication (from the organisation to its stakeholders), brands started to be built by a multi-directional set of conversations sparked by stakeholders' growing desire to participate (and by their having the means to do so). Consumers, influencers, suppliers and buyers began to share their inspirations, ideas, loves and hates with each other. They formed fan-based brand communities, created content for Wikipedia and YouTube and commented on brands on the burgeoning social media scene. Brand owners could still influence the world around them by constructing the brand and narrating its intended meaning, but the idea of control was becoming a mirage. For example, in the late 1990s and early 2000s, while LEGO was developing new products and communication campaigns, its customers (especially its AFOLs – Adult Friends of Lego) were busy establishing their own online brand communities, holding so-called Brickfests that took the brand in new directions (unforeseen by the company) and creating their own product adaptations.

**Second**: the Internet empowered stakeholders. In the pre-Internet world, organisations could present a façade which was difficult for outsiders to penetrate. A small cadre of managers wrote press releases, developed marketing campaigns and designed products and services. If they were well organised they could present a largely unified picture of a brand that aligned with perceptions of stakeholder needs. Inconvenient truths about the brand could be hidden away and selected virtues praised. With the development of the Internet – and the rise of social media – activists, NGOs and consumers could comment on, parody and criticise brands. As it has become easier to see behind the organisational boundaries and to share views and experiences, so it becomes ever more difficult for organisations to define brand meaning on their own terms. An interesting example of this change is the analysis by Vallaster and von Wallpach into the in-flight caterer,

Gate Gourmet.[54] The context for this study was an industrial dispute between Gate Gourmet and its employees. In a pre-Internet era, the struggle would have probably been played out by the Communication departments of the company and its Union. However, this dispute involved a diverse group of often impassioned commentators, including employees, customers, political interest groups and bloggers. Employees shared their personal experiences of hardship, the Unions commented on proposals, the media exposed underhand moves and everything was amplified by online bloggers. Vallaster and von Wallpach concluded: 'Brand management is no longer in the position to unilaterally define and control brand meaning but needs to perceive itself as one actor among many. All of these actors can take part in brand-related discourse and shape brand meaning depending on the resources they have at their disposition.' [55]

The change fostered by devices and networks created what Steve Jobs had referred to in 2001 as the emergence of 'digital lifestyles'. Jobs had seen the way his family and friends were increasingly using digital devices to listen to music and to photograph and film the things they found meaningful. Against this backdrop, in January 2001 at Macworld, he launched a new strategy, based around the idea of Apple as the digital hub for a digital lifestyle. The strategy led to the iPod, iTunes, iDVD, iMovie and eventually, the iPhone – devices and software that enabled people to share content with each other.[56] Along with the emergence of social media tools, people began to not only comment on, but also to contribute to brand meaning and development – especially if companies encouraged them to do so. In response, some brands did open themselves up, but others chose to maintain a penumbra of secrecy and largely rejected the idea that consumers could contribute anything of real value. In spite of the increasingly active role of some consumers, brand owners saw outsiders as passive recipients (and often still do) and lacking in the expertise to make valuable contributions – as suggested by this comment from an interview we conducted with a manager: 'I tend to think the new ideas have to come from visionaries in organisations who know their customers and are shaped into winning ideas by product managers who know their customers. I don't think they come from customers. They rarely come from customers.'[57]

**Third**: organisations have become polyphonic. While consumers and other external stakeholders were seizing the opportunity to make comments and share images about brands, so too were employees. Whereas once managers could present a simple picture of the organisation or the brand as a single entity, increasingly they had to recognise that organisations were more 'discursive spaces which are shaped by a multiplicity of voices, dominant and peripheral, which together make up a contested and ever-changing arena of human action.'[58] The cadre of press-releasing managers was supplanted by a loose collective of blogging and tweeting employees who expressed their sometimes quite divergent views about the brands they represented. On a positive note, this diversity enriched the experience of stakeholders by making communications more human and dialogic. For example, the Canadian business communications company Mitel has some 1,600 employees that work with social media. The company recognises that to be truly customer centric and to ensure that interactions reflect the values of the brand, employees need to both engage with the brand and have the freedom to interpret it. Each of Mitel's tweeting employees has been trained in the responsible use of social media and then trusted to do the right thing. Chief Marketing Officer Martyn Etherington says: 'Our social policy is simply at all times use your best judgement. There are no other rules. We expanded that a little by saying don't put anything on social you would not say to someone in person. Be respectful of our competitors and really focus on understanding and serving our customers better.'[59]

The downside of polyphony is that there is the potential for views expressed by individuals to run counter to the ideology of the brand. This sometimes is the result of misjudgement, but it is also the case that due to the permeability of the organisational boundaries, internal communications and conversations leak to the outside world.

A notable example of this was the firing in August 2017 of a Google employee who wrote an internal memo about workplace diversity, entitled 'Google's Ideological Echo Chamber'. The detailed memo argued in a cogent way about the political bias at Google and the lack of discussion that sustained the 'politically correct monoculture' but then veered into a contentious argument about gender traits. With seeming inevitability, the internal memo became external and Google's CEO, Sundar Pichai, argued that the views expressed ran counter to the code of conduct of Google. The Google memo and the furore it caused demonstrates how the more widespread expression of views can create tension and discordancy. Stakeholders might variously see Google as a repressor of free expression or a bastion of principles. Overall, given the rapid growth in the number of touch-points where employees and outsiders interact – particularly on social media – and the leakage of communications, the ability of the brand to manage its image coherently has been much diminished. (You'll find a case study of the Danish National Gallery based on this particular challenge by Line Schmeltz and Anna Karina Kjeldsen later in the book.)

**Fourth**: the validity of brands has long been based on a premise of trust. Some of the many definitions of brand refer to the idea that it is a promise. When we visit an Apple store or purchase and consume a can of Coca-Cola we draw on previous experience and associations that create an expectation on which the brand should deliver. The expectation can be specific to the experience itself but can also be coloured by broader issues, such as Coca-Cola's stance on social responsibility or Apple's environmental policies. The promise made by the brand through what it says must align with expectations and be delivered more or less consistently – otherwise the promise will be discredited. However, the very idea of the brand as a promise is questionable – for if value is created in the way the consumer uses the product, the fulfilment of a promise is beyond the remit of the organisation.[60] Nonetheless, the real issue here is connected to the points made above. Brands and their owners have traditionally relied on marketing communications to convey their promise, but as the number of voices talking about the brand increases and as stakeholders more easily see through the company façade, doubts emerge. Rather than accepting the seeming certainty of the advertising message, now we begin to doubt and question the trustworthiness of the claims made. In the 2018 Edelman Trust Barometer survey of some 33,000 respondents in 28 markets, 42 per cent of people said they didn't know which companies or brands to trust. Similarly, trust in business to do the right thing rests at only 52 per cent (43 per cent in the UK, 44 per cent in Germany and 48 per cent in the US). Uncertainty concerning the veracity of what is said is not confined to brands – government leaders, journalists and institutions of all types suffer a creeping scepticism about their claims. This lack of trust means it is ever more important that organisations try and ensure that they act responsibly and consistently in line with the idea of the brand.

## Towards a New Way of Thinking

The challenges outlined above suggest we need a new way of thinking about brand management. It is not exactly the case that past practices are redundant, as many are still relevant to the current context, such as the need to manage the interfaces between the organisation and its stakeholders.[61] However, there is a requirement to recognise that even interfaces (for example, the product, visual identity, in-store experience), while controlled to a large degree by managers, can be read in a wide variety of different ways and that the interactivity of networks and the permeability of the organisation necessitates a change in the models we use. One of the key issues here is 'Who owns the brand?' Conventional wisdom, as presented in marketing and brand management texts, says the organisation. And in one sense this is true. An organisation can sell, terminate and re-design its brand. However, the organisation cannot own the outcome. That is the province of the consumer. Brands only have value because consumers buy and use them. So we might ask whether in fact consumers own the brand. This is quite a popular idea because it shifts the perspective of how we think about brands towards consumers. It encourages companies to be less narcissistic and more aware of how they create value. Yet what the consumer owns is not the brand itself, but rather the experience of purchase and use. This is why Vargo and Lusch argued that we should see service as the fundamental basis of exchange, because it is the performance of the brand that creates value.[62]

In other words, it becomes apparent that the brand is neither owned by the organisation nor by the consumer, but rather it is created through the interactions and negotiations made continually between the organisation and its stakeholders and between stakeholders. This is something the German philosopher Martin Heidegger referred to as our 'being-in-the-world'. He argues that we do not live in a body, which then reaches out, but rather we are already involved and connected. We do not see an object as if we recently arrived from another planet, but rather we already have expectations, experiences and prejudices: 'when something within-the-world is encountered as such, the thing in question already has an involvement which is disclosed in our understanding of the world, and this involvement is one that gets laid out by the interpretation.'[63] This view of a connected individual and an organisation suggests we should not see two separate entities, but rather a space where the two fuse. More than this: once we expand the relationship from a simple dyad between the brand and the individual, we can begin to see a network of evolving connections and relationships. Consumers can be contributors, commentators, innovators and investors. They will often be employees themselves and also have relationships directly with users, intermediaries and employees in other organisations. In this context the brand is always in a state of 'becoming', as a spectrum of different meanings emerge from interactions. The implication of this is that while 'co-creation' can be used to describe a set of specific practices, in a broader sense it is the very essence of what a brand is, in a networked world.[64]

However, as the researchers Baumgarth and Kristal argue in their following contribution, the idea of brand co-creation is not completely new but rather builds on three theoretical roots or pillars of brand co-creation. Those will be described in the following boxed section.

## The three theoretical pillars of brand co-creation

*Authors: Carsten Baumgarth & Samuel Kristal*

### The paradigm of brand co-creation

The term brand co-creation describes a new paradigm in brand management that takes a stakeholder-oriented perspective on the brand building process.[65] It challenges the traditional perspective of brands as markers of identification and as a means of product differentiation.[66] Instead, co-creation argues for a new logic that views the brand and its construction as a social process consisting of multiple networked interactions between the company (who legally owns the brand) and various stakeholders.[67] In such a view, a brand becomes a continuously evolving vision that unites various stakeholders in the pursuit of a common cause and turns them into partners instead of targets.[68]

For the last 15 to 20 years, there has been a clear distinction in brand research between internal identity creation and external perceptions of brand image.[69] While both aim to capture a holistic view of the brand, they are traditional organisation-centric ideas of consumer behaviour[70] which have the potential to lead to dissonance between how managers perceive consumers' relationships with a brand and the reality of how consumers live, build and use brands.[71] Moving away from the organisation-centric idea, co-creation suggests that consumers and stakeholders are active brand co-authors of brand identity and carriers of brand meaning.[72] The fluid, flexible and organic nature of a brand means its identity can be influenced or even deflected in unintended directions by external stakeholders, as meaning is often built outside corporate walls where stakeholders interact and negotiate with each other on their own terms.[73] However, the idea of brand co-creation is not completely new. Rather, we can identify three theoretical roots or pillars of brand co-creation.[74]

### The three pillars of brand co-creation

Drawing upon publications that discuss the crucial areas for useful research into co-creation,[75] we have identified three thematic clusters and integrated them into a 'three-pillar' model of brand co-creation (see Figure 2.1). The pillars are (1) innovation management, (2) service marketing and service-dominant logic (SDL) and (3) consumer behaviour – the latter comprises the sub-topics of consumer culture theory (CCT), brand communities and user-generated content.

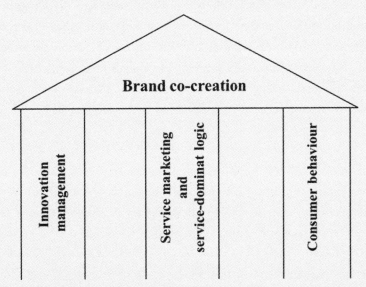

Figure 2.1 The three theoretical pillars of brand co-creation (adapted from: Baumgarth and Kristal 2015, p.16)

## (1) Innovation management

The traditional view of internally generated innovation and passive external stakeholders has increasingly been challenged by academics and practitioners as the benefit of collaborating with stakeholders in the development of innovative products and services has been recognised. Two streams within the field of innovation management in particular are regarded as forerunners of the co-creation paradigm. One of these is user-driven innovations in new product development.[76] The concept of lead user[77] and the toolkit approach[78] are two examples of this research stream. The second stream deals with open innovation processes.[79]

## (2) Service marketing and Service-Dominant Logic (SDL)

Another major precursor of current brand co-creation thinking can be found in the increasing importance of services and the shift from a goods-dominant to a service-dominant logic (SDL).[80] Central to service-dominant logic is the proposition relating to co-creation, which emphasises the active involvement and interaction of customers and other stakeholders. The argument is that companies can only offer 'value propositions', not value directly. The customer then co-creates value through value in use. This contradicts the classical idea of value being embedded in the product.

## (3) Consumer behaviour

This rather general pillar of brand co-creation in fact embraces three independent streams of research and theoretical perspectives. They are consolidated under one pillar because all three relate predominantly to consumer behaviour.

### Consumer culture theory (CCT)

Like SDL, consumer culture theory (CCT) is not a closed concept but refers to a family of theoretical perspectives on the dynamic relationships between consumer actions, the marketplace and cultural meanings.[81] Its fundamental argument is that meanings attached to products and services are negotiated and co-created between consumers, the company and their cultural environment, at various levels of market interaction. Consumer culture theory is also the theoretical foundation of the so-called cultural branding approach.[82]

### Brand communities

Researchers into brand communities were among the first to argue that a brand and its meaning is co-created through interactive and dynamic relations and negotiations.[83] Specifically, symbolic interpretations of brand-related information, plus personal narratives based on both personal and impersonal experiences with a brand, make a key contribution to co-created branding.

### User-generated content

The emergence and rise of the Internet and digital technologies have upset the symmetry of the provision and control of information, which for many years worked in favour of marketing managers.[84] Consumers have not only become increasingly empowered to interrelate with other consumers and with brands, but also to generate and share their own content, which has in turn led to a more participative approach to branding.[85]

### Final thoughts

It has been argued that branding is changing from an organisation-centric approach to a highly participative process between the organisation, consumers and other stakeholders. The meaning of the brand is no longer defined by a brand strategist in a rigid way, but by a variety of brand co-creators who conceptualise and even re-conceptualise negotiated brand meanings. A more fluid and open approach to brand building carries the risk that the brand is pushed in unintended directions and that brand owners are no longer able to protect and control their brands.[86] The consequence is that heightened participation externally fosters a need for participation internally. Brand managers can still have a strong influence on branding if they choose to become active participants in the process and are willing to create the conditions under which stakeholders can help in developing the brand.[87] Brand co-creation means that brand managers are still responsible for setting a clear direction. Instead of pre-defining a rigid brand identity, however, they need to define a proposition that offers a sense of direction but at the same time allows for reinterpretations.[88]

A consequence of a co-creational view of the brand is the collapse of the organisational boundary that separates the inside from the outside and the emergence of a culture that 'cannot be confined within the bounds of the organisation.'[89] The typical organisational chart has a hard border between the two: managers and employees with contracts on one side and consumers, investors, influencers, media and communities on the other. This again reflects an old way of thinking. In a co-creation perspective the boundary is permeable. In delivering a product or service, there is a whole network of suppliers, buyers and partners who contribute to the brand. Similarly, those working for an organisation come in many different hues – from the employed to contractors to advisors to volunteers. Interested outsiders take part in competitions to tackle organisational challenges promoted through such sites as the crowdsourcing platform Innocentive; small start-ups embrace speed-dating days with large organisations, such as financial software provider Intuit; and inventive companies contribute their skills and expertise to organisations that practice open innovation, such as the semiconductor company Intel. Some organisations, such as Mozilla – which created the email application Thunderbird and the web-browser Firefox – not only rely on their employees, but on more than 10,000 volunteers from around the world, who code, educate and promote, even while working for other organisations. Indeed, it is not employment that defines who should lead at Mozilla, but competence. It is often volunteers who oversee projects.

Similarly, as we will see in this book, consumers and other stakeholders participate in company sponsored co-creation communities and events, where outsiders and insiders mingle and create together on a more equal basis. Rather than imagining what consumers and suppliers might want, companies can ask them directly and provide the opportunity for outsiders to contribute solutions. In turn, this strengthens the bonds between employees and stakeholders. People who participate in online co-creation communities have more positive attitudes towards the brand and feel closer to it,[90] while managers and employees acquire deeper insight and connectivity to the value they create in the lives of others.[91] As the researchers Cova and Dalli argue: 'The more the customer is involved in the process of service production and delivery, the greater the perceived value and satisfaction…consumers (as individuals and as a group of interacting subjects) become partial employees and employees become partial consumers.'[92]

The model presented in Figure 2.2 indicates that the organisation has a permeable boundary such that there can be an ebb and flow of people and ideas. Each individual has their own experience of the brand, but there will tend to be clusters around common attributes resulting from coherence in the brand messaging. This is something the brand organisation tries to influence through the way it develops, presents and interacts with all the different stakeholders. And if it is receptive and open, it will learn from the process of interacting with others and allow them to enhance the brand. This is a process of discovery and self-discovery. As Heidegger reminds us, we can only

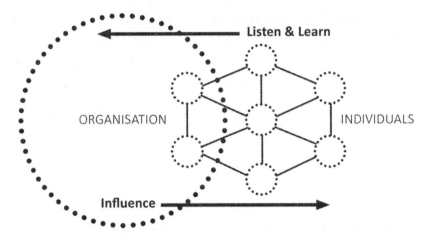

Figure 2.2 How organisations and individuals interact

know ourselves through our being with others.[93] Finally, we should note that contrary to some notions that the idea of a brand is fixed, from a co-creation perspective, the brand is in a continual state of movement.

## Co-creation in Brand Management: Benefits and Challenges

*Author: Stefan Markovic*

Since the early 2000s, co-creation has become more widely recognised in the field of brand management,[94] and researchers have investigated it in relation to various brand aspects including identity,[95] brand experience,[96] brand knowledge,[97] brand meaning,[98] and brand offerings (i.e. products and/or services).[99] However, regardless of which aspect of the brand is being co-created, the practice of co-creation is based on a common underlying mechanism: brand-stakeholder interactions. What this means is that without two-way interactions between the brand and at least one of its stakeholders (e.g. customers, suppliers, competitors, distributors, research institutions, government), we cannot speak about co-creation. From the brand management perspective, co-creation can be defined as an active, dynamic and social process based on interactions between the brand and its stakeholders to generate relevant brand-related innovations in terms of identity, experience, knowledge, meaning, offerings and other brand aspects.

The brand-stakeholder interactions on which the practice of co-creation is based are especially prominent in brand communities, both online (in forums and other social media) and offline (in workshops and meetings).[100] All brand communities share the characteristics of common consciousness, rituals, traditions and a sense of moral responsibility.[101] However, the rapid evolution of information technologies has given an emphasis to online brand communities which exceeds that of offline, because the former are not geographically bounded,[102] meaning that stakeholders around the world can participate in co-creation.[103] Thus, online brand communities enable a greater interconnectivity, in terms of both scope and intensity, among the participating stakeholders and between the brand and the participating stakeholders.[104]

One result of the active involvement of stakeholders in brand communities is that managers have lost a significant degree of power and control over their brands.[105] In such a scenario, managers cannot impose their views and strategies,[106] but rather have to try to support, foster and guide stakeholder discussions in brand communities.[107] Thus, managers should assume the role of 'network orchestrators'.[108] This calls into question various classic management assumptions,[109] challenges traditional power cultures,[110] and opens the door to receptive and participatory organisational cultures and to humble, inclusive and empathic leadership styles.[111] Now, managers can create an environment in which a wide set of stakeholders can contribute their insights, ideas and knowledge to the co-creation of different brand aspects. It is interesting to note here that customers can be even more knowledgeable about different brand aspects (e.g. brand offerings) than employees themselves:[112] there is a category of 'lead users' that refers to individuals who are highly knowledgeable and innovative.[113]

Customers, and especially lead users, are not passive recipients of the brand's innovations, but have the skills and expertise that permit them to undertake an active role in co-creation.[114] Every day, they are more informed, networked and empowered, and increasingly, there is the opportunity for them to participate in every stage of the co-creation process,[115] from idea generation to implementation.[116] Thus, instead of trying to figure out what customers may want by analysing market research data, brands should take advantage of the possibility to actively and directly involve them in co-creation.[117] This has potential benefits for both parties – customers and brands.

On the one hand, by engaging in co-creation, customers can obtain self-development, social, hedonic and financial benefits.[118] Interacting with the brand and with other customers with similar interests can be a stimulating experience.[119] Through such interaction, customers usually feel that they grow as individuals and develop new insight and understanding.[120] While some customers are concerned with financial rewards for their participation in co-creation, most are not.[121] Instead, most participating customers are intrinsically motivated and maintain their interest and commitment throughout the whole co-creation process.[122]

On the other hand, by embracing co-creation, brands can achieve a variety of organisational benefits, including better insights, more relevant ideas, a stronger feeling of connectivity with their customers, cost efficiencies, speed to market, reduced risk and competitive advantage.[123] Given these potential benefits from co-creation, a great number of specialised consultancies have been established, various brands have started to use customer immersion labs and many research agencies are offering co-creative approaches.[124]

However, despite all these potential benefits, co-creation can also generate some challenges for the involved parties. For example, who owns the intellectual property rights of the co-created outputs? Where does responsibility lie if the co-creation process goes wrong? What is the proper division of labour between the brand and participating customers? Can we talk of 'working customers' or is co-creation just free/cheap labour? What reward systems are equitable and relevant? What are the limits of involving vulnerable stakeholders (e.g., children)? Should the brand's and the participating stakeholders' expectations on co-creation be fully aligned?

Overall, given that co-creation is based on brand-stakeholder interactions, and given that these interactions can generate some challenges, brands should not engage in co-creation without taking into consideration certain universal moral standards. There are six universal moral standards that are relevant in the context of co-creation.[125]

- *Trustworthiness.* A co-creation process is trustworthy when the involved parties are honest and clear about their intentions, align their expectations, keep their promises and show commitment to the process.
- *Respect.* A co-creation process is respectful when it complies with human rights, when participants are not discriminated against, abused or undermined (e.g., used as free/cheap labour) and

when specific actions are taken to protect vulnerable stakeholders (e.g., children).

- *Responsibility.* A co-creation process is responsible when the involved parties are accountable for their actions, comply with their obligations and existing regulations, and support good practices and causes.
- *Fairness.* A co-creation process is fair when all participants are treated equitably and when the credits for successful outcomes (e.g., intellectual property rights) and the responsibilities for the unsuccessful outputs (e.g., costs) are properly distributed.
- *Caring.* A co-creation process is caring when the involved parties avoid causing unnecessary harm, make active efforts to help each other during the process and are concerned about each other's well-being.
- *Citizenship.* A co-creation process shows good citizenship when the involved parties do not only obey rules and laws, but are also concerned about the social and environmental implications of their actions.

## The Philosophy of Co-Creation

We would argue that co-creation is not a choice for organisations. Rather, it is the reality of how brands are connected to all their different stakeholders through networks of interest. However, organisations have the choice to embrace the idea and to take advantage of the opportunities afforded by co-creation or to reject it and adopt a more closed approach that relies on the vision of insiders. As Stefan Markovic argues, co-creation is effective because it delivers benefits to participants in the form of intrinsic and extrinsic rewards, and to organisations in terms of insights and ideas that help to build the brand. In this section we introduce four connected principles that underpin the philosophy of co-creation and enable organisations to get closer to their stakeholders.

## A focus on people

When we start looking at data, we stop seeing people. We use research to guide our judgements and forget about the people behind the numbers. However, we should remember that research data is abstract. It is not reality, only a reflection of it. Co-creation as a way of thinking tries to put the emphasis back on the human. It argues that we should not objectify consumers and other stakeholders, but instead adopt processes that encourage participation and close the gap between organisations and people.[126] Co-creation tries to create environments where people can feel free to express themselves and use their creativity. Co-creation works to encourage a feeling of equality and a willingness to share with others. This last point stresses the importance of a sense of inclusion – of overcoming the organisational tendency to be cynical about outsiders. A strong culture can encourage a sense of identification that cements the organisation together and encourages benevolent behaviour towards its members. Yet such a culture can also be negative, creating too much cohesion and resistance to the ideas of outsiders (especially if they come from a very different culture or background).[127] Co-creative organisations recognise the value of diversity and the value of different perspectives. They believe that involving people has the potential to generate previously unthought ideas.

Take LEGO as an example. It connects with others through the online communities that it creates, listening to fan-based communities, going to live events and using its brand ambassador programme. However, the success of LEGO is not simply down to these practices, but because it is receptive to the input of others. LEGO managers believe that there is valuable knowledge and expertise outside of the organisation that can inspire and legitimise the brand. This is an interesting counterpoint to LEGO as it was back in the early 2000s, when the culture was to a large extent closed to the outside world. The occasion that stimulated a re-think was the launch of LEGO Mindstorms – a high-priced set which provided the opportunity for customers to program the things they made. LEGO's assumption was that the product would appeal to teenagers, but there was another important audience that came in the form of technologically literate adults, who bought the product, hacked the software code and shared it online. Not surprisingly, LEGO were upset by this use of their intellectual property and the company threatened legal action. However, managers realised that it was somehow wrong to sue your own customers. For a while they did nothing, until they realised that there was an opportunity to learn from their customers and to involve them in new product development. First, they gave them the right to hack the software and then when it came to designing the second version of Mindstorms – NXT – the hackers were invited to Denmark to help develop the product. This was the catalyst for a shift in thinking and a recognition that openness could fuel the development of the brand.

## Being Open

One core principle of building brands is consistency. The rationale behind this is that inconsistent messages and actions lead to stakeholder confusion and a dilution of brand equity. If a brand says many different things, it becomes harder to pinpoint what it believes in. In the past, organisations went to great lengths to create processes, structures and manuals to help deliver consistency. However, in a context where brands are part of multi-valenced networks involving a great diversity of internal and external stakeholders, consistency is far harder to achieve. Now brand building requires organisations to both have a well-defined identity based on a pellucid statement of values that employees understand and internalise and the confidence to let go and allow others to re-interpret it. The philosopher Manuel DeLanda – referencing the work of Gilles Delueze and Félix Guattari – argues that you need structure if you are going to experiment with being open; find possible lines of flight; challenge linear ideas of causality. He suggests that 'Today our theories are beginning to incorporate nonlinear elements, and we are starting to think of heterogeneity as something valuable, not as an obstacle to unification.'[128]

LEGO illustrates the practice of a well-defined identity allied to openness. Customers have the opportunity to create new LEGO product proposals and submit them for approbation (by voting) by other customers at LEGO Ideas; independent artists and sculptors create art and installations made of LEGO; stop frame animators show how to execute short movies of LEGO characters and independent companies tailor-make LEGO mini-figures to order. These extensions of the brand – with the exception of LEGO Ideas – all run independently of LEGO. The company recognises that it is impossible to control the expression of the brand and that those who take the product and use it in new ways actually enrich brand meaning. This is not without risk, of course. People can take the brand and subvert it. And as Bal et al. observe in their study of crowdsourcing and brand control, weak brands can suffer from negative commentary.[129] However, LEGO has tried to ameliorate the threat by balancing openness with clarity. One of the new management's decisions in the 2000s was to re-visit the articulation of its brand (you'll read more about this in Chapter 4). The company, which had meandered away from its focus on the brick and a system for play, re-asserted its commitment to its heritage and developed a clear set of values to guide decision-making. This structure gave the company an insight into the areas where it needed to manage the brand and into where it needed to let go.

While clearly the practice of co-creation requires managers who believe in people and in being open, it also necessitates the mechanisms to enable participation. The tendency here is to immediately think of online interactions such as social media conversations and brand communities, but it is also necessary to consider the everyday experiences of visiting shops, the discussions over our latest purchase and the possibility of taking part in organisation sponsored events – whether they be primarily social occasions or opportunities for activism or workshops designed to evaluate or innovate. The initiators of these interactions can either be the organisation or its stakeholders, but it behoves the organisation to be an appropriate participant and to help ensure that the outcomes are valuable for all. As Venkat Ramaswamy and Kericam Ozcan point out, 'perspectives of both sides on creating brand value together must be addressed.'[130] From the organisational side the key opportunity is to facilitate learning, to uncover the needs and desires of stakeholders and to ensure the lessons are properly shared inside the organisation. It can also, depending on the ambition of the interaction, help to create innovative ideas. For the stakeholder – as we shall see in more detail later – the opportunity is concerned with learning, making a contribution and socialising.

When a community is initiated by stakeholders it tends to be based on a specific shared enthusiasm. Here, organisations can be listeners and supporters, but they have to remember that the community is not theirs to direct or control. The way interactions are managed must be at the discretion of the community members. When organisations host online brand communities, whether as permanent sounding-boards or for the purpose of a specific project, they can be more directive, but without a degree of freedom, participants can easily become demotivated. It is one thing to create the place to participate, but it is another to manage it with sufficient empathy for it to be productive.

## Building Trust
Whether individuals choose to engage with a brand depends on their interest – whether it is important to them – and whether there is trust between the brand and its stakeholders. As we saw in the Edelman study, trust can be in short supply. The point to emphasise here is that trust is not automatic. Rather, it is something that organisations need to earn by creating an environment in which people feel confident to express themselves and by demonstrating a willingness to learn from stakeholders and engage with them on a more equal basis. In an earlier study we did, based on the participation of 236 consumers in an online

community for 52 days, we learned that trust is the lubricant of social interaction and creativity – conversations grow and develop because of the emergence of trust.[131] This means you can't expect instant creativity or ask complex questions at the outset, but rather that you have to work together to build a safe environment. In the context of an online community, trust needs active facilitation, an appropriate level of freedom and regular feedback. In a study of some 246 communities, comprising more than 86,000 members, participation and engagement is determined by size (small is better) and being from the same place or using the same language (commonality is good). Otherwise the common attributes are: 'Exclusivity, intimacy, privacy, the opportunity to forge relationships with other members and with the sponsoring brand, high-touch facilitation, and the knowledge that one's voice is being heard.'[132]

We'll come back to the challenges of co-creation later, but for now, it's worth noting what undermines trust, which is when organisations fail to provide a proper response to the input they receive. When people give significantly of their time and their knowledge in an online community or in a workshop with managers, the trust they place in the organisation is that their contributions will be heard and noted. If the organisation only offers silence in return, then trust – and participation – will diminish.

## Becoming Humble

Managers are no longer the brand custodians they once were. Instead, they need to work with stakeholders and to encourage participation from within and without. This means less telling and more listening; less directing and more sharing. It also implies that co-creation must go beyond marketing and communications. Given the opportunity for interaction between stakeholders, all organisational members have to adopt a co-creation mindset so that it becomes an organisation-wide way of thinking and acting. The change here is that the organisation has to focus on its stakeholders and to help their self-development as well as its own. In a study conducted by Sylvia Von Wallpach, Andrea Hemetsberger and Peter Espersen, based on 29 in-depth interviews with LEGO AFOLs, curators, employees and managers (some of whom fell into more than one category), they looked at the way individual identities, and those of the brand, are constructed through the performance of language and practices. The study showed that the interviewees socially interact both online and offline in the process of enacting their identities. One of the conclusions that von Wallpach et al. came to is that managers should support the playful, creative and social qualities of interactions. As they put it: 'Encouraging brand performativity by creating and managing brands that engage stakeholders and speak to their identity development needs and by providing technology and places to do so are important managerial tasks for sustaining powerful performative brands.'[133] In practical terms this means directing the brand to a way of working which involves learning from, and with, others and accepting that internal experts may not always know best.

## Summary

This chapter has been designed to introduce you to a co-creation perspective on brand management. Co-creation is the reality of how brand meaning is created. A brand may make an offer, but it is the way consumers and other stakeholders use the brand and share their experiences online, and in conversation, that defines the meaning for each individual. This means seeing brands in a different way from that presented in many brand books. Instead of imagining a brand as something the organisation owns and communicates about, you have to shift slightly and look at a brand as a connected network of interests. In this picture, the organisation influences the network, but the members of the network also influence each other and the organisation. It's not as neat as a linear model. It's messy. But it better reflects the reality of brand building.

## Reflections/questions

1) Think of a brand that truly focusses on people. It could be a local shop, a favourite hotel or an international brand. What does it do that gives you the impression that it is focussed on people? And in one sentence, how does that make you feel?
2) Which brands do you know that give you an opportunity to participate in their development? How do they do that (e.g. by online poll, brand community/panel, informal discussion)?
3) Are there any brands that you especially trust? What does it take for you to trust a brand? And are there any brands/organisations that you wouldn't trust?

## We recommend the following reading to expand your learning experience:

Ind, N. & Coates, N. (2013). 'The meanings of co-creation', *European Business Review*, *25*(1), 86–95.

# CHAPTER THREE

# Why individuals and organisations co-create

## In this chapter ...

Co-creation can deliver benefits for both organisations and individuals. From the organisational perspective, the opportunity exists for companies to connect to people and to explore together with them how their brands can be more relevant and desirable. This requires a willingness to open up the organisation and encourage participation. From the individual perspective, the opportunity is there to engage with brands and to influence their development. Here, we stress the importance of the 'co' (which means 'together, with') and suggest that it is in the act of participation with a brand that new meaning is created. Co-creation in this sense is rooted in a relationship more than a transaction. Indeed, co-creation does not require the act of consumption – people are quite capable of sharing their views on brands and helping to create new ideas without consuming.

This chapter poses two questions. First, why do individuals choose to participate? Second, why do some companies choose to encourage the involvement of stakeholders in brand development? Before we launch into the answers, pause and reflect on these questions – what would be your initial response?

In this chapter, we will concentrate on company-initiated co-creation. This story involves both online communities and events, and will feature a co-creation event with a story about the restaurant and leisure brand Hakkasan. It will also use research we have conducted into the motivations of companies and individuals to challenge some existing convictions about motivations and to provide an insight into the ways in which value is co-created.

## Learning Objectives

After reading this chapter you should

- understand that the practice of co-creation should create value for both the individual participants and the brand;
- appreciate that most people are motivated to co-create by intrinsic factors connected to self-expression, making a contribution and socialisation (extrinsics largely play a symbolic role);
- understand that organisations see co-creation in different ways, ranging from a market research tool (albeit one that offers depth) to a strategic innovation method;
- realise that managers should view co-creation as a form of gift exchange and structure the process accordingly.

## Why do individuals participate in co-creation?

In answering this question, we first have to understand the different methods used in co-creation practice. Each of the methods employs a different process, but what makes them co-creative is that they involve interaction between participating individuals and between individuals and the brand. In other words, insights develop and meaning emerges because of multiple interactions. The first type of co-creation is similar to the example of LEGO online fan groups mentioned in the previous chapter. These naturally occurring communities are built on the appeal of sharing ideas and experiences with like-minded others. Naturally occurring communities, which can include everything from car brands to sports clubs to rock bands, are largely self-organising and require committed evangelists to establish and run them. Here, the motivations are to do with socialisation and meaning-making – what the researchers Muniz and O'Guinn describe as the most important element of community: consciousness of mind. In other words, the sense of being connected both to the brand and to each other.[134] As these communities are owned by their members, organisations can listen to them, learn from them and support them, but they cannot direct them. They can, however, become more involved with these communities by inviting members to take part in projects, as Alfa Romeo has done with their Alfisti fan community, and as Fiat has done with the development of the Fiat Mio.[135] But fans, while highly motivated, are not always typical consumers and do not necessarily make for the best co-creators.

A second type of co-creation practice involves the use of open challenges or competitions, in which the organisation is more explicitly involved in directing the process by inviting outsiders to develop new concepts by asking them to solve a problem. Orange Telecom has established a community called 'Imagine with Orange', where would-be entrepreneurs can submit ideas and discuss the contributions of others. Orange then works with those entrepreneurs whose ideas are selected to build them into business concepts. The motivations to participate here are concerned with self-expression, peer recognition and economic reward. Nicolas Bry, a senior VP at Orange Innovation Marketing Technology and the Founder and Leader of Imagine with Orange, says: 'We say that the community is shaping the innovation because it directs as well the most relevant ideas.'

The third type of co-creation practice is company-initiated, either in the form of online communities (more than 60 per cent of the biggest brands in the world have these) or physical events, such as workshops. Here, the company defines a task and invites selected participants to take part. Generally, these type of communities and events are not open to the public, but are enclosed spaces where managers and individuals work together. The typical size of online communities is in the range of 300 to 500 people – enough to generate insightful discussions while still maintaining a sense of community. Events can range from a few to up to 100 people. Company-initiated endeavour is a managed process, and because of its more explicit commercial orientation, you might imagine that the prime driver for participants would be economic reward. This is certainly what managers think, but as you will see, this is not the case.

Managers tend to assume that if you want individuals to participate in a company-initiated event or online community, then it comes down to money. This assumption derives from two beliefs. First, managers link this form of co-creation with their experience of traditional market research techniques, such as focus groups and in-depth interviews, where the interactions are transactional. For example, in a focus group, people are asked to spend an hour or so together with a moderator and a room full of strangers sharing their opinions on an issue that has been decided upon in advance. Afterwards, people are paid for their attendance and sent on their way. The organisation sponsoring the research has no obligation to share the findings of the research or to consult further – indeed to do so would impair the objectivity of the process.[136] Second, managers tend to believe in the power of money to incentivise. As Stanford Professor Chip Heath observed in four different studies, people consistently suffer from extrinsic incentives bias, in that they believe others are more motivated by extrinsic factors than they are themselves.[137] Managers are too easily swayed to use money and other extrinsic incentives to engage people and to solve problems – even though what matters more than money is a fair process rooted in engagement, explanation and expectation clarity.[138]

This assumption about the importance of extrinsics is not surprising, given the historical focus on rewarding people for their productivity and the seeming importance of pay when it comes to executive salaries and labour negotiations. The belief is that money determines behaviour. Indeed, a transaction-based approach works when you ask little of people. If you want consumers to tell you whether they prefer advertising campaign A over campaign B in a focus group, or have them complete a questionnaire, you don't really need engagement. If the task is basic then people think, I will exchange my time for a specific reward. The difference with co-creation processes is that it asks for more. It asks for knowledge and creativity. It asks for commitment. And it asks for time – people could be involved for several months in an online community. Or work for several weeks as ethnographic researchers. Or take part in an intense two-day workshop with managers. In these contexts, a transactional approach is insufficient. It requires a relationship.

The use of the word 'relationship' in the context of branding is fraught with danger. People clearly do have an emotional connection to brands and in some cases a strong desire – just observe the passion of sneaker-heads on YouTube and shoppers desperate for H&M x Balmain.[139] Yet marketers easily over-egg the 'relationship' a brand has with its customers.[140] It is hardly a relationship when you see an advertisement for Pepsi-Cola and you buy and drink the product, even if there is some residual emotion derived from communications and past experience. Relationships require commitment and trust.[141] They are built on listening and two-way communication. To be successful, relationships also need sincerity. In sum, both sides in a relationship should treat each other for what they are rather than what they might get out of it. This is similar to the argument of Immanuel Kant when he writes that every human being 'exists as an end in itself, *not merely as a means* to be used by this or that will at its discretion.'[142] Yet marketers continue to advocate this idea of relationships by lumping individuals into segments to be communicated at and monetised. The orientation often originates from a sense of utility rather than from a respect for others.

## Looking at Motivations

The linguist and philosopher Noam Chomsky argued that any human being 'is not only capable of, but is insistent upon doing productive, creative work, if given the opportunity to do so.'[143] Consumers and other stakeholders do want the stimulation of doing productive, creative work in online communities and offline workshops. The research of Edward Deci – a Psychology professor – and Richard Ryan provides evidence for this. Deci and Ryan conducted a series of studies during the 1970s, 80s and 90s that explored the relationship between intrinsic and extrinsic motivations. Core to their argument was what they called Cognitive Evaluation Theory,[144] which was based on the idea that people have innate psychological needs for competence and autonomy and that these underpin intrinsic motivation. The implication of the theory is that rewards will affect people based on how it alters their perceptions of self-determination and competence. As well as their own research, they conducted a meta-analysis of 128 studies into the effects of extrinsic or tangible rewards on intrinsic motivation.[145] The analysis provides some interesting insights:

- verbal rewards (i.e. positive feedback) can have an enhancing effect on intrinsic motivation – but only when they are unexpected. When they are expected, they do not provide the affirmation of competence that people seek, but rather seem to be an attempt to control behaviour;
- deadlines and imposed goals tend to undermine intrinsic motivation, whereas the provision of choice and the acknowledgement of feelings improve it. This finding reflects a desire for autonomy and a rejection of control;
- intrinsic motivation 'energises and sustains activities' by delivering spontaneous satisfaction when people are free to choose what they do. It is expressed in such activities as play, exploration and challenge seeking that people often do for no extrinsic reward and reflects the desire for autonomy;
- tangible rewards – even when offered as indicators of good performance – can typically decrease intrinsic motivation for interesting activities;
- while rewards can control behaviour, the primary negative effect is that they undermine people taking responsibility for themselves;
- context matters: the relevance of different intrinsic and extrinsic rewards depends on the activity, the participants and the culture.

Other studies affirm these points about the seemingly strange nature of motivations and rewards. For example, Frey and Götte found in a study of volunteering, which is dominated by intrinsic motivation, that as soon as you introduce monetary rewards it reduces people's desire to do voluntary work.[146] Similarly, in a study of a children's day-care centre, Gneezy and Rustichini found that parents would sometimes arrive late to collect their children, which meant a teacher would have to stay behind. When the researchers introduced a fine on late-arriving parents, one might have expected that parents would act to avoid the fine, but the opposite happened. Late arrivals went up significantly.[147] Both of these studies emphasise the point made by Deci: intrinsic motivation drives a set of behaviours based on the desire for autonomy and that the introduction of extrinsics tends to make things transactional. We reduce the amount of time we give to volunteering if it becomes paid and we leave children at a day-care centre when we move from a relationship to a transaction.

When it comes to the online communities that typify a large portion of the practice of co-creation we see much the same evidence. Johann Füller, drawing on Deci and Ryan's work on self-determination, conducted a research study involving 727 people that found four differently motivated groups that engage in virtual co-creation:[148]

- reward-oriented consumers: highly motivated; have an interest in innovation but underlying this is a desire for monetary rewards;
- need-driven consumers: participate because they are dissatisfied with existing solutions on the market;
- curiosity-driven consumers: curious to learn;
- intrinsically interested consumers: score on every motivational aspect connected to innovation and have low expectations of monetary rewards.

What is interesting about these different groups is that, with the exception of the reward-oriented consumers, monetary rewards are not significant. It is the intrinsic rewards connected to feedback and recognition that drive behaviour. The reward-oriented group does show a high level of interest in activities, but only as long as the monetary incentive is there. It also seems to be the case that the quality of material this group produces may not be as high as it is in other fields of research, because the subjects are motivated to deliver the quantity of contributions that generate the rewards, rather than something more meaningful. Füller observes that 'intrinsically interested consumers not only show the highest motivation, but also are highly qualified due to their knowledgeable and creative personality. In other words, consumers who are more creative (and, as a consequence, are more qualified for co-creation activities) are also more interested in co-creation projects.'[149] The final point that Füller makes, referencing a study of 216 innovation and marketing managers, echoes the challenge of incentives bias. These managers believe consumers' motivations come down primarily to offers and financial compensation. Intrinsic motivation and 'fun factor' are rated lowest. In other words, the exact opposite of what does actually motivate most consumers.

## The Gift of Co-creation

Inherent to the ideas of Deci and Ryan, Füller and others is that people want to commit themselves to a purpose; to do something they consider meaningful, to contribute to a brand or cause that they have some affinity with, and to connect with others. It is these intrinsic motivations that drive the quest for fulfilment in co-creation. However, the focus on intrinsic motivation does not fit so well with the principle of market exchange upon which branding sits. In a market exchange economy people sell their services for an agreed price that meets both their individual needs for an extrinsic reward and the needs of the organisation for relevant insight and ideas – which is exactly how traditional market research functions. Yet with co-creation, where intrinsics dominate, we need to move away from a market exchange mindset to one based on the gift. Here, we can draw on the highly influential work of the French ethnologist Marcel Mauss, who in his 1923/1924 essay on The Gift (*Essai sur le don: Forme et raison de l'échange dans les sociétés archaiques*), argued that a gift economy was distinctively different from exchange, and was built on three different obligations: the obligation to give, the obligation to accept and the obligation to reciprocate.[150] Mauss' point was that a gift is never truly free, because it is imbued with the identity of the giver and implies a response. Whether one is making a physical gift or gifting one's time and knowledge, one gives part of oneself in the giving.

The point of difference between a market exchange and a gift exchange is that in the former, the tangible or intangible becomes the property of the acquirer – a company manager buys the insights generated from a focus group based on a contractual arrangement and has no further obligation to the participants. In the latter, the gift comes loaded with the commitment of individuals who still retain an interest in its use – here, a manager has an implicit obligation to respond through a counter-gift. As the gift is 'never completely separated' from the giver and in turn from the receiver's response, it has an almost 'magical' property.[151] Indeed, part of its magic is its power to create a sense of solidarity – this is something that Mauss observed in his study of different ethnic groups who built relationships around gift exchange. Gifting creates momentum and deepens relationships, as gifts flow back and forth. It generates the social capital that ties individuals together.[152] Hyde, in his book, *The Gift*, which builds on Mauss, writes: 'Because of the bonding power of gifts and the detached nature of commodity exchange, gifts have become associated with community and with being obliged to others.'[153]

To put Mauss' ideas into play in co-creation, we have to remember that a) community participants are mostly motivated by intrinsic motivations connected to doing meaningful things and to socialising with others (they want to develop their competence and they want to have a reasonable degree of freedom); and that b) organisations want to generate relevant insights by tapping into people's experience and knowledge. To realise a) and b), participants have to be willing to gift their time both to each other and to the community sponsor, and organisations have to create a space where the exchange can take place and reciprocate by being as open as possible and providing active facilitation with proper feedback, both during and after a process. Of course, theory is one thing and practice another. So, the question is, can Mauss' gift exchange really be applied to the world of co-creation and communities?

## 'Come back for ribs': some thoughts on building a customer value exchange

*Author: Nick Coates*

Picture yourself on a balmy, sun-kissed day in Los Angeles. At a swish hotel, with fabulous views. The shimmering sprawl, familiar from many movies, stretches out as far as the eye can see. Crisp white linen adorns the terrace loungers. Dappled shadows dance on the surface of the pool. And all manner of cocktails, crisp Californian whites and bourbons call suggestively from the award-winning bar.

But at 8.00 a.m. none of this is uppermost in your considerations. You have other, more pressing, questions flooding your mind as you prepare for kick-off. T-minus 60 minutes.

- Will they come?
- Will they play ball?
- Will the CEO turn up?
- Will he be happy?
- Will my opening spiel get a laugh?
- Will they warm to a British accent?

And more prosaically

- Do we have enough Post-its?
- Does my hair look neat?

It's another day, another city, another workshop, another topic, another bunch of workshop participants. The bizarrely up-and-down life of an innovation consultant. Today's fare? Hakkasan (the Michelin-starred Chinese restaurant brand that's now a global group of nightclubs, dayclubs, bars and restaurants).

So why all the questions? Because today we've invited 20 LA high-rollers (from wealthy doctors to fashionistas) to spend the day with us shaping a brand strategy. And despite months of planning, we have no idea whether our carefully crafted invitation, co-creative format, choice of hotel and breakfast with the CEO will do the trick. Yes, we're offering a 'thank you' (money) plus a voucher for the Beverly Hills Hakkasan. But these people don't need the money, and it's rationally not nearly enough to cover their day rate.

Fast forward five hours and, with the session going great guns, full of sparkling conversation and hands-on creativity, we're all feeling much better. Among our guests is a millionaire cosmetics entrepreneur and doyenne of the LA art world. Shortly after lunch she comes up to apologise for having to leave early (a funeral calls). But then she says to us, 'Why not come back to my house tonight? My husband can cook you all special ribs!' So that's what we do. And we end up spending a surreal and wonderful evening in her Beverly Hills mansion.

The point is this: why would a millionaire give up valuable time to show up to what is essentially a market research exercise? And why would anyone show up to anything like this? It can't be the money – and realistically, in most cases, it won't be.

We need to figure this out because, in the Western world at least, we live increasingly in a knowledge and service economy, where insight, intelligence and intuition are power. But also, where consumers have more and more control, and more alternative outlets for their time and skills, and where the gig economy is growing. Here, creativity is a more and more prized asset and, as Clay Shirky has shown, there is a massive, and often untapped, cognitive surplus available for all kinds of personal, commercial and societal gain.[154] If we believe in innovation and brand-building becoming more 'customer-inspired', we need to work out the motivational puzzle.

If we are to talk about commercial co-creation – as opposed to sister disciplines like mass collaboration (Wikipedia) or naturally occurring communities – we cannot start with the assumption of *purely* intrinsic motivation. Yes, there are degrees of interest, and yes, it is our role to make the driest of topics – from toilet tissue to Polyfilla – intriguing. But most people don't get out of bed in the morning to help Aviva (an insurance company) understand retirement. This isn't a hangout for Justin Bieber, or Harley-Davidson fans, although there are lessons from them and their admirers that we can learn. It's different.

On the other hand, economists, with their rational models and focus on extrinsic motivation, tend to largely miss the point. Their view is a blind alley, a dead-end in the engagement labyrinth. Cognitive psychologists, social scientists and anthropologists have long known this to be an incomplete model of human behaviour and motivation. The evidence from behavioural economics and social media activity shows people are willing to devote large chunks of their life to connecting with others.

This brings into focus the question of what we like to think of as a 'value exchange': a theory of engagement based on gift-giving and reciprocity. It is our belief (from 15 years' experience of co-creation, both online and in-person, but also from formal research into co-creator motivation) that we need to avoid the transactional trap (what we like to call 'cash for questions') and concentrate instead on building relationships between participants and between brands and participants.

For us, three rules seem fairly constant:

1) **Intrinsic > Extrinsic**: social glue and relationships matter most
2) **Habit > Hook**: what gets you there doesn't keep you there
3) **Space Counts**: each challenge needs a bespoke space and value exchange design

If we want to move beyond opinion research, or the fake laboratory of the industrialised version of the focus group, and if we want to ask not just for opinion, or feedback, or candour, but also creativity (time, effort, thoughtfulness, ideas), we need to think differently about this value exchange. So, we use two frameworks in sequence to think this through.

The first poses a simple question: based on this challenge, what kind of space do I need? For space, read not just online or offline, but also emotional and interactional.

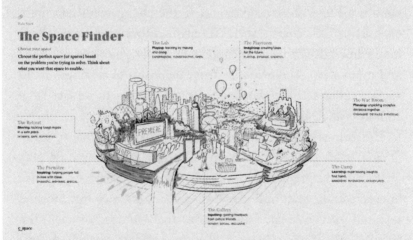

Figure 3.1 The Space Finder (Source: C Space – customer thinking toolkit)

We ask ourselves:

- **What are the qualities required in this space?** What should it enable? Authenticity and vulnerability? Creativity and energy? Diversity and debate? Reflection and thoughtfulness?
- **What concept/analogy can I draw on to brand and shape the space?** Is it a camp (more experiential)? A war room (more strategic and organised)? A gallery (an interactive space for constructive feedback)? Or a playroom (to explore new possibilities without judging)?

This tool helps us define the tone, the physicality, the branding and the type of activities – it creates a clear direction. And in turn, it helps us frame the value exchange necessary to enable the outputs and interactions we need to solve the challenge at hand:

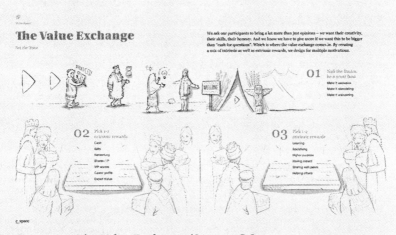

Figure 3.2 The Value Exchange (Source: C Space – customer thinking toolkit)

In the Value Exchange we pose another set of pretty simple human-centric questions:

- Why would they care?
- Do I know what they value?
- What can I ask for?
- What do I have to give?

And then we think through the optimal blend of extrinsic and intrinsic rewards, making sure to dial up the intrinsic side of the equation (since it is easy to overlook).

## So, what does this all mean in practice?

Well, going back to LA, it's clear that some of the intrinsic reward design took us beyond money into VIP (money can't buy) territory. By inviting customers to a one-off 'breakfast with the CEO' we generated a sense of FOMO. By sending a beautifully-designed invite on premium card stock we played to their desire for exclusivity and anchored an expectation of pampering. The co-creative format itself offered both the promise of networking and of impact (if the CEO is listening, I can have an influence). And by leveraging a brand that they cared about, we engaged their sense of purpose, progress and identity. Because we let them wax lyrical about the 'Cod in Champagne Sauce', we fostered a real sense of listening and caring. The money really had very little to do with it, beyond making them feel we weren't taking advantage of them.

But our participants come from all walks of life and all cultures, and the challenges and subject matters vary enormously, from the mundane to the sexy, the one-off to the ongoing, the present and the future, the tangible and the intangible. Here are some of the ways we've found that build the intrinsic set of rewards that help balance the value exchange and create more energy, engagement and ideas.

## Make space together
Routinely in workshops and in the set-up phase of a community we talk openly about what the space should be like, but we also ask for feedback on what people are enjoying, or struggling with. It's also important to make space for reflection and relationship building, not just for content.

## Build a sense of authorship
We are *homo narrans* – storytelling apes. People respond well to the sense of themselves as authors and storytellers. So we make sure that around 20 per cent of questions are member-generated/open-ended. This not only surfaces blind spots which become opportunities (our work with Jaguar Land Rover on making their vehicles more dog-friendly), but also creates a sense of purpose and agency.

## The longing for belonging
One of the most powerful drivers of participation in the exchange is the sense of learning and companionship. Many communities act both as insight and idea generating spaces, but also as a form of self-help. Audiences that are cohesive in terms of identity, such as teachers, people living with cancer or mums are obvious examples where swapping tips, empathising about difficult situations and learning are core drivers. But the best co-creative spaces, even on supposedly dry topics such as finance, can become learning spaces if spiced up with content on trends, the future, and on the best and worst experiences to which one might be exposed.

### Jump first (to build confidence)

When we needed to understand intimate shaving behaviours, our facilitator Zehra created a 'shaving yoga' photo-sharing activity where people could take selfies in shaving poses. Semi-naked. And, of course, no one would have shared if Zehra hadn't gone first. Never ask for something you wouldn't do yourself. Helping people do more than they thought possible makes them realise their own courage and creativity.

### Demonstrate impact

We often hear that people want to shape the brands and the world they engage with. It's a powerful reciprocal gift that goes beyond the sense of speaking into the void of traditional feedback channels. So for ongoing customer-communities, one demand we make of our clients is to show up in person (through a video introduction as a minimum), but also to give feedback on impact in the business through updates and blogs (even 'we've decided to do nothing' is useful feedback).

These are just some of the ingredients for building a more reciprocal value exchange – one that refuses to treat participation as a transaction, precisely because we need more than transactional input. In the 'Age of You', consumers have more choice and power than ever, but they are also bombarded by requests for data. Co-creation, in the flesh and through online communities, provides a safe space for people to give more of themselves and receive more than they expect. This virtuous cycle, which is the fruit of planning and tailoring, constitutes the fuel for a new relationship between brands and their customers.

If you read 'come back for ribs', it should be clear that co-creation is about relationship building, but you might also wonder whether a session with 20 high-rollers in Los Angeles is reflective of the general approach to co-creation. So to show how co-creation works in other contexts, we conducted some research among three large, long-established company-initiated online communities in consumer goods, diabetes and high blood pressure products, and private health (private hospitals, physiotherapy and gym services). Each community had been running for some time and had adopted principles designed to maximise participation and encourage involvement. These involved providing high levels of facilitation, a good degree of freedom for participants to explore issues, emphasis given to intrinsic rewards and minimal use of financial rewards. We invited the community members to take part in a research exercise and 178 participants from the three communities joined. The research showed that:

- most people are dominantly intrinsically motivated: they want to contribute to something they find valuable and interesting, and to have the opportunity to express themselves and to develop their knowledge together with others;
- participants give their time and knowledge and expect to receive in return feedback on what has happened to the ideas developed by the community. The reciprocation is important and when we asked, 'Do you think the people and brand(s) behind the community should tell you how they are using your insights and ideas?', Ninety-seven per cent of people said 'yes';
- there is positive feedback on the balance between moderators, community members and the brand in setting direction and tone. Notably, 97 per cent of participants believe that they have been treated fairly by the moderators, who clearly play a vital role in creating a positive culture and in helping to humanise the community;
- there is a perceived benefit in learning from other members. Our research showed that people used words such as 'reading', 'sharing' and 'learning'.

Overall, even though these communities are for commercial organisations and include customers and non-customers, there is a high level of participation in activities (between 64 per cent and 72 per cent). In the language people use they are also surprisingly passionate (although not uncritical) and it is clear that for some the community comes to play an important role in their lives. They may not start out as fans, but they come to exhibit some of the same attributes as people in fan communities. What becomes important through participation is the sense of connectedness to others and what Deci and Ryan refer to as competence – the sense of self-development that comes from interactions. In this research study, it is notable that it is the sense of community that seems to matter more than its purpose. When we started the study, we anticipated that the most committed participants would come from the diabetes and high blood pressure community, but it turned out that the consumer goods community was equally committed, if not more so.

Co-creation can be a gift for consumers, but it also brings many advantages to organisations. Before we discuss them further, let's take a look at those consumers who are at the forefront of this relatively new form of engagement: millennials.

## Millennials and co-creation in the world of Web 2.0

*Authors: Francisco Guzmán & Eric Kennedy*

What influences consumers' willingness to take part in co-creation? Brand co-creation has exploded in the past few years and has become a critical marketing process through which brands engage with their consumers and, ultimately, build stronger and more long-lasting relationships. The co-creation process has found particularly fertile ground in the digital world, where direct and immediate interaction between brands and consumers is possible. Spearheading this relatively new form of engagement are millennial consumers – digital natives, who have taken to heart the task of shaping the brands they love and that share their values. Millennial consumers are not only a large and powerful voice in the digital world, representing over 30 per cent of the United States population – two fifths of those in work[155] – but are also economically valuable. By 2025 they will have an estimated annual net income worth of over 8 trillion US dollars.[156] Therefore, understanding the attributions millennials make about brands, the nature of the attributions and their outcomes – in terms of co-creation and perceived influence – is critical for allowing social media marketers to strategically position their brands to engage in co-creation.

Within this context, we conducted two research studies among millennial consumers, specifically designed to understand if their perceived ability to influence a brand affected their desire to co-create with it. In the first study, millennial consumers were asked to identify technology brands they felt they were able to influence and not able to influence. In the second study, an experiment was conducted to assess the impact that perceived brand influence has on co-creation, attitudes towards an advertisement and purchase intention. Formally stated, we hypothesised:

H1: Consumers' willingness to engage in co-creation is positively affected by their perceived ability to influence a brand.
H2: Consumers' attributions about a brand are positively affected by their perceived ability to influence a brand.
H3: Consumers' attitude towards the advertisement is positively affected by their perceived ability to influence a brand.
H4: Consumers' purchase intention is positively affected by their perceived ability to influence a brand.

Brand co-creation tends to happen naturally as consumers engage with the brands they love. However, as co-creation is increasingly viewed as an effective marketing process, designed to increase consumer engagement, more firms are making explicit efforts to motivate consumers to participate in co-creation. To differentiate these two different paths to co-creation, we coined the terms 'prompted' and 'non-prompted' co-creation. Prompted co-creation happens when a brand makes a marketing message with an explicit call to consumer action, while non-prompted co-creation implies no explicit call to action for consumers by the brand.

After receiving the results of the initial two investigations, we developed two additional studies to examine the impact of prompted versus non-prompted co-creation messages on consumers' perceived ability to influence a brand. Specifically, we explored the question of whether the consumers' perceived ability to influence a brand has a direct impact on the effect that a prompted co-creation message has on their willingness to co-create; their attitude towards the advertisement; their purchase intention and the attributions of the brand. Formally stated, we additionally hypothesised:

H5: A prompted co-creation message from a brand that a consumer cannot influence is negatively associated with consumers' willingness to engage in co-creation.

H6: A prompted co-creation message from a brand that a consumer cannot influence is negatively associated with consumers' attitude towards the advertisement.

H7: A prompted co-creation message from a brand that a consumer cannot influence is negatively associated with consumers' purchase intention.

H8: A prompted co-creation message from a brand that a consumer cannot influence is negatively associated with consumers' attributions about the brand.

Two studies were conducted to explore these hypotheses. In the first study, 424 consumers (51 per cent female) recruited through a Qualtrics panel participated in an online survey. The consumers were asked to provide the names of five brands they could influence and five brands that they could not influence. The resulting lists of brand names were sorted by frequency and the 25 most frequently named brands from each question were randomly listed in a subsequent survey. A different set of 388 consumers (51 per cent female), also recruited through a Qualtrics panel, were presented with the list of 50 brands from the previous study. These respondents were asked to assign to each brand a score of 1 to 5, with 1 being 'unable to influence' and 5 being 'able to influence'. The results revealed two groups of brands, representative of multiple industries – including the beverage, fashion, automobile, retail and technology sectors – based on consumers' perceived ability to influence them. From these groups, two brands were chosen: Samsung from the 'able to influence' and IBM from the 'unable to influence' groups.

In the second study, 170 millennial consumers (aged 18–29; 64.7 per cent female) participated in an online survey. Subjects were randomly assigned to one of four manipulated social media posts/conditions: 1) a prompted co-creation message with a brand perceived as influenceable (Samsung); 2) a prompted co-creation message with a brand perceived as not influenceable (IBM); 3) a non-prompted co-creation message with a brand perceived as influenceable (Samsung); and 4) a non-prompted co-creation message with a brand perceived as not influenceable (IBM).

After checking that our prompted versus non-prompted co-creation manipulations were successful (participants in the prompted co-creation condition had a stronger perception of being asked to engage in the social media post than those in the non-prompted co-creation condition), we continued with the analysis of our hypotheses. The statistical analysis we conducted confirmed hypotheses one to four, and seven and eight. In other words:

- consumers' willingness to engage in co-creation is positively affected by their perceived ability to influence a brand (H1);
- consumers' attributions about a brand are positively affected by their perceived ability to influence a brand (H2);
- consumers' attitude towards the ad is positively affected by their perceived ability to influence a brand (H3);
- consumers' purchase intention is positively affected by their perceived ability to influence a brand (H4);
- a prompted co-creation message from a brand that a consumer cannot influence is negatively associated with consumers' purchase intention (H7);
- a prompted co-creation message from a brand that a consumer cannot influence is negatively associated with consumers' attributions concerning the brand (H8).

Our results demonstrate the power of millennial consumers' perceived ability to influence a brand in terms of their brand attributions, attitudes and willingness to engage. When a brand is actively seeking to engage in co-creation, consumers' perceived ability to influence the brand can override a call to action from the brand, limiting the ability for co-creation to occur. Our results also offer new insights as to when co-creation will and will not occur, how perceived ability to influence a brand can affect attitudes towards the advertisement, purchase intention and co-creation and how prompted co-creation does not necessarily have a positive outcome. If a brand is perceived as being unable to be influenced, not only will consumers not engage in co-creation, but attitudes towards that advertisement and purchase intention will also decrease and the consumer will ignore the call to action for co-creation and will not try to co-create with the brand. Conversely, millennials have a higher purchase intention with brands that have more likelihood of being influenced. Finally, if the consumer perceives the company as being resistant to influence, he or she is unlikely to engage in co-creation.

Given the size and influence of millennial consumers in today's market, and given their high level of participation in social media platforms, it is important for brands that wish to engage with this consumer group to understand that how consumers perceive the brand is important for success. Brand managers must strive to create a perception of a brand that is open to engagement with consumers and consistently prompts co-creation by allowing consumers to give input and help shape the brand. Consumers should become comfortable with the idea of the brand asking for, accepting and implementing feedback from them. To foster this potential relationship, brands should adopt a culture that is welcoming and friendly to all consumers. This sense of an accessible and caring organisation that is seen to be open to consumer influence encourages engagement with the brand. Once the brand successfully engages consumers, then the attributions made concerning the brand will likely be associated with the perceived ability to influence it, which in turn will have a positive outcome on co-creation, attitudes towards the advertisement and purchase intention. The implication is that a transparent and balanced dialogue between parties is crucial for co-creation.

## Why do organisations co-create?

The second question we posed at the beginning of this chapter was: why do some companies choose to encourage the involvement of stakeholders in brand development? One answer to this question is that they have no choice. If a brand is a mash-up created by consumers, bloggers, retailers and other stakeholders as well as by organisations, then co-creation is simply what happens. It's the way brand meaning is created. Yet we can also note that the building of tools that enable interactivity is a conscious choice. Not all organisations make that choice. Luxury brands such as Burberry and Balenciaga are very active in their use of social media and the involvement of influencers, but they do not generally involve consumers in designing products. Part of the appeal of these brands is the vision of the designers rather than the collective input of consumers. Other more mainstream brands are tepid in their attitude towards co-creation – partly because they view it as another form of market research, rather than as a way to enable active consumer participation. Generally, these brands want insight into the attitudes and lifestyles of consumers and other stakeholders, but believe that it is managers and employees that deliver creative solutions.[157]

For those organisations that see co-creation methods as a form of market research, the approach is one of distance.[158] They do believe that spending extended time with customers will provide greater depth than other methods of analysis, but often feel the need to have the ideas that come out of the process validated afterwards by quantitative research. This reflects an uncertainty about co-creation and the way it seems to flout traditional research rules and also about the need to build a business case inside the organisation. The pressure falls on Insights and Research Managers, who often lead the process, to persuade line managers of the potential value of involving customers in this way. As the focus here is derived from market research, the common belief is that internal experts should determine the ideas and that customers and other stakeholders should comment on and validate them. This inevitably closes down the range of creative possibilities and also limits the freedom of participants. When we asked managers about their expectations of co-creation, they did not talk about customers creating new ideas. Rather, they use words such as 'inspire', 'work up', 'refine' and 'test'. An interesting corollary of this approach lies in the fact that organisational infallibility is sometimes confounded by reality. Organisations believe they already know everything that is relevant and important when developing ideas and are surprised when consumers see things differently.

In contrast to the advocates of the value of market research, there are organisations that use co-creation strategically. Rather than creating distance between the organisation and the consumer, they see consumers and other stakeholders as partners and creators rather than just validators. Consequently, these organisations tend to be more willing to share and be more open to possibilities. They don't assume they already know the answer, but rather listen and learn with others and allow ideas to evolve through discussion. The attitude of managers in this group is noteworthy, not least for the emphasis it places on equality. There is a belief that outsiders really do have valuable knowledge that can benefit the organisation. As an Insights Manager from a technology company said: 'The knowledge that our customers have about the business is phenomenal...their understanding of our operation is as good as lots of people who work here, it really is incredible.' Whereas the market research orientation leads to co-creation becoming rooted in Insights and Marketing, the strategic one tends to be based on an organisation-wide system that embraces a variety of departments. It can be the case that senior executives are enthusiasts for co-creation. But engagement is also sometimes the result of an evangelist, who pushes the organisation towards co-creation.

The strategic view and the market research view are the two ends of a continuum along which organisations can be positioned. At one end are the sceptics who argue that consumers are good for helping to refine the way the brand is positioned or how it is communicated, but not for creating anything that is profound. At the other end are the believers, who can point to evidence that consumers and other stakeholders really do deliver meaningful insights that generate new opportunities that are strategically important. Organisations at both ends of the continuum are consistently surprised by the engagement and enthusiasm of community participants. The business area does not seem to be significant in determining a particular position on the continuum. Rather, the determinants seem to be the perspective of the business and its degree of openness to the world.

An interesting example of this more open approach comes from the sportswear brand adidas. The spur for them to become co-creative came from a presentation by Silicon Valley managers on how the concept of open source works. This resonated with adidas, because the brand had long practised a form of co-creation. The company's founder, Adi Dassler, had a long history of working with athletes to create tailored sports products. Dassler would observe athletes, talk to them and then build products that met their needs. Once they had worn the shoes he created, he would want them back because he wanted to see the wear and tear. He used a combination of empathy and experiment to create a business based on industrialised craftsmanship. After Dassler died in 1978, the company became more closed and inward-looking. However, in 2015, with a new CEO and marketing director in place, adidas set out a new strategy called Creating the New. This gave emphasis to a particular audience that they called 'creators' – athletes and influencers who help shape the world – and to three inter-connected points of emphasis: an open source approach, a focus on key cities and speed. Rather than seeing co-creation as a method of gaining insight, adidas made it a central element of its whole strategic approach in order to enable it to get closer to consumers.

To execute the strategy, adidas built partnerships with organisations and individuals. For example, a high-profile range called Yeezy was developed in conjunction with American rapper Kanye West while a new range of shoes and clothes developed from recycled ocean plastics was established together with an NGO called Parley for the Oceans. Collaborations were established with a broad range of retailers and designers, from a high-end Japanese leather-goods craft-shop to Savile Row tailors. In the six key cities chosen as a focus by adidas, designers worked with runners to co-design shoes suitable for each urban environment. Adidas also encourages 'creators' to work with employees to develop new designs and at the Brooklyn Creator Farm people from diverse backgrounds regularly come together to explore and experiment with new ideas and create new concepts.

As a result of its open, co-creative approach, adidas has become a more dynamic and creative organisation. The benefits it derives from this approach are also typical of other businesses who use co-creation successfully. These include:

- deep insight – by spending time with stakeholders, advocates of co-creation become adept at looking beneath the surface of people's views to better understand their latent needs and desires;
- lab-like experimentation – simple experiments can be conducted through other research means, but co-creation affords the opportunity to conduct more complex experiments where people can be involved in analysis and discussion of alternative scenarios, and in the development of service and product prototypes;
- exploring new markets and audiences – managers can often seem very confident that they know everything about current markets and audiences, but to understand the opportunities in new geographies or categories, there is a need to understand points of continuity with, and divergence from, existing behaviours;
- identifying trends – co-creation can provide a window into customers' lives by engaging with what they do, rather than simply relying on what they say they do;
- generating new concepts – most traditional market research tools focus on generating opinions about new or existing concepts based on thinking that has already been done by managers. Co-creation also offers up the opportunity (even if there is often management cynicism about it) to initiate and develop fresh ideas;
- building internal engagement – because co-creation encourages managerial participation, it can enable managers to perceive the issues that really concern stakeholders, and in doing so help them to overcome taken-for-granted truths.

## Summary

To better understand and manage the practice of co-creation, organisations need to develop insights into the motivations of their stakeholders. Online communities, events and workshops only function optimally when managers move away from the perspective of 'what can we get out of this?' to 'how can we create benefits for everyone that participates?' The fulfilment of this question requires the construction of an exchange in which participants gift their time, knowledge and creativity in return for proper feedback and involvement from the brand. Co-creation based on a gift exchange model both enhances the solidarity of the group or community and creates the trust that is necessary to enable creativity to flourish.

## Reflections/questions

1) Which activities do you enjoy most? Think about what your motives are – are they more intrinsic or extrinsic? If they are intrinsic, what would happen to your motivation if someone paid you to do the activity?

2) When you give someone a gift what do you feel? Does it bring you closer to them? Do you expect them to reciprocate?

3) Do you think co-creation has negative aspects? What do you think could be done to make co-creation fairer?

## We recommend the following reading to expand your learning experience:

Ind, N., Iglesias, O. & Markovic, S. (2017). 'The co-creation continuum: From tactical market research tool to strategic collaborative innovation method', *Journal of Brand Management*, 24(4), 310–321.

# CHAPTER FOUR

# Organising for co-creation

## In this chapter...

When managers want to move beyond the confines of the organisation and involve other stakeholders in the creation of value, the process has to be well-structured. Many writers argue for the importance of diversity in processes, both to avoid the conformity of group-think and to spur new ways of seeing things. But diversity also invites divergence. When you choose to involve perhaps several hundred people in a co-creation process, or invite business partners to develop an idea, you can tap into a broader base of knowledge and skills. But you have to cope with digressions, disagreements and contradictions. And you have to assess and analyse the resulting flood of data that emerges. Then it might start to look easier and neater if you can go back to just having a few experts – informed by market research – sitting in a room and working things out for themselves. It's certainly an appealing option for a hard-pressed brand or innovation manager. Nonetheless, this neat approach can easily suffer from mistaken assumptions and a tendency to objectify consumers and other stakeholders. The message of this chapter then is that co-creation is about both freedom and order. Organisations need a clear and transparent governance process and the cohesion provided by a strong brand identity before encouraging stakeholders to participate in the development of the brand and the enriching of its meaning. Kasper Rørsted, CEO of adidas, illustrates this when he says: 'We are clear about the borders of our brand, because the brand is sacred to us. But we also recognised that if we have only the inspiration and creativity of people within our own organisation, we miss a lot of what's going on in the marketplace.'[159]

Here, we will look at how a brand creates a border (or framework) for co-creation and at the requirements of managers in embarking on an open process. We will examine the problems that can occur and the requirements of leaders when it comes to establishing an effective process. The example that will illuminate the opportunities and challenges of this is offered by the French electricity transmission system operator RTE (Réseau de Transport d'Électricité) and specifically, the role played by its innovation lab, Open Studio, which demonstrates the virtues of openness and the importance of listening – of working together with diverse stakeholders to innovate and ensure future relevance.

## Learning Objectives

After reading this chapter you should

- understand that brand identity should drive a co-creative approach to brand management;
- realise that the active participation of stakeholders can energise and develop the brand;
- understand the importance of establishing at the outset an effective governance process (the idea of co-conception);
- appreciate that co-creation requires internal commitment and external engagement.

## Preparing to Co-Create

Co-creation is rooted in the principle of getting close to customers, start-ups, researchers, influencers and partners – the network of people and organisations who create brand meaning and value. As we saw in Chapter 3, for those brands that see co-creation as a transactional process, the demands on the organisation are not so onerous. Co-creation is in such cases another item in the market research toolbox, which can be used reactively when requests come from managers to generate insights into stakeholder attitudes and behaviours. However, when co-creation is seen as a strategic method of brand building, which involves a partnership with external stakeholders, the management of the process needs to be carefully considered because it has the potential to have a more profound impact on the direction of the brand. Here, managers not only need to think through the role external stakeholders can play in building a brand, but also the way to best manage internal expectations.

The starting point for any brand is to know itself – to understand the history, philosophy, beliefs and values that define its unique identity (see Chapter 6). The traditional perspective in classic marketing texts is that a brand identity is stable and enduring. The identity is determined by managers who then control its expression over time. This idea has been accepted because managers focus on what is actual and observable, which tends to be fixed, rather than on the dynamic processes that lie beneath. As should be obvious by now, we would argue that while indeed some elements of the brand identity endure, brands exist in the world and are subject to the influence of all stakeholders as they assume new shapes. The brand identity is constantly negotiated between what is intended by the organisation and what is experienced or enacted by stakeholders. In other words, the brand identity itself is co-created. As a consequence, 'managers will have to give up the idea of control over a brand and accept instead a fluid, uncertain world where a brand evolves in dialogue with others.'[160]

This dynamic view of identity might suggest that there is little point in a brand owner agonising over defining its beliefs and values when stakeholders are going to prod and push them in new and different directions. However, the opposite is true. If managers are willing to let the brand go and accept or indeed encourage stakeholders to adapt the brand, it makes sense to have a clear idea about what you stand for, so that it can inspire and guide internal and external audiences. As an illustration of this, in a study by researchers in Denmark of a Nike online brand community called NBRO, which was started by young runners but received sponsorship from Nike, the differences between intended and enacted brand identities are very evident.[161] Nike has a distinctive identity that is rooted in its past, the beliefs of its founder and its consistent expression of itself as a performance brand through its products, services and communications. Customers – and indeed the members of the NBRO community – wear Nike because they identify with what Nike is perceived to stand for. Consequently, NBRO members mirror the intended Nike identity in their language and behaviour, but there are also deviations from the Nike identity that reflect the collective community identity of NBRO and also some voices of resistance to the commercialisation of the community. The researchers observed that the identities are different, but not conflictual. What Nike has learned (as we also saw with LEGO) is that they should interfere as little as possible in the community – however tempting it might be to do so – and allow members to enact its identity in a way that is relevant and meaningful for them.

From the organisational side, the brand has an identity whether the organisation has thought consciously about it or not. It is there in the assumptions, beliefs and practices that define the brand. Nike's identity is different from adidas' because of the different corporate cultures and experiences of the two companies. There may be some similar perspectives because they operate in the same industry, but each brand has a unique (if fluid) identity. Normally, as brands grow and develop, they move from an implicit idea of the brand, where the identity is sensed, to a more explicit one, where the identity is articulated. During the early years, a brand's identity may strongly reflect the enduring beliefs of the founder or founders of the company: the founders' beliefs still remain important for adidas and Nike, even if their meaning has evolved. However, as the influence of a founder diminishes over time, so the brand identity may change to adapt to a new reality.

To understand and define a brand's identity, we need to look inwards and outwards (we'll look at the process of doing this in the coming chapters). To turn inwards involves an organisation looking self-critically at itself in order to uncover the attributes that define what the brand is and what it means. The challenge presented by this is that brands are often complex: there may not be one brand identity, but several co-existing identities, based on the different interpretations of organisational members or departments. Getting to the hidden, taken-for-granted attributes that underpin the identity requires digging in the form of workshops, interviews, surveys and discussions. It requires questioning and challenging assumptions. The goal is to unearth a set of ideas that best represent the brand identity and that fuse together the past, present and future. Ideally, the ideas should convey what is distinctive about the identity. But equally important is a sense of authenticity. The underlying issue here is that simply creating a set of words that try to describe the brand's identity will achieve very little if employees, partners and other stakeholders don't recognise their validity. As several studies have shown, the words used to articulate the identity of a brand need to have a clear link to the past if they are to have legitimacy. They also need to help realise the brand's strategic ambitions.[162]

While you could argue that a brand identity is a reflection purely of an organisation's internal beliefs and attitudes, it would be wrong to do so. As the social psychologist George Herbert Mead pointed out in relation to people's individual identities, we are formed both by who we are and by how others see us: 'the individual finds himself acting with reference to himself as he acts towards others.'[163] Viewed this way, a brand's identity is formed by its interactions with the world and that experience is re-absorbed by those who work with it. This means that a brand also needs to understand how it is seen by its key stakeholders. This requires the brand to acquire insights into the perspectives of customers, partners and employees. The standard way of doing this involves embracing qualitative and quantitative modes of research. However, the process can also be co-creative. Brands can involve both their internal and external stakeholders in online communities and events as a means of both creating interaction and searching out the relevant uniqueness of the brand identity. For example, when Kraft Foods (now part of Kraft Heinz) decided to think about its identity, it saw clear benefits in a participative process and over an eight-month period involved some 10,000 employees online and offline to help make that reconsideration possible. Additionally, Kraft hosted a series of large group events in Chicago, Paris and Shanghai that brought internal and external stakeholders together to help the company better understand the role of food in peoples' lives and the perceptions of Kraft that those people shared. The process was designed to ensure and enhance business relevance and employee engagement.[164]

While a participative, co-creative process can seem a slow way to define a brand identity, it does have important virtues. First, it helps to ensure that the resulting words do actually reflect the reality of the brand, rather than wishful thinking about what the brand could be. Second, the participation of employees and key partners legitimises brand definition. Third, through participation, people come to understand the idea of brand identity and what it means (in the case of Kraft, six months after launch, 94 per cent of employees thought the process worthwhile and 83 per cent knew what the work was designed to accomplish). Participation means that companies can avoid the trap of having to use a lot of time and money by subsequently trying to sell the brand identity to sometimes uninterested employees. Fourth, by being inclusive, the brand identity is more likely to reflect the totality of the organisation in all its different activities and geographies. Collectively, a co-creative process can create the potential for a brand identity definition that is robust, credible and inspirational. Whether it realises its potential comes down to how the identity is used in practice.

## The Brand as a Framework

The words that companies use to define brand identities are an attempt to narrow down what is unique about the company. Yet we should note that the meaning of words is not fixed – indeed it is co-created by people as they use language to guide decisions and take actions. For example, the LEGO brand identity is defined by various statements, but includes these values that were developed in the early 2000s: trust, self-expression, active fun, playful learning, endless ideas and a positioning of the 'power to create'. These values were an evolution of what had previously existed rather than a radical re-working and were designed to reconnect people to the company's past as a way of charting a new course for the future that was more focussed and to provide employees with a shared sense of direction. To uncover the meaning of the words, LEGO (among other initiatives) sent its employees to its own brand school where they could play with LEGO bricks, learn about the company's identity and work with translating the values it celebrated into practical actions.[165] However, the values (along with the mission, vision and promises) do not prescribe behaviour but rather inspire and guide it. Imagine yourself in the position of a LEGO manager, having to choose between product ideas. How would you do it? If you were to adhere only to prescribed values, you would probably discuss with your colleagues which ideas best align and you would be able to filter out ideas that were clearly not creative or did not stimulate learning or the other qualities cherished by the company. But you would still perhaps have several that could fit with the values. The values do not give you the answer, but they do give you the basis of a conversation.

## Co-conception

With the brand identity providing the framework, an organisation can seek to enrich its brand by involving its stakeholders. Of course, as noted earlier, interested customers, partners and employees will participate in research whether the organisation plans the process or not. People will discuss ideas together, write online comments and even take part in events or brand communities. In each case managers should think about how to engage with these interactions and support them. For savvy brands, these occasions provide opportunities to learn about their stakeholders' views, to share positive feedback and to try to manage criticisms. However, brand owners can also take a more proactive approach by seeking to engage others in co-creation through initiating events, competitions, online communities and innovation labs. As testament to the effectiveness of this opening up of the organisation, a study of 329 Research and Development scientists and engineers working for a major international business 'found strong evidence that openness to external sources can have significant benefits for the ability of individuals to generate new and valuable ideas for their organisation.'[166]

This move to open the brand to the involvement of others is not without risks and requires an effective process of governance. The starting point should be an internal agreement on the rationale for using co-creation – whether it be the need to ensure that the voice of key stakeholders is heard, to co-opt the specific expertise of outsiders, to speed up the innovation process, to improve performance or to enter a new market segment or develop an existing one. For example, the global software company SAP uses a Co-Innovation Lab global network to foster and speed up co-innovation with its ecosystem. Started in 2007 in Palo Alto, California, the SAP Co-Innovation Lab (COIL) now operates in more than 15 locations around the world. It provides capable and productive spaces where the industry's top minds can work together on the most pressing business challenges customers face, bringing together the elements needed to make co-innovation among partners and customers successful. Kevin Liu, North America Head of the lab, notes that the scale and complexity of a large enterprise such as SAP can be off-putting to outsiders. Over time, the lab has learned how best to structure processes and to balance the needs of business compliance with agility to help partners, especially smaller ones, navigate the SAP structure and to try out new ideas with SAP. Liu says: 'A framework is important, from legal to infrastructure to engineering support to the process flow, to go to market. You need a framework to put it all together. On top of the framework you need business relevance. If you want to do a co-innovation program, one way or another it needs to contribute to your business. COIL uses co-innovation as a service platform that covers all the key elements of a co-innovation project and makes it easier for the SAP ecosystem to create and enable high-value, co-innovated business solutions.'

One aspect of the process that Liu emphasises is the need to avoid the common mistake of jumping into things – you need to spend time at the beginning of an endeavour in order to properly think through possible problems. This is something that Pierre D'Huy, Chair of Innovation and Permanent Transformation at French business school EDHEC and co-author of *'L'innovation pour les nuls'* (Innovation for Dummies), also emphasises when he says that you can't co-create until you have sorted out the process of co-conception: what is the challenge or opportunity you are trying to solve, who is the sponsor; which stakeholders are you going to involve and how, and how will you judge the results? D'Huy argues that you have to be explicit and honest about the process at the outset if you are to realise the potential of co-creation. You need to be clear about the rules of the game and the means by which things will be evaluated. As he suggests: 'Decide those in peace time and not when everyone is at war and panicking.' In practice, these 10 points can help managers handle the co-creation process:

1) **Define the scope of the problem/opportunity**. The task here is to define a question that is strategically relevant to the business and framed in a human-centric way that will engage participants. This means managers have to be able to empathise with and understand the motivations of their stakeholders. Sometimes the scope will be major, such as deciding together with potential customers the

business strategy of an organisation, while at other times the scope will be more specific, such as deciding how we should design our latest service experience.

2) **Manage expectations**. There is nothing more frustrating for people than to be invited to take part in an exercise only to realise that things have already been decided or that nothing significant is likely to happen. Organisations can involve people through 'hackathons', brainstorming sessions, communities and other mechanisms. Managers see value in such activities as they provide a means of burnishing the corporate reputation and generating ideas.[167] Participants take part, often for little or no financial gain, because they are motivated largely by intrinsic rewards. However, as we saw in Chapter 3, participants can be disappointed when the organisation fails to provide proper feedback on the ideas developed. So there is an ethical issue here: a business has to ensure it has the right level of management support to deliver on the expectations of people. This does not mean that all ideas will be implemented, but rather that there will be a fair process of consideration and that adequate feedback will be provided both on the ideas that progress and those that don't.

3) **Freedom to explore**. Co-creation projects will often have a senior manager who acts as a sponsor. It is their job to ensure the scope of the project is set at the right level and to act as an arbiter at agreed key decision points. A good sponsor will give direction and provide support, but will also give people the freedom to develop their ideas. This means resisting the temptation to sit looking over the shoulders of the participants. The sponsor has to ensure that the right people are involved in the process and then trust them to do the right thing.

4) **The right people**. The question of who should participate in a given process is driven by the nature of the problem/opportunity. If the problem is technical, such as when NASA wanted to investigate how to improve the predictability of solar particles in space, then participants need a reasonable level of knowledge about the field

(the solution in this case was provided by a retired radio frequency engineer, who improved prediction accuracy concerning the nature of particles from 55 per cent to 85 per cent).[168] If the goal does not require specialist knowledge, as when generating new yoghurt flavours or developing a check-in service for a hotel chain, then the target would either be an existing and/or potential customer. Those managing the process also have to decide not only who to involve, but when to involve them. There are some examples – such as the development of the Volvo XC90 car – where customers were involved throughout,[169] but it is often more typical that co-creation is used at certain points, with early stage ideation being the most frequent.[170]

5) **Define the process**. The process is not the responsibility of the sponsor – as D'Huy says, 'the how is not their business.' The process should set out the clear targets for each phase so that all participants know what is expected of them and what the anticipated results will be. However, even if the process has a clear structure, there should also be a recognition along the way that circumstances will change and that there will be a need to re-plan. A good creative process will challenge the boundaries that have been set – which means that those running it have to make judgements on when to say 'no' and when to adapt.

6) **Keep moving**. There is often a temptation in these processes for people to want to re-visit previous decisions. Involving diverse people in a process means being prepared to be open to diversity of ideas. Inevitably, many of these ideas will be discarded, but it is often hard for people to accept that their cherished idea is not chosen – they will then try to resurrect it or suggest that perhaps some wrong assumptions have been made. The key here is to allow full and honest debate on ideas as they emerge, but then also to impose discipline when a decision has been arrived at.

7) **Work with hypotheses**. This point connects to the second, in that those running a process have to stress that there can be no guarantees as to its outcome. There will be senior management support for

the process and there will be proper feedback, but the decision to proceed with an idea will lie outside (and be based on) the needs of the business, the alignment with the brand and the availability of resources. D'Huy says: 'we are not taking decisions at all, we are working with hypotheses…things that are not yet.'

8) **Build a partnership.** When an organisation involves outsiders, whether business partners or consumers, there is a power relationship at work, because the organisation that initiates the process has influence over the direction of interactions and controls the flow of knowledge. However, co-creation works best when participants are willing to share and to treat each other as equals. The implication here is that the initiating organisation should be as open as possible and allow stakeholders to influence the process of co-operative undertakings.

9) **Keep it legal.** When co-creation involves business partners and suppliers, organisations need to be able to share findings and aspirations without fear. From the perspective of a start-up that engages with a larger organisation, there is often a concern that openness will lead to an idea being stolen, while for the larger organisation, there is the concern that they may be contaminated by learning something that they are already working on. Liu says a fair co-innovation program needs to protect both sides by creating a level playing field: 'The lab provides a legal framework that protects intellectual properties for all participants in the lab, and it even takes it one step further by having its infrastructure framework hosted outside the company firewall in a de-militarised zone – a neutral environment for SAP and its partners to work together'.

10) **The culture counts.** The successful practice of co-creation depends on the involvement of motivated participants. This means that whether a manager is working with an online consumer community or a co-innovation lab with business partners, attention needs to be paid to nurturing a space where people have sufficient freedom to explore together. Attention has to be paid to facilitation – particularly to listening to people and inspiring them to participate

in proceedings. It's important to note that the tone is set at the very first meeting – this is where people get a sense of what it will be like to work together. However, the sense of togetherness needs to be maintained by creating a supportive culture. Without active and committed participation, co-creation simply collapses.

## How RTE is co-creating its future

Much of the focus of co-creation falls on consumers, yet if all stakeholders contribute to the value of a brand, then we must also pay attention to how co-creation affects partners, suppliers and buyers. In this section, we will look at how a business-to-business brand, RTE, has opened itself up to influence, and be influenced by, others. RTE was established as a Transmission System Operator (TSO) in 2000 and is responsible for the management of the French high-voltage electricity transmission system, which at 105,961 kilometres of lines is the largest in Europe. Given that the company is a regulated monopoly, one might wonder why it needs to even think about its brand and why it needs to innovate. The answers aren't immediately obvious, but the need to innovate is being driven by the rapid change in the energy ecosystem that has arisen from the emergence of the direct consumption of renewables, such as solar- and wind-generated power and the introduction of energy storage systems, such as lithium-ion battery plants. To help RTE engage with this changing environment, the company established an innovation lab called Open Studio.

The change in the ecosystem also points to the relevance of the brand, because it means that the future for RTE will be both competitive and co-operative. To attract and retain employees, engage with trade unions, build a positive reputation with the media, attract business partners and create a connection with end consumers, RTE will have to co-create a brand that is open and relevant and appealing to its diverse stakeholders. As part of this process, RTE has been re-stating its values – solidarity, transparency, daring, performance, efficiency, leadership – as a way to build on its past and to project into the future. The values are designed to reflect the core of RTE, but Open Studio also helps to stretch their meaning and give them momentum. Essentially, the goal of RTE's Open Studio is to transform the organisation by opening it to new ideas and influences. Gwenaëlle Lemarchand of Open Studio says that the idea of the lab emerged as a way to learn about, and participate in, the energy ecosystem: 'The idea was to change this way of looking at the world outside of RTE...to look at RTE with the eyes of new people who are changing the way we produce and we consume. And to experiment with them. To try to find ways we can co-design, co-concept some new services.'

Open Studio is small (six people) and has no fixed base – it moves around yearly to visit different incubators. And not surprisingly, it has faced scepticism from managers who question why the company is working with other companies to facilitate the direct consumption of energy. Executives sometimes question what the Open Studio is doing and why is it outside the core business? However, key to the studio's continued existence is the visible and active support of the CEO, François Brottes, and the clear benefits of co-operation. An intriguing facet of the studio is that it not only delivers on the explicit technological benefits that it anticipated, but also in other areas connected to processes and people. In the technological arena, the studio has partnered primarily with direct consumption start-ups to act as a guarantor and to provide forecasting services based on RTE's data analytics. This helps start-ups to establish their credibility and provide a quality service. In return, RTE has developed a data platform built on the information coming from the partners on direct consumption, which improves the ability of RTE to better balance production and consumption. However, RTE has also learned from start-ups in other ways. A well-established company such as RTE with over 8,000 employees and a protected market struggles to move quickly. Within the organisation, plans have to be highly detailed, with each phase fully designed, before a process can be initiated.

This is fine within a steady market state, but less than desirable when there is rapid change. Open Studio learned from the businesses it was co-located with about lean processes such as smart testing and building rapid prototypes. Similarly, the studio has learned about the importance of people. While the original focus was on innovative ideas, Open Studio began to learn from start-ups that while a good idea is one thing, turning the idea into reality requires committed, engaged people and a good quality of working life. Lemarchand notes: 'Our first approach was technical and then little by little, and by talking to people, we understood that the human area was often forgotten. When you look at all the great technical innovation, often at the very beginning there was some human resources innovation that made people able to innovate in technical fields.'

Part of the power of Open Studio has resided in its ability to influence the practices of the main organisation by sharing their experiences about partners and customers. They meet with around 1,000 employees a year and through the data they acquire, they explain how the energy transmission business is changing. They point out that RTE will have to adapt to new circumstances and employees will have to become more creative and entrepreneurial. This could seem threatening (and for some it clearly is), but the message is that employees have the opportunity to improve the quality of life inside RTE, to work in new ways and to design the jobs of tomorrow. There is some scepticism about whether the company is serious about such radical change and whether a small innovation team has the legitimacy to deliver it. However, with the backing of the CEO, training programmes to support people who want to develop and a network of 'corsairs'[171] to subvert the system, change happens. RTE's corsairs (numbering about 300 people) are working to change the processes and culture of the company in order to encourage people to be more open to innovation and to stimulate entrepreneurships. Lemarchand says that the viral and localised approach of corsairs challenges the traditional way of working with initiatives mandated from the top down: 'What we like is when things are spread in a viral way…If something is being tested by a small team in the South of France, we think they are the most credible to explain to a team just near them how it works…this way of working is very new for RTE, but it works.'

## Building consensus for co-creation

The work of RTE's Open Studio demonstrates the power of a small group of committed people to deliver change and affect a corporate culture. However, to assume that this change is welcomed by all would be mistaken. In RTE, some managers resist the ways of working that Open Studio and the corsairs are pushing because they upset the traditional hierarchical structure and the certainties of the past. Similarly, the trade unions, who often have a powerful position in French organisations, are wary of co-creating the future with managers. The idea of liberating employees to define new roles; to work together in fluid teams; to create peer-to-peer reward systems and to develop innovation projects, subverts the 'us versus them' relationship with management and makes the role of the union less clear.

Perhaps not surprisingly, as organisations open themselves up to a co-creative approach, tensions emerge. In closed structures, people's expectations and positions are more precisely defined. One's identity is determined in relation to others' by roles and achievements that exist within the cultural framework of an organisation. However, in an open organisation, there are valuable opportunities to learn from those with different knowledge and skills. Organisations as diverse as the consumer goods company P&G, and space exploration agency NASA, have enjoyed considerable benefits from an open approach (accelerating innovation, improving success rates), but they have also found that employees can show resistance to openness because it makes them feel vulnerable. In the instance cited earlier concerning the retired radio frequency engineer who solved the problem of accurately forecasting solar activity, we applaud him as a hero. But now put yourself in the position of a highly qualified NASA engineer, who had failed to find an adequate solution. How do you feel? If your identity is rooted in your formal position and expertise and you see yourself as a problem solver in the field of solar activity, you might feel quite uncomfortable. NASA found a mixture of responses among their own people from those who embraced the idea of co-creating to those who were deeply resistant to the prospect. To overcome this resistance, NASA has tried to shift employee perceptions away from thinking about solving problems and closer to seeking solutions – recognising the need to acknowledge the potential input of others in a process. The organisation also worked on trying to perforate the boundaries between the inside and the outside by communicating the benefits of openness, and by involving employees in events and meetings that would enable them to work with others.

As well as encountering resistance from internal experts, managers can also reject opening up the organisation and the practice of co-creation that is often a feature of such openness. We have seen some of these factors in the RTE case, but additionally, people balance the benefits of co-creation with arguments about the relevance and effectiveness of ideas from outsiders and also with the challenge of innovation overload (too many ideas competing for scarce resources). In the case of the former feeling, it seems that the strength of internal cultures can lead to a sense of otherness that fosters the perception that the ideas of outsiders will not add to the collective knowledge of those inside. The argument here is that the experience and knowledge of employees trumps the diversity that other stakeholders can bring.[172] This view, however, is not supported by the extensive research on open innovation and consumer creativity. External stakeholders may not always have the depth of knowledge of insiders, but neither do they suffer from the blinkers of a corporate culture. If an organisation has the nous to open itself up and nurture the opportunities that connectivity affords, then new ways of seeing can emerge. As Steve Johnson argues in his book, *Where Good Ideas Come From*, it is not that crowds are wise, but rather that connected people become smarter. The second argument about too many ideas might be regarded as a sign of success, but there is often a tension between the needs of running an organisation efficiently day-to-day and experimenting with innovations. There is a danger of losing focus and over-stretching resources in the search for the new. However, most industries do not operate in a stable environment, but rather one where change is constant – and that means embracing a spirit of on-going adaptation. Co-creative organisations understand that they will generate many more ideas than they can use, but they also know that they can bank as yet un-used ideas that can either come to life in the future, or in combination with other ideas.

## A new managerial approach

In the quest for an effective approach to co-creation, we argue for a new management approach – one that is rooted in a transformational leadership style and that is humble.[173] What does this mean? A transformational leadership style recognises the dominance of intrinsic motivation and the value of emotional engagement. While transformational leadership normally focusses on how to generate the commitment of employees, in the context of co-creation it can be expanded to involve both internal and external stakeholders in the process of building a brand. Felicitas Morhart, who has both researched the area and trained leaders in transformational leadership, argues while the goal might be to turn customers into fans, you have to turn employees into them first.[174] In essence, this requires employees to support the brand by acting consistently in line with the values and standards of the brand and also to strengthen the brand through voluntary behaviour. A manager can nurture this by articulating a powerful vision and stimulating pride in the brand; by acting as a role model; by empowering people to deliver the brand and by coaching employees in their roles as brand representatives. When a transformational style is consistently applied, it helps to ensure that the interactions between the organisation and its stakeholders both align with the brand and are human-centric. Alignment is a result of employees projecting the brand through their statements and behaviour as a consequence of identifying with it, rather than an outcome of simply following instructions. Human-centricity occurs because employees are empowered to deliver something of value to stakeholders by way of discussions that are increasingly unscripted. Similarly, customers and other stakeholders have the opportunity to span organisational boundaries and become active participants in brand development and creating innovative ideas.

To make a transformational approach work in co-creation, managers have to be humble. It requires a move away from a desire to control relationships to a belief in partnership and an ability to empathise with others by engaging with a third-person perspective.[175] For this to be realised, managers have to be both capable of the imaginative mental activity that allows them to understand behaviour and of believing that external stakeholders can make valuable contributions to their endeavours. This suggests that managers, in spite of all their expertise, have to realise how much they don't know. It argues for the importance of listening, a willingness to enter into a conversation with an organisation's stakeholders and for the value of knowing how to share and to learn.

## Summary

This chapter has shown that if a co-creation process is to realise its potential it needs to be carefully planned and executed. Co-creation implies letting go of the brand and empowering stakeholders to help shape and develop it, but this freedom needs to be accompanied by order. Organisations therefore need clarity about the brand and to establish a framework for this freedom that is rooted in the brand identity. Effective co-creation also involves managing the process of involving others by paying attention to setting and meeting expectations. The examples of SAP and RTE illustrate the value of a co-creative approach while recognising the barriers that have to be overcome.

## Reflections/questions

Choose an organisation that you think could benefit from the practice of co-creation. It could be a retailer, a public transportation system, an arts organisation or a service business. Have a look at its online profile and then how consumers use it.

1)  Define the key question you want to investigate.
2)  Work out who you would involve (e.g., customers/non-customers/ experts).
3)  Outline the method you would use to generate insights.

## We recommend the following reading to expand your learning experience:

Morhart, F. (2017). 'Unleashing the internal fan community through brand-oriented leadership', In Ind, N. (ed.), *Branding Inside Out: Internal Branding in Theory and in Practice*. London: Kogan Page, 33–50.

CHAPTER FIVE

# The co-creative brand management system

## In this chapter ...

Throughout this book, we have argued that to build and manage a brand, an organisation needs to be open to its stakeholders. Marketing and brand managers have to give up the idea of total control over a brand and accept instead a fluid, uncertain world where strong brands are co-created together with others. But that doesn't mean that a brand doesn't need an active and strong management to set direction, inspire people and to help build customer-based brand equity. This requires a certain management philosophy and a way of working – a model – that gives a structure to how to build brands in a participative world: this structure and model is what we mean by 'the co-creative brand management system'. This model, like many other brand management models, divides brand management into several building blocks and is designed to guide brand managers in their decision-making. At first glance, you might feel that our model strongly aligns with other well-known and established models that aim to organise the brand management process. But if you take a deeper look you will realise the differences. First, the three parts of the co-creative brand management system are deeply connected and, unlike other more traditional models, are not organised in a step-by-step-process in which one project stage follows the other. In other words, it is not a linear model but a fluid one, in which actions and influences have diverse impacts. It is an example of what Ramaswamy and Ozcan refer to as networked

106

interactions within the frame of an assemblage that can move in different ways.[176] Second, the model is co-creative, in that it is both directed by managers and interpreted and redefined by stakeholders. Third, the system differs dramatically from others in terms of the way in which the different model parts come to life, asking which co-creative activities and instruments could and should be selected and used in order to analyse, define, implement and control the brand. In this chapter we will provide an overview of the co-creative brand management system and illustrate it with a case about the logistics company TNT. In Chapters 6 to 8, we will discuss the building blocks of the system in greater depth.

## Learning objectives

After reading this chapter you should

- understand that brand management involves much more than following a gut feeling;
- know some of the models that leading authors have proposed to help structure the brand management process;
- be able to broadly explain the co-creative brand management system;
- have the knowledge to plan and structure a brand management process for a company.

## What makes a company successful?

You might instinctively answer this question by arguing that what a company needs is a superior competitive product or service. Just think of long-established companies such as Mercedes, American Express or Coca-Cola, or even of some younger entrepreneurial companies such as Facebook, Tesla or Airbnb, who solve customer needs in a superior or unique way. However, there are also many examples of excellent products that failed.[177] Just think of the map provider MapQuest, rated the number-two mapping service in the US in 2015; think of Black Berry, the go-to device of the business world, and for many the first smartphone; and think of MySpace, which was named one of the 50 best websites of 2006.[178] A good product or service seems to be a necessary but not sufficient condition for market success. If so, what is sufficient? Thousands of books have been written to answer this ultimate management challenge, but 'the' recipe for enduring business success has not been discovered.

Root around in the different management disciplines and you will find various philosophies on how to manage a business successfully. Often, authors see the different strategic orientations a company could follow as an explicative variable for determining success.[179] A strategic orientation can be interpreted as a hidden compass that navigates the company through good and bad times – a kind of code of behaviour that managers and employees will relate to when facing business decisions.[180] Drawing on this, some researchers argue that it is a customer-centric organisational culture that fuels success and enables the organisation to adapt in tune with customers' needs and desires. Such a philosophy is called 'customer' or 'market' orientation. Procter & Gamble, for example, has been described as a company with a high degree of market orientation. When the company introduced the male razor Mach 3 under the Gillette brand (one of the many brands within P&G's huge brand portfolio), they invested around $680 million on market research and product testing, with the goal of generating deep insights into customer behaviour and incorporating them into their strategies.[181] Other researchers, and now we are moving closer to the overall theme of this book, would argue that business success is related to a company's ability to build and maintain strong brands. This way of thinking is also called brand orientation – a philosophy which can be described as an 'identity-driven approach that sees brands as a hub for an organisation and its strategy'.[182] In organisations with a supposedly high brand orientation, such as Apple, Porsche,

Wimbledon (yes, a tennis tournament can be a brand) and Burberry, management focusses on the brand's identity and core strengths and doesn't lose sight of its origins. Over time, these organisations manage to build a strong brand equity. Which raises the question: what exactly is brand equity?

## Brand equity

Kevin Keller, who was one of the pioneers of the concept, defined customer-based brand equity (CBBE) as 'the differential effect of brand knowledge on consumer response to the marketing of the brand'.[183] In everyday terms, this means that brand equity expresses how a product or a service is seen with and without a brand name attached. Brand equity describes the difference between the two – the evaluation of the benefits of the offering when you know the brand versus your evaluation of the benefits of the offering when you don't. A simple and oft-cited illustration of high brand equity can be found in the cola industry. Research has shown that in blind taste tests, when consumers do not know the brands involved, Pepsi often beats Coca-Cola. In open tests, when consumers see what they drink, a majority favour Coca-Cola. This demonstrates that Coca-Cola, compared to Pepsi, has higher brand equity.

A key point about Keller's model is that it is 'customer-based', so it aims to see the value of the brand through the customer's eyes. In the CBBE model there are four stages, at the base of which lies awareness (or as Keller calls it, salience). A customer must know and remember the brand as a first stage in building a product's identity – without that awareness there is no possibility of brand equity. To build equity, brands also have to deliver on an additional three stages. The second stage has two elements. The first element is concerned with products or services that perform to customers' expectations. The second element is concerned with creating imagery that engages customers from a psychological and social perspective. The third stage focusses on realising positive customer responses on the basis of both their opinions and evaluations of the brand (judgements) and their emotional responses to it (feelings). The last stage concerns the concept of resonance: developing a close relationship with customers that can lead to attitudinal and behavioural loyalty. Strong brands work at all stages, because their customers not only know about them, but also find they meet their functional and emotional needs. Strong brand equity can lead to high brand value (the financial value of a brand) because the more loyal the customer, the greater the certainty of future cash flows from the brand.

The power of brand equity is that it nails the idea that customer attitudes and behaviour are a vital element in understanding why companies are successful. The downside is that it is one thing to develop a strong equity, but quite another to keep it. How companies might build and maintain brand equity is the theme of the next sections.

## The Blueprint of Brand Management Models: Aaker's Brand Identity Planning Model

A brand needs to be actively managed – rarely is brand success just the result of luck (although sometimes it is) or the gut feeling of a marketing genius who follows his or her intuition. Numerous authors have tried to find a 'golden rule' of branding or a 'path to success' that could be applied or followed by companies to build and maintain brand equity. A lot of these approaches are phase models that divide brand management into different steps. Many of them are based, in one way or another, on the PDCA-Cycle (plan–do–check–act or plan–do–check–adjust), which is an iterative four-step management model for continuous improvement of processes and products. It has often been described in business literature and extensively used in practice.[184] The basic idea of the PDCA-Cycle is that activities need to be planned, which includes the setting of clear and measurable goals, before they are embarked upon. When implemented, there should be a monitoring of the activities to see if they meet the pre-defined objectives. If necessary, adjustments need to be made that will lead to a new planning of the activity. The PDCA-Cycle approach has influenced various brand management authors who have recommended using models that consist of four, five or even more phases. Most of the proposed models include an analytical phase where information about the image of the brand is collected and interpreted and markets are analysed; a strategic phase where central elements of the brand, such as the brand core and brand positioning, are decided by management; a phase of implementation where the appropriate measures to bring the brand to life are employed by marketing specialists and a final phase in which all actions are reviewed and perhaps adjusted.[185]

One well-known PDCA approach is David Aaker's *Brand Identity Planning Model*, which was first published in the 1990s. The model was one of the first of its kind and provided a blueprint for most of those that followed.[186] Aaker recommends that the first step of brand management should be a Strategic Brand Analysis, which comprises Customer Analysis, Competitor Analysis and Self-Analysis. The objective of the Customer Analysis is to identify the relevant trends in the market, to better understand the motivation of customers, to find out about unmet customer needs which could be served in the future, and to better understand the various market segments. The Competitor Analysis is needed to identify other market players and to understand their brand images, to learn about their strengths and weaknesses and to uncover any potential vulnerabilities. The Self-Analysis is a look inwards to get a clear view of the brand's existing image: its heritage, strengths, capabilities and organisational values.

Based on the outcomes of this first phase of the model, the identity of the brand should be defined by management in a second step, the so-called Brand Identity System. This element of the Brand Identity Planning Model analysis includes considering the definition of the Core Identity, which is described as 'the central, timeless essence of the brand', and its Extended Identity, which is more flexible and consists of grouped attributes 'that provide texture and completeness'.[187] This second phase should be completed with the formulation of a Value Proposition, which sums up the functional, emotional and self-expressive benefits of the brand from a customer viewpoint. In the third and last step of the Brand Identity Planning Model – the so-called Brand Identity Implementation System – a brand must be positioned, executed and tracked. Aaker sees Brand Positioning as a sub-set of the brand identity that is actively communicated by the company at a clearly defined target audience in order to provide a competitive advantage. The Execution involves establishing the definition of various measures, including the definition of brand symbols and metaphors as well as of communication activities. Finally, Tracking needs to be undertaken to see how successful the measures were in meeting the goal of bringing the brand positioning to life.

Aaker – and the writers that followed him with similar models – made significant contributions to the understanding of the brand management process and to the development of brand management as a discipline. Their main achievement was that they largely dispelled the view that a brand is merely a labelled product or symbol that can be created through advertising. Aaker, in particular, made it very clear that a brand is about substance: that it offers specific benefits that enable a brand to be positioned as a problem solver, friend or advisor. This view suggests that a brand is more than just the concern of a marketing or communications department, but rather must involve a holistic management approach.

While the brand management models of the recent past have been widely taught and used by organisations, most of them also have one central deficiency: they emphasise the dominance of managers as the definers and implementers of the brand and implicitly assume that brand managers are in control of the brand management process. The customer is largely seen as a passive recipient of communication, who does not participate in the brand planning process. For example, when looking at the Brand Identity Planning Model, it is noteworthy that the involvement of different stakeholder groups only takes place in the first phase of Strategic Brand Analysis. Here, insights into stakeholders' attitudes and behaviour are sought as a means of tailoring the brand to the needs and desires of different segments of a potential market, but this is not an invitation for outsiders to collectively shape the brand. In all subsequent steps, it is the brand owner or its representatives who give meaning to the brand, position it and implement appropriate measures to secure its effectiveness. Co-creative activities are not planned – neither in the formulation of a strategy, nor in its implementation. There are no feedback loops foreseen in the model. Overall, these models are managerial – concerned with what organisations do. They reflect an idea of brand identity as stable and enduring, in which the responsibility of managers is to create the discipline to maintain the brand's identity as it is designed to be implemented. Whatever happens at the implementation stage has no, or only a minor, influence on the Brand Identity System. If you agree with the idea that we presented in Chapter 2 concerning the way in which consumers have moved from passive to active participants in the development of brand image, then you will see that the brand management models of the past are problematic.[188]

## The Co-Creative Brand Management System

In a co-creative world, brand management is an enduring brand-related negotiation between different stakeholders where insights are continuously generated and interpreted, the brand's identity is simultaneously shaped and adapted and brand meaning is created through the actions of all participating parties. Building on this co-creative view, our model, which is introduced in Figure 5.1, emphasises that brand equity is generated within three basic brand-related activities which all occur at the same time. Successful companies use an open and participatory approach to generate the right brand-related insights and interpret them, and to transform those insights – while permanently challenging them – into a brand strategy while also adjusting and implementing that strategy (like a rubber band that is flexible but always comes back to its original form),[189] together with others to create brand meaning. Therefore, the first building block of our so-called Co-Creative Brand Management System is termed Generating and Understanding Brand-Related Insights. In the tradition of Aaker, and as we have already argued in Chapter 4, this includes conducting analysis of the brand-related views of internal and external stakeholders, learning about the positioning of competitors, understanding customers' central reasons for buying a particular product and considering how these things could change over time. Also, within this element of the model, the success of the brand management process is monitored and the resulting information serves as an instrument of brand control. Accordingly, the monitoring informs all the brand-related activities that may be adjusted during implementation. Useful instruments here include traditional quantitative and qualitative market research methods, such as customer or employee surveys, interviews and workshops; and 'deep approaches', such as ethnography and 'netnography'. To measure a brand's success financially – as a point of reference to measure improvements as the brand management process evolves, or as a source of information to initially feed the Co-Creative Brand Management System – brand valuation procedures can be used.

To understand or define a brand's identity, we need to look inwards and outwards. When brands are in the early stages of development, they often reflect the ideas and aspirations of a founder or founders, but over time the brand identity evolves as different stakeholders enact it and contest it. This process tends to lead to refinement, enrichment and clarification of the original intended identity, rather than to radical change, but there is still a sense of movement. Consequently, in the second building block of our model, Designing and Adjusting Brand Strategy, we reflect this fluidity by focussing on the brand's strategy: on

Figure 5.1 The Co-Creative Brand Management System

where the brand comes from, where it is now and its ambitions for the future. In a sense, this is about brand identity and intent – about what the brand will and won't do. But we argue that it is not only brand managers who define brand strategy. Management may take a first attempt to do so, but various stakeholders must be included in the process and participate in the development. This will become obvious when looking at the Hakkasan case presented in Chapter 7.

The third building block of our model has a co-creative perspective. Co-Creating Brand Equity is about implementing the brand strategy with the help of various stakeholders. It is more explicitly about the way people interact with the brand and how consumers build value with the organisation. In Chapter 8, we will discuss in more detail how brand value is co-created. This includes looking at a debate about the changing role of marketing communications in a world dominated by social media; a consideration of the role of events, storytelling and brand communities in brand building; and assessing ideas about how to co-create value with employees.

To help you understand the basis of the model, the following case illustrates a comprehensive and multi-phased brand management project for a global company from the service industry.[190] The case explains the different steps within the project and the instruments that were used to collect data, to define the brand's strategy, to co-create brand meaning and to control brand success. The strictly separate project phases, their description and the dominance of the management team reflect a time when brand identity was defined according to a more linear and traditional understanding of brand management. The high level of participation of various stakeholders and the willingness of the marketing department to partly give up control of the brand experience points to an emerging, more co-creative approach. In our eyes, this is what makes the case useful: it illustrates the transition from a perspective that sees the brand as organisationally controlled to one where different voices are emerging and gaining influence. In practice, it will often be necessary to make compromises in order to get decision-makers on board.

## The case of TNT Express

In 2007, the German subsidiary of the global logistics company, TNT Express, topped an industry survey of the strongest brands in the German parcel market. This was a surprise to everyone in the industry. At the same time, the company achieved one of its best financial results ever. This was even more remarkable, since Germany was not the home market of TNT (DHL, with its global headquarters in Bonn, Germany, had a very significant market share), and in earlier image rankings the company was an also-ran, way behind DHL, UPS and some local providers. What had happened?

Management attributed the new status as an admired brand partly to a branding project that started in 2003. In September of that year, the company specified project goals, established a steering committee and set a plan. In the following months, over 1,400 actual and potential customers, employees (including drivers) from all levels and departments were asked to state their opinion about the TNT brand. This was partly done via telephone and personal interviews and partly by way of workshops. The overall perception of the brand 'TNT' was quite positive, but strongly dominated by industry-typical generic characteristics like 'fast' or 'reliable'. Additionally, for employees the brand was largely shaped by the so-called 'TNT Spirit', as well as by high customer orientation. On a scale between 0 and 100, using a methodology that the market researchers who facilitated the analysis developed, the TNT brand achieved an overall rating in the low seventies. Perhaps more important than the score though was that the analysis helped to develop a common understanding of what the brand was all about and, consequently, set the ground for a deeper discussion about the brand's future positioning.

In the next project phase, which was termed 'defining the brand identity', the executive team analysed the results of the research in Brand Identity Workshops. The task of those workshops was to get a clear view on the brand's identity and to set the ground for a brand book in which the identity was clearly written down. During the process, in an attempt to include a more co-created view of the development of brand identity, the discussions were extended from the senior to the middle management and to so-called control groups. The control groups were formed of apprentices of the company. The idea was that this would ensure that the objectives developed at management level were in fact connected with the daily business and had relevance on the shop floor. When the brand book with the newly formulated value proposition was almost finished, but before it was finally decided upon, it was once again challenged and improved by a group of external partners (customers, advisors, marketing practitioners from other industries).

In the third project phase, where the focus of the project shifted from strategy formulation to implementation, 300 employees, drawn from all functional areas from the branches and from headquarters, were asked in 27 Brand-Value Conferences how the newly defined brand values could be integrated into day-to-day business. They were also asked to comment on the new value proposition and to provide proposals for brand-related projects. The idea of those projects was to define ways to bring the brand's core and its values to life. More than 40 long-term projects and immediate measures were identified. Accordingly, the executive team decided to establish a programme management plan to install project groups and to implement the proposals. The results of the projects were regularly monitored in board meetings. Parallel to the implementation process, an internal communication campaign was elaborated and executed, involving many different communication channels. For example, employees were sent packages with freshly printed brochures and various little gifts and gimmicks, all of which related to the new brand positioning. These shipments included a self-adhesive package tape saying 'Why say no when you can say no problem?' Employees were asked to use the tape and take a picture of it being used, which could be posted on an internal platform. The best photos were subsequently rewarded. The result was a plethora of photos showing employees using the tape in a challenging, humorous or everyday context to bring the brand to life. The marketing department didn't try to control this process. Rather, it just let people do what they felt was most appropriate. Mostly, this was positive, but there were also some marginal initiatives, like the driver who took a photo of a competitor's vehicle wrapped in the tape. Nonetheless, the idea allowed employees to get involved in the implementation process in their own way and to interpret the brand on their own terms. Some months after the kick-off of the internal campaign, an external campaign was launched to reach out to actual and potential customers via national print advertisements.

In the following months and years, market research about the brand was intensified and the brand became a permanent area of consideration, not only in the boardroom but throughout the whole company. Brand-related Key Performance Indicators, like brand awareness, brand sympathy and brand clarity, were defined and audited regularly. About four years after the project had been started, with the goal being to track progress and change measures if needed, the initial brand survey was repeated with the same questions and the same process. Though the overall rating of the TNT brand had now climbed to the mid-80s, the results also showed that some adjustments should be made regarding the brand's value proposition.[191]

## Learnings

There are several aspects of the case of TNT Express that seem interesting for our purposes. First, even if the project followed a clear roadmap, including the phases of brand analysis, identity definition, implementation and control, several feedback loops were integrated to ensure the project's success. Think about the workshops with apprentices to ensure that management's decisions were grounded in day-to-day-business, or the discussions with external partners before the new brand book was published. Through those measures, the connection of the brand to employees and customers was strengthened. Second, the involvement of various stakeholder groups also meant that brand management lost a degree of control of the brand management process. Think about the marketing department that developed a creative way to enable employees to express their personal connection with the brand. Third, in bringing the new positioning to life, an internal campaign was designed first and only then were marketing communication activities targeted at external markets. This supports the idea that brand management is an inside-out activity, which means that a company should focus on internal stakeholders to help build its brand before considering traditional marketing campaigns. And fourth, brand management is an ongoing process of attempting to align the brand's identity with the brand's image.[192]

# Reflections/questions

1) Think about a project that really mattered to you – for example, writing your student thesis, renovating where you live or starting a small business. How did you proceed? How did you manage the project? Can you find differences from, or similarities to, the way a brand management project should be managed?

2) Saint Augustine, an early Christian thinker, once said: 'You can ignite in others only the fire that burns in yourself.' How does this relate to co-creating brands?

3) Where would you expect hidden resistance, or even open opposition, to involvement of various stakeholder groups in the brand management process? What are the reasons for such opposition?

## We recommend the following reading to expand your learning experience:

Da Silveira, C., Lages, C. & Simões, C. (2013). 'Reconceptualizing brand identity in a dynamic environment', *Journal of Business Research*, 66(1), 28–36.

Zednik, A. & Strebinger, A. (2008). 'Brand management models of major consulting firms, advertising agencies and market research companies: a categorisation and positioning analysis of models offered in Germany, Switzerland and Austria', *Journal of Brand Management*, 15(5), 301–311.

# CHAPTER SIX

# Generating and understanding brand-related insights

## In this chapter...

Informed decisions and actions lie at the heart of successful brand management. Therefore, brand managers need a clear view as to which kind of brand-related insights are needed to initiate and inform the co-creative brand management system. We argue that to build a strong, long-lasting and flexible brand strategy at least three questions must be addressed: 1) What competencies are strongly connected with our brand? (This question reflects the need for authenticity in brand management); 2) How do our competitors position themselves in the market? (This question relates to the search for points of difference from other, similar offerings); 3) What, now and in the future, are the needs of consumers and society? (This last question points at the relevance of brand-related associations, and at their long-term sustainability, as a means of defining the brand's future direction.) In discussing these three basic questions, we will show how brand-related insights can be generated and interpreted using various sources of information, such as quantitative and qualitative research, workshops and observations. More specifically, we will focus on two related research methodologies which have proven to be very useful in the context of co-creation: ethnography, where the observer actively participates in the process and systematically analyses impressions through observation and questioning, and 'netnography', where the methods of ethnography are applied to communities on the Internet (brand communities). Furthermore, we also introduce the reader to the concept of brand valuation. There are many alternative approaches to valuation, but here, we will focus on one brand valuation approach. The insights generated in this building block of the co-creative brand management system do not only serve as an input for formulating a brand's strategy, but also as a means of controlling how a brand develops.

## Learning Objectives

After reading this chapter you should

- Understand why knowledge about a brand's history, as well as about its current reputation, is important for designing a brand's strategy – and be able to ask the right questions to collect the necessary information to do this;
- be aware that brand managers have to be familiar with the strategies and actions of their competitors to be able to lead a brand in a unique and targeted way;
- know that successful brand managers implement their strategies based on the existing and potential needs of their customers;
- understand why it is relevant to take central technological and societal developments (mega-trends) into account when developing the strategy for a brand;
- be able to explain some of the most important current mega-trends and understand how they impact the management of brands;
- be aware of various methods that help to generate and understand brand-related insights (specifically, you should be familiar with ethnography and 'netnography' and know how these methods can be used);
- understand the basics of brand valuation.

## What kind of insights are needed?

Whether managers are introducing a new brand to the market, or repositioning or extending an established brand, they need insight. This can be generated through traditional research methods, but it is common when working with a co-creative mindset to involve relevant stakeholders in the process (as you will see in the examples given later in this chapter). Acquiring insight is concerned with building knowledge about the image of the brand from the viewpoint of internal and external stakeholders (of employees in the former case, of customers and non-customers in the latter) as to the positioning of the competition, the current and future needs of consumers and the developments within an industry and society. However, the most important thing is perhaps to understand the brand itself — its deeper meaning and central strengths.

The first phase of the brand management system, which we call 'generating and understanding brand-related insights', involves analysing the brand and its markets. This phase should provide answers to at least three basic questions: 1) What does our brand stand for in the eyes of various stakeholders and how could this current position be used as a starting point for our future brand strategy? 2) How do our competitors position themselves and how can we differentiate our brand from theirs? 3) What are the current and future needs of customers and society? The following sections offer some basic ideas about how to collect and understand the relevant information. A good starting point here is to use a brand valuation process. There is nothing specifically co-creative about attaching a monetary value to a brand or brands, but the process has some important benefits. First, in some organisations brands struggle to command credibility. But when a monetary value is attached to them, senior managers start to take notice. Second, brand valuation is adept at pinpointing the relevant strengths and weaknesses of a brand. It can tell us, for example, that our brand is strong among young urban consumers but weak outside main cities, or that (for a B2B brand) we are strong among large companies but weak with start-ups. It can also show that in our portfolio of brands, we have some that are powerful and others that fail to command real loyalty. Third, although the accuracy of valuation can be questioned – it depends how good the assumptions and data are – it does nonetheless provide a measure against which received wisdom can be questioned and progress can be judged.

## Interbrand's brand valuation methodology

There are various consultants and researchers who offer brand valuation methodologies, but here we will focus on perhaps the best-known one.[193] In the later 1980s, the consultancy Interbrand developed a process that brought together thinking from accountancy practice and brand management to assess the financial value of a brand. Their timing was good, because the move coincided with a growing recognition of the importance of the value of intangible assets, such as brands. As other consultancies have entered the field, so Interbrand has re-designed its methodology. Interbrand is well-known not only because of its pioneering role, but also because it publishes a list every year of the 100 'Best Global Brands' in terms of their financial value.[194] The list is a good piece of reputation building and is widely referenced, but the interesting aspect here is the methodology that Interbrand uses to help companies generate valuable insights into their brand eco-systems.[195] Let's have a closer look at the building blocks of their model.

Like other competing processes, Interbrand's method requires a brand to segment its market into like-minded groups. The rationale for this is that different market segments will behave in different ways. This is obviously true if we look at different stakeholder groups such as retailers and consumers, but it is also true of consumer groups. Lumping consumers together might make things easier but it can also reduce the robustness of the analysis, so there is merit in segmenting consumers into groups that have similar behaviours. Once an accurate segmentation is achieved, there are three modules that need to be applied to each segment. The three model modules are 'financial analysis', 'role of the brand' and 'brand strength'. The complete process provides a brand valuation for each customer segment and through combining the segments, an overall brand value.

The first building block of the model is the financial analysis. The key indicator here is the economic profit of each segment, which shows the operating profit of the customer segment after taxes, reduced by the cost of the capital invested in the business activity. To do this analysis, a company needs a financial forecast of the economic profit for the next five years. Estimates of the brand's financial performance beyond the forecast period can also be included in the model. The discount factor is determined based on the average cost of capital of the company.

The role that the brand plays in the purchasing decision process is reflected in the second component of the brand rating process. The 'Role of Brand Index' (RBI) measures the percentage of the purchase decision that is attributable to the brand compared to other purchasing-related factors such as price, product characteristics or customer service. The information gained from the financial forecast is now merged with the RBI. The discounted future earnings, calculated on the basis of the forecasts of the economic profit, are corrected by the RBI so that only the brand-induced share is considered for further analysis.

In the analysis of brand strength, the third component of the brand rating process, the brand's ability to build loyalty and generate demand and profitability in the future is calculated. The brand strength is measured on a scale of 0 to 100 and is based on the evaluation of 10 criteria, which Interbrand believes are crucial for a strong brand. They include the following (see Table 6.1):

Table 6.1  Interbrand's 10 brand strengths (Source: Adapted from https://www.interbrand.com/best-brands/best-global-brands/methodology; accessed 6 March 2019)

| Internal Criteria | External Criteria |
| --- | --- |
| Clarity: clarity about what the brand stands for (values, positioning, proposition); clarity about target audiences; clarity customer insights and drivers. | Authenticity: the brand promise is experienceable and rooted in the company history as well as a well-grounded set of values. The brand meets the expectations of customers. |
| Commitment: internal bonding with the brand and a belief internally as to its importance. The extent to which the brand receives support (time, influence, resources). | Differentiation: perceived as being different compared to the competition. |
| Governance: the degree to which the organisation has the required skills, and an operating model, for the brand that enables effective and efficient deployment of the brand strategy. | Presence: to what extent is the brand present in the market and how intensively do people talk about it in traditional and social media? |
| Adaptability: can the brand adapt to market challenges and take advantage of corresponding opportunities? | Engagement: the degree to which customers and consumers show a deep understanding of, active participation in, and a strong sense of identification with the brand. |
| | Relevance: the degree to which the brand meets the needs, wishes and buying criteria of the customer across all relevant demographic and geographical segments. |
| | Consistency: the extent to which the brand is experienced consistently across all key points of contact. |

The strength of the brand is determined by the analysis of existing data, surveys and expert judgements compared to other industry brands and leading global brands. The brand strength correlates negatively with the degree of risk associated with the financial forecast. In other words, the higher the brand is rated, the lower the risk of future non-expected returns. The argument is that a strong brand has more loyal customers and thus carries a lower financial risk – because the probability that the predicted cash flows will be delivered is higher. The specific link between the brand strength score and the brand-specific discount rate can be described by an S-curve.

The monetary brand value is now calculated by applying the brand-specific discount rate, determined on the basis of the analysis of brand strength to the brand's future revenue, which was itself determined in the financial forecast. As a result, you get the present value of the brand-specific income by segment. This reflects the brand's ability to successfully meet future challenges and to actually generate the expected returns.

The brand valuation approach of Interbrand is widely used. Its advantages are obvious. First, the approach takes into account behavioural and financial variables to identify a monetary brand value. Second, it is able to measure brand strength among different segments (consumers, retailers) and to compare them with the overall brand strength. Third, when analysing brand strength, Interbrand considers external but also internal perspectives, which, in the latter case, involves recognising employees and their attitude to the brand as a significant driver of brand strength. Fourth, there are data on many companies already rated by Interbrand. This allows for good comparability with competitors. Fifth, the approach receives a high level of acceptance at the decision-maker level. Sixth, the approach results in a monetary brand value.

However, some elements of the approach can be criticised. The procedure is not transparent in every respect, which becomes obvious when determining the brand-specific discount factor based on the indices of brand strength. In addition, it is not always possible to ensure that the Brand Strength Score's rating is objective (using expert judgement) and that the dimensions of brand strength are independent of each other. It can also be very difficult to make reliable forecasts of the economic profit of a brand and sometimes there are challenges in segmenting economic data in line with brand segments. Finally, the cost of obtaining all relevant data for non-listed companies can be relatively high.

## The three basic questions of brand analysis

Despite the criticisms of brand valuation approaches, assigning a financial value to an intangible asset (such as a brand) can be a good starting point for brand analysis, especially because the methodology can provide interesting insights. However, brand valuation is just a tool. The wider goal, as noted in the introduction to this chapter, is to understand the deeper meaning and core strengths of the brand itself by collecting information that inspires its future development. Therefore, let's consider in more detail the three basic questions (mentioned at the beginning of this chapter) that must be answered in this phase of the co-creative brand management system: 1) What does our brand stand for in the eyes of various stakeholders and how could this current position be used as a starting point for the future brand strategy? 2) How do our competitors position themselves and how can we differentiate our brand from them? 3) What are the current and future needs of customers and society?

## How is the brand perceived by its stakeholders?

While many brands have a long history, others are newly minted. Whether the history is long or short, to understand a brand's actual and potential positioning in a market it is valuable to have a thorough analysis of the past. Understanding where a brand comes from is important both as a means of appreciating the strategic options for the brand, and for understanding the potential use of authenticity. This has implications for the brand both internally and externally. Employees are more likely to support brand strategies that they perceive as authentic[196] and consumers long for authentic experiences, which are often derived from their sense of the brand's history.[197] Christoph Burmann and his colleagues explain our preference for authentic brands as follows:[198]

> In recent years, the authenticity of a brand has increasingly gained in importance as a lever for differentiation. This is due to the severe loss of trust as a result of the non-authentic behavior of many brands, e. g. in the banking sector, the food industry and the energy sector. While a vague brand positioning leads to a reduced credibility of the brand promise, an authentic brand guarantees for the 'genuineness' of the brand promise. Authentic brands use this to strengthen the trust placed in them. Brand authenticity is therefore a determining factor that comes before trust.

The importance of authenticity is particularly notable in the context of new products offered by established companies. Today, when managers consider the broadening of a brand's offer, access to formal knowledge is not the most significant barrier they face. In principle, many companies have the technological know-how to produce and sell many more products than they do today. Would it be so bizarre if Apple built washing machines or if Mars marketed a yoghurt? Washing machines are probably no more complicated than computers and Mars undoubtedly has excellent connections to retailers to place a new yoghurt on the supermarket shelves. And even if those companies didn't have the necessary skills and resources today, they could undoubtedly quickly acquire them. However, the key question is not so much whether a company objectively has such capabilities, but whether we, as consumers, believe that they are able to satisfy our needs in a way that is superior to the competition. Miele builds good washing machines. Could Apple build better ones? Danone is a successful marketer of various yoghurt brands such as Activa or Actimel. Could Mars better market a new product? It is the lack of authenticity, not so much our missing trust, in Apple or Mars that probably would make such products a failure.

The history of a brand, what it has achieved in the past and what it is or was known for, can be an inspiration for its future. Building on the past certainly creates authenticity. Take, for example, the German premium watch brand A. Lange & Söhne, which manufactures models that can cost up to 100,000 euros or more.[199] Since the launch of the brand in 1994 the watches have been regarded as among the best in the world. The interesting thing here is to consider how a newcomer from Germany managed to succeed in an industry dominated by Swiss companies, mostly with long histories? In part, it is because A. Lange & Söhne does itself have a long history that goes back to 1845. Unfortunately, the company's factory was destroyed by bombs in one of the last nights of the Second World War. And then in 1948, the Soviet administration nationalised the company and the A. Lange & Söhne brand disappeared. Only with the fall of the Berlin Wall in November 1989 could Walter Lange (the son of the brand's last owner) and the successful watch manager Günter Blümlein realise their dream and revive the brand. Although there was nearly 50 years between the death of the brand and its resurrection, Lange and Blümlein were confident that the consumers and fans of the A. Lange & Söhne brand would connect with its heritage. To position the brand, the two entrepreneurs used several cues to point at the company's history. For example, the brand refers to its Saxonian heritage while the brand's founder, Ferdinand Adolph Lange, is introduced as the originator of Saxonian precision watchmaking. The visual appearance of the brand also signals a traditional, long-established company.

In addition to the example of A. Lange & Söhne, cases have been written about how brands such as LEGO, Tiffany, adidas, Carlsberg and Burberry have tapped into their past to uncover the essence of their brand and develop strategies that create a clear point of difference from their respective competitors. Some researchers have noted that the past can create what is called path dependence (a cage that limits strategic choice),[200] but others note that properly used, the past can liberate and enrich the brand through path creation.[201] The researchers Kaplan and Orlikowski note that developing a strategy 'thus involves constructing and reconstructing strategic narratives that reimagine the past and present in ways that allow the organisation to explore multiple possible futures'.[202] The luxury fashion brand Burberry provides an interesting illustration of this idea.[203]

Burberry is a well-known and successful luxury fashion label with nearly 500 outlets and more than 10,000 employees. The company was founded in England in 1856 by 21-year-old dressmaker Thomas Burberry. The brand became famous for its outerwear – partly through official endorsement as an official supplier to the British royal family, and partly through the endorsement of celebrities, such as Humphrey Bogart. The clothes were seen as stylish because of these connections, but also practical as the coats were worn by British officers in the trenches (hence the name 'trench coat') in the First World War and by the members of Sir Ernest Shackleton's Antarctic expeditions. In a newspaper advertisement from 1926, Burberry was praised as 'The King of Weatherproofs'.

Despite this long and successful history, by the early 2000s the brand was struggling. Over the years, the regional distributors and licensees had been granted a great deal of freedom in terms of the design and product range. This resulted in a confusing and regionally diverse range of Burberry products, which included such trivial items as dog leashes. There was no consistency in the offer and Burberry was represented in more and more distribution channels. The brand offered something for everybody, but not much of it was distinctive or exclusive. Outerwear, the segment with which the Burberry story started, represented less than 20 per cent of the company's global business. The result was that the brand was diluted. Many customers no longer perceived Burberry as a prestige brand and its growth lagged considerably behind its competitors.

In 2006, Angela Ahrendts, a fashion manager who had previously worked at Donna Karan and Liz Claiborne, joined Burberry as CEO. After meeting with management and staff, and studying important milestones and learning about the history and culture of the company, she and her chief designer, Christopher Bailey, decided to reinforce the Burberry heritage but at the same time to modernise it. Using craftsmanship and Britishness as the core values, they set about creating a modern and innovative interpretation of those values to produce a modern luxury brand. The iconic trench coat was the symbol of the new focus on the brand's heritage. The product was typically British, but in spite of its aura, it wasn't sold at a premium price. Ahrendts raised the prices of the trench coat, initiated new innovative designs and made sure that it was always visible in the display windows of the stores and on the first page of Burberry's webpage. Visit the online shop and you can still see (as of 2019) the main categories 'Men', 'Women', 'Kids' and 'The Trench Coat'.

With a stronger focus on the brand's heritage, supported by a courageous restructuring process which touched all areas of the business, Ahrendts and her team succeeded in turning round the failing luxury fashion brand. By 2012, 60 per cent of the business was apparel. With outerwear counting for 50 per cent of the apparel business, revenues and operating income had doubled and Burberry was the fastest-growing luxury brand. Once her mission was complete, Ahrendts left Burberry in 2014 and headed for Apple.

## Analysis of a brand's heritage

The example of Burberry and A. Lange & Söhne shows how important a company's heritage can be. Burberry's trench coat is a symbol of the brand's enduring meaning and a core part of the brand. Similarly, the founder of A. Lange & Söhne, Ferdinand Adolph Lange, has been the spiritual essence of the newly founded brand and has helped to bring the company back to life. As brand consultant Achim Feige says: 'A brand is a value creation system that is charged with values and peak performances, which can then be marketed.'[204] The question though is how can brand managers find out about those values and peak performances? To discover what a brand stands or could stand for, we need both to understand the internal perspective, i.e. that of the brand's management team, its shareholders and the company's employees, and an array of external assumptions, i.e. the view of customers, the general public and suppliers. Questions that need to be asked in reference to both perspectives include the following:[205]

- What is unique about the brand?
- What is the brand known for?
- What made the brand successful in the past?
- What achievements of the brand are remembered by customers and society?
- What special competencies does the brand have that cannot be found (or that can only rarely be found) at competitors?
- Which customer and societal problems can only be solved by the brand?
- What distinguishes the brand from other brands?

But how to collect all this information? Let's start with the internal perspectives. Companies can easily forget what they know and corporate memories can be selective. For example, adidas long believed that the first runner wearing shoes (designed by the founder, Adi Dassler) to win an Olympic medal (bronze) was at the 1932 Olympics in Los Angeles. This iconic event was presented in official stories about the brand. However, in preparing a history book about the brand in 2009, researchers discovered that a runner in Dassler spikes had won gold at the 1928 Olympics in Amsterdam. Similarly, following the death of Adi Dassler in 1978, when the company was keen to focus on the future, it decided to reject its past. Dassler had an extensive collection of worn shoes, and also of notebooks covering more than 50 years of ideas. As these were no longer seen as relevant they were put into storage and forgotten. Some 30 years later, when the company re-appraised the importance of its past and established a history management department to build and curate an archive, the material was rediscovered and used to inform the company's strategy and a selection of his thoughts was published as a book.

The example of adidas illustrates that the past can be hidden from view (although today, with an archive of 90,000 items and 10,000 images, it is very visible and actively informs the development of the brand). This means that you may have to dig for information, but past products and communications can contain important brand-relevant information. Sources can include current and past marketing materials such as brochures, advertisements and TV commercials and other information that can be found in company archives. Sometimes, companies have a brand museum (adidas has a Walk of Fame), where the history of the brand is displayed. In addition, long-term employees and managers can be asked about the milestones in the company's history, special achievements and other typical brand characteristics. It is valuable here to involve in the process as many employees as possible, both in order to collect rich information and to increase the acceptance rates of the later results. Therefore, interviews should be conducted with representatives from as many departments and hierarchical levels as possible. If they are approachable, the shareholders should also be represented in interviews, discussions and workshops.

To illustrate the practice of learning about oneself and building internal insight, we can turn to the Frankfurt-based company WISAG, which employs 23,000 people and offers services in the fields of aviation and facility management. The goal here was to uncover what differentiated WISAG from the competition and how these attributes might be strengthened. To find out how WISAG was seen internally, the company undertook a comprehensive brand survey, involving employees across all functions and hierarchical levels, and conducted 10 intensive workshops with some 100 people from the shop floor. During the workshops the employees had three tasks:

1) Design a poster or mood board (a collage of text and/or images) to describe what is unique about WISAG.

2) Develop a code of conduct that lists the things a new colleague at WISAG should definitely do and should by no means do.

3) Write a story in a fairy-tale style ('once upon a time ...') based on anecdotes from their working life.

The workshop outputs helped the company better understand the WISAG brand from the inside. WISAG then turned to external audiences to survey B2B customers and potential customers. The whole process fuelled discussions within the decision bodies of the company, including the union councils, resulting in a major repositioning of the brand and the definition of three basic values: 'appreciation, commitment and colorful'.[206]

## Conducting external research

The internal view must be complemented by an understanding of the perceptions of external stakeholders. Often organisations will use quantitative methods which measure constructs like brand image, brand personality or brand associations. To do this, brand researchers have developed reliable scales which often need to be adapted to the specific needs of a certain industry.[207] Based on those scales, market researchers offer a variety of proven methods and tools to collect representative data. This is likely to be particularly valuable if the results are to be presented to company-wide decision-making bodies (supervisory boards of stock exchange-listed companies), who usually prefer to base their decisions on large samples. In most companies, customer surveys will be done on a regular basis, and this data can be used if it contains brand-specific information. Additionally, methods of sentiment analysis are often used to analyse social media communication and to specifically uncover the tone of voice of consumers when they talk about specific brands on social media. Sentiment analysis refers to the use of artificial intelligence to evaluate large quantities of written text.[208] With the help of sentiment analysis, for example, a hotel brand's management could find out if the service when checking in or out was perceived positively, neutrally or negatively by consumers who commented about their corresponding experience on social media. However, it is not always necessary to collect representative data from large samples. From a brand management perspective, it is about finding answers to the previously mentioned questions. Therefore, it can be more valuable to conduct qualitative research (for example, through interviews, focus groups or the use of the diary method, where consumers report their own perceptions and observations), which can give greater depth of understanding and may be more appropriate when conducting exploratory research, where there are a greater number of questions to address.

As a way of generating insight and reducing risk, quantitative and qualitative techniques are widely used. In 2017, the global turnover of the market research industry was more than $45 billion. These techniques offer a tried-and-tested way of working and can deliver valuable insights into the attitudes and behaviour of external stakeholders in particular. Not surprisingly, every marketing and brand course will devote considerable attention to the practice of market research. However, in spite of the prevalence of market research in business, there are some challenges with it, which you should know.

First, traditional market research can be effective in testing and evaluating concepts developed by the organisation, but it is less good at idea generation and involving stakeholders. To maintain scientific credibility, researchers aim to be objective and to keep a distance between the researcher and the subject of research. The goal here is neutrality – even if in practice this is hard to achieve. Yet the problem is that this focus on objectivity means it is harder to uncover people's latent needs and to explore new ideas together with consumers. This tends to make surveys, focus groups and interviews good for looking back, but less useful in exploring future possibilities.

Second, market research results are necessarily abstract. Conduct a study and you can obtain insight into how people might behave, but 'people', or even a subset of them, such as 18–22-year-old males with a penchant for online gaming and in full-time study, is an abstraction. The challenge here is that we mistake the abstract for the real. In planning a brand strategy or managing a brand promotion, managers will refer to the abstraction as if all those in that segment will behave in a like-minded way. It takes away individuality in order to secure the convenience of predicted common behaviours. This in itself is not a problem, because the act of thinking involves abstraction and ignoring difference. But it is important that managers remember that research is an abstraction.

Third, market research findings can easily be forgotten. Research is mostly commissioned by insights and market research managers to address a particular issue or gap in knowledge raised by organisational managers. The research is conducted, the findings presented and in time these things are forgotten. It is not unusual to find that organisations don't know what they know. Knowledge exists in pockets in the market research department or in the experiences of frontline staff, but it is not shared across the organisation. Mostly, this is a case of organisational forgetting, but it is also the case that sometimes research and knowledge is distorted by giving emphasis to some things and suppressing those that do not fit with managerial intent or the strategic story.

The above arguments are not designed to undermine the value of market research, but they are intended to suggest that when it comes to co-creating brands and involving stakeholders, some research principles and practices can get in the way. One way round this is to take a different view of stakeholders. In a two-stage study by Swedish researchers into the uses of co-creation and traditional research techniques, they argue that organisations need to see customers as active contributors with relevant knowledge and skills. Whereas traditional research can uncover manifest needs, it is less successful when it comes to unearthing more deeply rooted needs and desires, not least because the research is conducted on the organisation's own terms.[209]

In a co-creative approach, more innovative ideas are likely to emerge, especially if the research is conducted in people's own environments. The co-creation approach shifts thinking away from the rules of research to the rules of people. It is a human-centric approach that goes deeper by way of a willingness to encourage participation.[210] The Zaltman Metaphor Elicitation Technique (ZMET), for example, is a patented qualitative research method that builds on the interaction between researchers and participants, and is often used to better understand consumers' perceptions of brands. The technique was developed in the 1990s by Gerald Zaltman at Harvard Business School. It is a procedure that brings thoughts and feelings to light that would stay uncovered in most traditional research settings. Participants in such studies are asked to collect photos, drawings or pictures that represent their overall attitudes towards the brand or that remind them of concrete brand-related experiences. In a second step, those pictures are interpreted by the researchers, often together with the help of the participants.[211] This latter step makes the endeavour co-creative.

Out of the many innovative research techniques that exist, here we will outline how two methods – ethnography and its online variant, 'netnography' – can be used in co-creation. In this book you will find examples of organisations – such as hospitality group Hakkasan, IKEA and the Canadian healthcare provider, Mayfair Diagnostics – that use ethnography, 'netnography' and other immersive practices to define and build their brands.

## The Practice of Ethnography

Go and watch people standing at a bus stop. Or observe them as they cook dinner at home. Or even go and take part in the meetings of an outlaw motorcycle gang. Market researchers wouldn't normally do these things. You'd send out a questionnaire to ask people about their travel experience or bring family cooks into a focus group to spend an hour talking about how they shop for and make food. And you'd probably leave the outlaw motorcycle gang alone. Ethnography, though, is different. As the sociologist Karen O'Reilly says, whereas quantitative studies are based on a positivist view that seeks structural patterns and laws in the data, 'ethnographic research and analysis emerge from an interpretation of the motivations, thinking, and ideas that generate the patterned mosaic of social life.'[212]

Ethnography aims to look at people in context, so rather than asking people what it's like to cook dinner, you sit and watch them in the kitchen and ask questions. You try and stay open to possibilities. Instead of deciding before you start what the issues are, you decide on a research quest and learn as you go along. If you have trouble imagining what this is like, just look at an immersive television journalist such as Louis Theroux (who has been making documentaries since the late 1990s) and how he tackles often difficult subjects in context and with seeming naivety. Theroux doesn't judge the people he talks to, no matter how uncomfortable their ideas can be, but rather he listens and asks open questions. Of course Theroux's presence, and that of the camera and sound crew, does affect how people behave, but ethnography accepts that the researcher is involved, even while they try to be detached. Ken Andersen of Intel describes ethnography like this: 'Unlike traditional market researchers, who ask specific, highly practical questions, anthropological researchers visit consumers in their homes or offices to observe and listen in a nondirected way. Our goal is to see people's behaviour on their terms, not ours. While this observational method may appear inefficient, it enlightens us about the context in which customers would use a new product and the meaning that product might hold in their lives.'[213]

To help stay open to new ideas, the practice of ethnography aims to follow people and their interests, rather than guide or control them. This method is known as iterative-inductive, which means that the researcher begins with as few preconceptions as possible. The inductive (as opposed to deductive) method is concerned with allowing theories to emerge as a way of explaining what is being observed, rather than with using theories to frame a certain way of seeing. This process recognises that we cannot jump from blissful ignorance to knowledge but that as we participate, observe, listen, talk and think, we are in a loop of learning, forming judgements and testing them as we go along. This iterative process combines both discovery and analysis as we inch towards deeper insights. The implication is that conducting ethnographic research requires Theroux-like naivety. Within social science research this is known as an 'emic' approach. In simple terms, an emic approach tries to see the world from the view of the insider. So, to take the example of the outlaw motorcycle gang, the approach would aim to adopt the perspective of the gang member and to observe their actions and thoughts as if one were also a gang member. The contrasting approach is known as 'etic', whereby the researcher tries to see the behaviours of the observed group in the context of a wider environment. Inevitably, there is bias involved here because the researcher pays attention to some things more than others, but the combination of an emic and etic approach provides for both a rich description of the behaviours of people and the ability to uncover the meaning behind their behaviour.

A further distinction of ethnography is that it is not simply about what people say. Most obviously, it can be about what they *don't* say. Listen to a politician when asked about a difficult issue and the things they avoid saying, or think about that bus queue and the lack of any dialogue between people standing next to each other. Sometimes this not saying is a result of deliberate evasion (as in the case of the politician), but at other times it can be the product of a lack of reflection or perceived lack of importance. Often, we work round the challenges of daily life – signs we don't understand, software that doesn't do what we expect it to, forms that frustrate us, household products that are inefficient – without saying anything. The role of ethnography is to uncover these hidden issues by watching people's lives *in situ*, looking at the rituals they adhere to and their interaction with artefacts. If a company wants to generate insight into how to develop a new vacuum cleaner, for example, it could conduct a focus group in an office and ask people what they do when cleaning at home, or conduct a quantitative survey about which machine people use, how often they clean and what they find to be the most difficult cleaning problems. However, they could go and spend time with people in their homes and watch them as they clean, all the while taking photographs, making notes, asking them why they do what they do, discussing their challenges and imagining with them better solutions.

From a co-creation perspective, ethnography's value derives both from the depth of insight it offers and from the ability to involve customers and other stakeholders in the process. In ethnography, depth comes not necessarily from large numbers, but from the searching, probing approach that it encourages. Ethnographic researchers are sometimes also afforded the time to dig deep (something that can easily become comprised in commercial contexts). Remember the outlaw motorcycle gangs. Here's Christian Schmid from the Technical University in Dortmund, talking about his experience of studying them:

As I proceeded to attend some hardcore biker events I would soon come to the conclusion that it was never an option for me to operate undercover and infiltrate this lifeworld (complete participation). I decided that I would continue to try to recruit volunteers I could interview. After a year's span of desperate attempts and attendance in numerous meetings (a form of participant as observer), I had finally gained the trust and established rapport with a few bikers that allowed me to build a theoretically informed sample of 20 interviewees ready to cooperate.[214]

It is also not the case that only researchers can do ethnography. Stakeholders can as well. For example, the telecom company Orange recruited some 40 of its customers to be ethnographers – to go out over several weeks and observe the behaviour of friends and family and their use of mobile telephony. The process then fed into a workshop, where the customer ethnographers and Orange managers worked together to create new ideas. The approach required some basic training to conduct the ethnographic research, but when consumers are asked about participating with brands, they like the idea of learning new skills and they particularly like the idea of becoming part-time ethnographers.[215]

Ethnography challenges some traditional research practices through its willingness to encourage participation. Customers don't need to be kept at distance. They are quite capable, if well supported, of expressing opinions and creating solutions. It's also the case that ethnographic research can help a researcher pinpoint the role of a brand in people's lives and bring that to life through the tools of ethnography, such as photos, videos and rich descriptions of the environment in which events take place. Ethnography is not about validating choices, which is where other forms of research are more valuable. It is about inspiration. It can help bring the experience of consumers to life for senior managers and it can enable researchers to see new meanings and new possibilities – especially when researchers are effective in conveying the context in which their research has been conducted. Take this description by Robert Kozinets of his experience of attending the highly participative Burning Man festival – an annual cultural event held in the Black Rock Desert in Nevada. From his words you can see, hear and smell the festival:

> The sun beats down. My shoes scratch over the parched and crumbling floor of fine dust. It is dinnertime, and the smell of charcoal and cooking food joins with the omnipresent alkali scent of desert dust and burning kerosene. The clanking throb of hundreds of generators melds with the sounds of distant music, rhythmic drumming, and shouts. A walk on the wild side, the Burning Man festival is a radical departure, a feast for all the senses. I pass people in intricate costumes, with butterfly wings, helmets, huge hats, strange hats, body armor, leather bondage outfits, historical costumes, alien costumes.[216]

The description focusses on the experience of physical interactions – what then are we to make of the role of online ethnography? This area of activity, which involves immersing oneself in online cultures, is known as 'netnography' and was pioneered by the Burning Man participant Robert Kozinets. Rather than paraphrasing his ideas about the subject, it seemed to make more sense to ask him to write down the ideas himself.

## Netnographies of the Future

*Author: Robert V. Kozinets*

### Prognostication

From time immemorial, people have dreamed of being able to access the future. Indeed, as Clifford Pickover's delightfully quirky book *Dreaming the Future* makes clear, human beings have used an almost inexhaustible variety of methods to try to ascertain what is coming next.[217] Have you ever heard of kephalanomancy? That's the burning of a piece of carbon on the head of an ass to predict the future. How about onychomancy? Divination by observing the reflection of the sun on a person's fingernails, of course. And haruspicy? Obviously, it's a pre-Roman method of divination that involves studying the shapes of animal guts. And Pickover has scores more.

Slightly more scientific, one would hope, but perhaps equally peculiar in name is netnography. Netnography is the use of various qualitative research methods to study social media in a way that maintains the complexities of its lived experience and cultural qualities.[218] Netnography is, in short, a series of six sometimes overlapping 'movements', where movement 4 is considered optional by many researchers (but is often desirable):

1) Initiation: formation of a research question or business problem that needs solving, and can be solved through social media data; formation of criteria for data collection.

2) Investigation: focussed search for rich sources of social media data, followed by evaluations and real-time reading of that data, evaluation of the quality of the data for the research purpose and the saving of the most relevant, criteria-meeting data.

3) Immersion: reflective practices that capture the personal experience of relevant social media use from the researcher perspective; performed individually, but often combined later with the work of other collaborative researchers.

4) Interaction: data elicitation from relevant social actors through (usually online) interview, research web-pages, digital diaries or other methods.

5) Integration: combining analysis (coding and pattern matching) and interpretation (meaning making and holistic connection and reconnection) of the entire dataset in search of answers to the questions or problems posed in 1.

6) Incarnation: communication of research findings in a relevant format; the clear answer to the question or problem posed in 1.

As this short section will describe, a number of contemporary companies and researchers use netnography to forecast the future needs of consumers. I say, with a touch of irony, that netnography is slightly more scientific than cromniomancy (divination using onion sprouts, of all things) because, as we should always remember, prognosticating inevitably involves guesswork. Nonetheless, it is often necessary.

## Netnography as Oracle
In an early work, I described motivated social media influencers as 'devoted, enthusiastic, knowledgeable and innovative' and noted that, in their public displays of 'enthusiasm, knowledge, and experimentation' with products and consumption 'they can provide information similar to that from "lead users".'[219] Lead users are, of course, the leading edge, highly motivated consumers who are used in lead user analysis to predict and generate ideas for desirable future innovations. According to Eric von Hippel's founding definition, lead users are 'users whose present strong needs [that] will become general' in future times, thus providing an accessible crystal ball for managers and others who are interested in structured modes of market divination.[220] Although von Hippel devised his term to talk about customers and marketplaces, his concept may also be applicable to other situations and needs, such as those involved in political or general social trend forecasting.

In my research, to illustrate the lead user qualities of social media participants, I chose one social media group, a newsgroup/bulletin board, that discussed coffee online.[221] I examined this online group of coffee enthusiasts, looking for situations, events, conversations and people who were driven by strong needs for development and pushing the boundaries of what was then possible for coffee culture. The objective of the marketing research study, determined in the initiation stage, was to inform future coffeehouse retailers and others who might benefit from the development of innovative new product ideas. Looking back at the study, which was conducted almost two decades ago, it is interesting to note that some of the influencers who were present on that newsgroup are still active influencers today. For example, Mark Prince, who was on the [alt.coffee] group that I investigated from 1998 to 2001, still Tweets and blogs and runs the Coffeegeek.com website.

## Influencers and Lead User Omens

What the netnography of this dedicated group found was that coffee marketers had barely even begun to plumb the depths of taste, status and snob-appeal that were waiting to be explored by discriminating coffee consumers. Putting the future predictions into press, I forecasted that retailers like Starbucks still had a major opportunity to develop connoisseur coffee markets with offerings such as 'new brands and blends of beans, new means of delivering the freshest of fresh beans (online and offline), new means of roasting, new bean roasting services, new espresso and cappuccino machines, new forms of education and instruction, new coffee tasting clubs, and new types of cafés'.[222] And, indeed, those netnography driven predictions about the future of coffee retailing have proven to be as robust as a good robusta coffee blend.

In 2016, Starbucks launched Starbucks Reserve, an ultra-high premium coffee market offering that features large selections of branded and blended beans, new means to roast coffee (including a 22-foot bronze roasting cask that folds and unfolds like a flower in bloom), new coffee preparation mechanisms, education sessions (including coffee tasting 'flights' with explanatory cards), coffee tasting menus and both expansive and extraordinary themed retail environments (such as the reportedly $20 million Starbucks Reserve in Milan, which features augmented reality experiences and was described by *Cosmopolitan* magazine as 'Disneyland for coffee lovers'). Starbucks Reserve has been a major success, reportedly earning as much as 300 per cent more revenue per square foot than a regular Starbucks. The Starbucks concept has clear echoes of the lead user recommendations from 14 years before.

## Developing Netnography for Future Prediction

Other researchers have followed up on my initial idea that netnographic research can be effectively used to identify social media sites devoted to particular user and consumption groups and to study the most forward-looking needs and innovative solutions that they propose. In 2010, Belz and Baumbach were one of the earliest to explore the usefulness of netnography as a way to identify lead users.[223] They noted that the traditional ways to screen for lead users are time-consuming, expensive, rely upon self-assessment and also tend to be inefficient. Their research demonstrates that netnographic research, on the other hand, can be performed relatively quickly, at low cost, use organic or naturalistic data and be highly efficient. In fact, their research revealed that focussing on social media conversations that are coded as 'ahead of trend' and 'dissatisfaction' can provide 'a high discriminatory power' to separate out the future-predictive lead users from their less-predictive peers.[224] Following this logic, the same sorts of principles used to identify influencers in the social media sphere can also, it seems, be employed to effectively locate motivated users. Lead users can help us discern the shape of future demand in different markets. In some cases, the two groups – influencers in social media and lead users – may even be one and the same.

Here is another example of a development of these initial, coffee-grounded ideas and examples. In 2015, Brem and Bilgram found netnography to be an effective method for identifying lead users in commercial projects.[225] Their conclusions about the role of social media in forecasting offer new insights, most notably that 'the more profound and elaborate the identified needs' are for the project, 'the easier it is to find lead users' using techniques such as netnography.[226] This conclusion is highly advantageous. One might consider it easier to conjecture future needs for rather mundane and simple matters. However, according to their findings, netnography actually reveals subtle and sophisticated needs better than it does ordinary ones. Why would this be so?

## Collective Intelligence in Networks of Desire

The reason netnography is effective at elaborating sophisticated needs is attributable to an underlying cultural principle in which the sum of social media participants' comments is more valuable than the individual comments themselves. Social media groups devoted to particular topics are a type of social organism. We could call them a collective, too. Or an assemblage with unique new capacities. Within these groupings, people share their fascinations and amplify each other's knowledge, creativity and interests. An awareness of this collective principle has been baked into netnography since it was originally devised to further the study of the passionate and creative posts of online media fan communities devoted to complex, intertextual entertainment properties such as *The X-Files*, *Star Trek* and *Star Wars*. The similar ability of other social media groups gathered around particular topics to amplify desire, solve complex problems and extend creativity in a directed manner has been noted and termed 'collective intelligence' by Pierre Lévy.[227] The phenomenon was further explored in the context of creative online groups by media scholar Henry Jenkins in his influential *Convergence Culture* work.[228] Kozinets, Patterson and Ashman later developed some of these ideas into notions of 'networks of desire', which are assemblages of technology and people that act as directed desire amplifiers.[229] As Brem and Bilgram's work suggests, all of these related notions pertaining to collective intelligence also can usefully be applied to the idea of using social media groups as lead users.[230] These groups can be deployed as directed crowdsourced groups in netnographic interviews and can also use existing organic conversational groups as sources of future-looking intelligence.

Providing a third example of the netnographic extension into oracular conjecture, a 'foresight' process was also developed by Zeng, Koller and Jahn.[231] Combining 'Radar groups' (which are similar to focus groups), Delphi studies and the netnographic research coming from the identification of high-quality social media data, Zeng et al. construct what they describe as a 'pragmatic and robust foresight approach'.[232] The authors note that the collaborative work undertaken by the group members constitutes an important element of the quality of the marketing research study's results.

## Divining Netnography

Because social media is both unstable and destabilising, netnography is best thought of as a shifting collection of research practices and inclinations towards social media data. What it was in 2002, in 2010, and even in 2015, it is no more. In the current moment, netnography is a collection of 25 distinct research operations that cover the collection, analysis, interpretation integration, and communication of social media data – as described and detailed in the elaboration of the six movements of netnography above.[233] Among the practices in the optional 'movement 4' of the netnography process are active data collection methods that elicit data through various modes of interview, constructed research web-pages, digital diaries, and mobile ethnography techniques.[234] Each of these can lead us to work in different ways with engaged groups of social media posters and in directed ways that transcend the mere observation of organically occurring posts and replies.

When we collect data from relevant social media actors, we view these engaged people as the influencers and insight brokers that represent, or speak for, much larger groups. Their conversations may end up becoming mainstream, or will perhaps always stay marginal. If we are to use these conversations as fuel for future divination, then it is incumbent upon us to attempt to establish in advance what is potentially most meaningful from what is not. After we find those sites and conversations (and I use the term 'conversation' loosely, as these conversations might be conducted through photographic images, hashtags, video, screenshots and/or emojis), we must evaluate the ideas we consider to be of particular interest.[235] We must cross-validate the conclusions they offer us with other methods and types of reliable data, such as well-designed and well-executed surveys and market tests.[236] We must cross-check our findings carefully before we commit, invest or communicate.

Divination using structured netnography might help us to discern the shady shapes of the future a little bit before they actually take form. It might be slightly more helpful in this task than using flower petals to conduct anthomancy, or casting yarrow stalks to build hexagram patterns. Maybe...

## How do our competitors position themselves?

Generating insights into internal and external perceptions of the brand is important, but is it enough to develop a brand strategy? Remember that in Chapter 5 we argued that a brand's strategy should encompass where the brand comes from and where it is now (what we define as brand identity), and its ambitions and intent for the future. This implies that for brand managers, it is not enough to have a solid understanding of the brand: you also need to differentiate the brand in a relevant way. This means we need to know more.

In a world where consumers face thousands of branded messages every day, brands that are different from others receive more attention, are more memorable and communicate more efficiently. Of course, that differentiation cannot be just guesswork; it needs to be built on solid foundations and it needs to matter to consumers. Take Ryanair, a brand that has a distinctive low-cost focus that is built into its decision-making and is communicated through a lucid, price-focussed tone of voice in its advertising (the preferred channel is aggressive email-marketing). Or take Nespresso, which has built unique experiences around its brand. Just visit a Nespresso store, experience the special atmosphere (which it built around a positioning as the Louis Vuitton of coffee) and have – as a Nespresso club member – one of the complimentary coffees and you will find out what we are talking about. Or take Lush, a cosmetic and retail brand with unique values that – unlike many other cosmetic brands – focusses on handmade and pure cosmetics that appeal to people who want to buy ethical products. It's a brand with a very explicit (and authentic) position and it's hard to think of a competitor that really lives by its principles in the same way.

However, a brand cannot distinguish itself from others if brand managers are not aware of the context in which they compete and of the positioning of their competitors and their strategies. From a managerial viewpoint, it is therefore important to obtain accurate information about other market players and identify those areas that offer the biggest potential for differentiation. A manager needs to know the perceived strengths and weaknesses of competitors and be aware of their positioning in consumers' minds. We can pose such questions as:

- Why do consumers buy, or decide not to buy, competitive products?
- What stories do competitors tell about themselves in online channels (such as Facebook and other websites) and offline channels (such as brochures)?
- How do competitors communicate? How do they position their brands in their online and offline advertising? What tone of voice and what pictures do they use? What colours and fonts are part of their corporate design?
- How are they seen in their markets? What is their reputation? Is their image aligned with their communication activities?

The best source of information regarding the perception of competitive brands is the consumer,[237] and therefore brand managers should discuss with their target groups how they perceive comparable offerings. This is also a valuable way to pinpoint who their key competitors might be. This might appear obvious, but the fluidity of industry boundaries means that competitors can come from surprising places – think of the transition of Google and Apple away from their core businesses and the way they surprised incumbent brands. Consumers are able to provide useful insight as to the nature of the competitive set – in other words, about which brands they consider in their buying decisions. The research process itself can be done at the same time as the self-analysis of the brand – consumers then not only answer questions on the brand in focus but also on competitive brands. Again, the methods used can be of a qualitative or quantitative nature and can include ethnography, netnography and online communities. The research should always include people who have different relationships with brands: users are likely to have a different image of a brand from users of other brands, or from non-users. Other stakeholders, such as suppliers, buyers, retailers and sales people, should also be researched and regular communications material assessed (this means considering Internet presence, communication in social networks, advertisements, television and radio, billboards, annual reports, case studies, newspaper articles and sponsoring activities).

Apple is a good illustration of how a company can position itself based on good insight, because it made the value of distinction quite explicit in its communications. From 2006 to 2009, Apple ran a comparative campaign of Apple v. PCs called the 'Get a Mac' campaign. In the advertising, the Apple Mac is represented by a hip and unflappable actor, while the person playing the PC is more conservative and clumsy, though not unlikable. In one of the first spots of the series, the Mac character admits that PC is good at business stuff like spreadsheets, but points out that he's better at 'life' stuff like photos, music and movies.[238]

## Looking to the future: the needs of consumers and society?

A solid brand strategy is based on the functional, social and emotional benefits that motivate consumers to buy and use a brand today and in the future.[239] Functional benefits are primarily instrumental, in that they help to meet practical needs and are often associated with problem solution or problem avoidance. Social benefits, sometimes also called symbolic benefits, allow us to connect with others, to express who we are and to make our role in society visible – to ourselves and to others. Emotional benefits refer to feelings that occur when using the brand that could be characterised by emotions like joy, desire, excitement, love or optimism.

Today's consumer needs can be analysed with the help of more or less standardised customer surveys that are regularly conducted in ongoing marketing research activities. Various sectors, industry bodies and consultancies also publish studies. This research into existing and changing customer needs and desires in, for example, the fashion industry, the automotive industry and the retail industry helps us to understand the dynamics of a particular area. Additionally, ethnography and netnography can again help to provide deep insight into customer behaviour.

None of this work means that brands should simply follow where markets are going. Some brands, such as Tesla, Apple and Patagonia, pay attention to their customers, but they also lead. They don't try and run against key societal trends; they intuit them and build on them. This helps to make brands more attractive. For example, a company that discovers that one of the major trends in their industry is the increased use of the kinds of technology that enable customers to track the process of service provision could use this insight to position itself as a technologically advanced and transparent company – assuming it is supported by the company's competencies and that it differentiates the company from competitors. The following example of the brand GLOSSYBOX demonstrates how a successful brand strategy can be built around a key societal trend.

## Unboxing GLOSSYBOX

*Author: Judith Meyer*

What makes the GLOSSYBOX subscription box full of cosmetics so successful?
Around the world the subscription box business is booming. In Germany, for example, you can pay between €14.95 and €29.95 a month and have everything delivered to your door, from food (brandnooz, Vegan Box) to mothers' products (Mamibox) to cosmetics (GLOSSYBOX).

The Berlin-based GLOSSYBOX, which started in 2011, now operates profitably in 10 countries, including France, the US and the UK, and has some 3,000 employees.[240] The business model of GLOSSYBOX follows that of the American brand Birchbox. Customers regularly receive a box filled with five beauty and wellness products – some in miniature, some in original size. The range of GLOSSYBOX products is already relatively segmented and appeals to digital native consumers with different versions such as the 'Expert' box, 'Beauty School' edition, 'It's all about love' edition and a 'Strong & Beautiful' box.

## Trends – wonderful breeding grounds for the brand

GLOSSYBOX subscribers spend up to €180 per year without knowing which products they will actually receive. Which means there is a risk of getting products they don't really want. What then motivates customers to subscribe to such a grab bag? And why is the brand successful? One key success factor is that GLOSSYBOX actively uses trend insights to meet customer desires. In particular, it pays attention to three trend areas (influencers, making-life-easy and experience) and it uses customer feedback to constantly optimise its product range.

## Influencers are still considered credible in the cosmetics sector

In the cosmetics industry private individuals have become highly influential as opinion leaders and the demand-determining power of bloggers has often been skilfully appropriated by companies. For example, the most successful German blogger and YouTube star Bibi, from 'Bibis Beauty Palace', has been adopted by the leading German drugstore chain dm, who include her products in its assortment planning. GLOSSYBOX also uses the reach of bloggers as a recommendation channel. Before each monthly box is sent out, bloggers and YouTubers are provided with advance deliveries of new offers so that they can draw attention to the new GLOSSYBOX offer through sneak previews. The authenticity of their recommendations is enhanced both because they try out and comment on the products and because they are considered experts. This makes them ideal brand ambassadors.

For millennials and Generation Z, influencers are the most important channel. Young people between the ages of 21 and 36 are the first generation to grow up with social media. They sympathise with bloggers from their age cohort and as enlightened buyers doubt the credibility of large corporations.[241] Too often they have already been disappointed by scandals and unfulfilled promises of performance.

## Subscriptions make life easier

One of the observed mega-trends is that the proliferation of choice in many market segments has led to a desire among consumers for brands to just make things easier for them. Rather than be confronted with the difficulty of choosing between one brand and another, or between one set of product features and another, consumers would like brands to make the choice for them by curating the brand offer. This is particularly noticeable in the body care industry, where there is an abundance of brands, products and innovations. The benefit for consumers is that rather than investing time and money identifying products, brands like GLOSSYBOX do it for them. The selection of products a customer receives is based on a completed beauty profile. When the consumer takes out a subscription they are also asked questions (about their preferences, product categories used, skin type and style), which helps to build a profile that matches the person to the products. GLOSSYBOX determines the pre-selection of suitable products and contributes to reducing the complexity of everyday life. In addition, the product samples reduce the frequent mis-purchases in the cosmetics sector and allow people to try something before making a commitment.

Up to this point the success of GLOSSYBOX is comprehensible – but also easy to copy. So, what is the actual performance of the brand? The 'aha factor' on which the positioning is successfully based?

## Creating an experience to savour

Included within the GLOSSYBOX subscription each month are five products, an experience and a surprise. The feel and aesthetics of the box are therefore just as important as the selection of the products themselves. The highlight of this is the unpacking of the box – the 'unboxing'. Here, tension is driven to its maximum: the moment of surprise is delayed and several layers have to be opened: the box, another smaller box, a bow, the tissue paper. Nothing is left to chance, which shows that the company is well aware that unpacking is a decisive moment. Even a logo sticker, for example, delays the moment of opening. Then, last but not least, the five products reveal themselves.

The enclosed product card communicates special features and value, which is designed to create a sense of reward. The brand packaging contact point delivers not only a simple box of cosmetic products, but a beauty experience – a feeling of giving oneself a present.

## Using feedback

Too often, brand managers only take care of the first contact point (a TV spot, say) when it comes to selling a product. Downstream contact points, on the other hand, are often neglected. GLOSSYBOX avoids this problem by contacting customers after purchase (this is a downstream brand contact point) and seeking their input. GLOSSYBOX uses the insights from this to constantly optimise its product range and to give feedback to the brand manufacturers whose products were shipped in the boxes.

There are trends and there are mega-trends. The latter are emphasised here because they are concerned with the future direction of societies and cultures.[242] Mega-trends can be defined as social, technological, economic, environmental and political developments, which – in contrast to fashion or industry trends – are largely cross-cultural in nature and reflected in many areas of life. Mega-trends are scientifically researched and regularly reviewed with regard to their topicality. The Hamburg-based think tank and consultancy Zukunftsinstitut identifies 12 mega-trends that inter-connect with each other:[243]

1) 'New Knowledge Culture': today, people handle information differently from before. Knowledge is generated in decentralised structures and openly shared, and innovations are generated co-creatively. Knowledge is no longer elitist but for everyone. A new focus is lifelong learning.

2) 'Urbanisation': more and more people live in cities. Cities are developing into major activists and important problem solvers in our lives. Urban life equates to a hip lifestyle and generates new ways of working and thinking.

3) 'Connectivity': everything is networked – both in terms of people and of things. Connectivity is changing our lives and helping to establish a new digital lifestyle.

4) 'Neo-ecology': a greener lifestyle changes personal buying decisions, social values and behaviours. An ecological orientation and a capitalist way of life can fit together. Corresponding target groups such as the LOHAS (Lifestyle of Health and Sustainability) can be tapped into, to exploit this phenomenon.

5) 'Globalisation': globalisation is the oldest of the current mega-trends. Global interdependence is increasing and global relations are becoming more intensive. But at the same time, a strong counterculture has become visible. People attack globalisation and withdraw to their private life.

6) 'Individualisation': this mega-trend is a cultural pattern in the Western world but is spreading globally. It affects the structures of our societies, our values, our consumption patterns and our everyday culture. It is about freedom of choice. Products are tailored to individual needs. There are more and more choices.

7) 'Health': wellness and health are taking on a new meaning in people's lives and are of central importance. Health and satisfaction are inseparable from each other. And people are more self-confident when dealing with health authorities because through the Internet they have easy access to once-hidden knowledge. Health-oriented people want to live in healthy environments and demand to do so constantly.

8) 'New Work': working life and individual self-realisation are not opposites. They condition each other. Furthermore, digitalisation and the use of intelligent machines increase our need for purpose in life and work. New work focusses on the potential of all humans.

9) 'Gender Shift': changed role patterns and breaking gender stereotypes has led to a radical shift in perceptions of gender in economy and society.

10) 'Silver Society': all around the globe people are living longer and the buying power of older people is increasing. Ageing is no longer seen as a restriction, but is rather understood as a new space for development. This is turning into a new mindset as society says goodbye to youth mania.

11) 'Mobility': the world is mobile. Innovation and changing needs are the engines of new forms of movement and travel.

12) 'Security': we are always alert – one crisis follows the next. But this is only our perception. We live in a very safe world, but we strive for security like never before.

As consultants Dave Florin and his colleagues argue, relevancy, which they define as the role that a particular brand plays in consumers' lives, is becoming more and more important.[244] This is because today's consumers are more willing, and have more technical means than ever before, to tune out messages that do not resonate with them. Relevance can be achieved by absorbing major societal developments in a brand's strategy. Those trends should be known and analysed when a brand defines its ambitions and intent for the future. The car manufacturer Audi, for example, established an interdisciplinary think tank called 'Audi Innovation Research' (AIR) that is dedicated to providing answers to the three global mega-trends, 'urbanisation', 'digitalisation' (what we called 'connectivity') and 'sustainability' (what we called 'neo-ecology'). At offices in Germany, China and in the US, various experts are analysing those trends and searching for their implications for the Audi brand.[245]

Another example of a company that is searching for insight into the future is the Swedish homewares brand IKEA. It uses a variety of different research tools to try to uncover how people feel about their homes and to pinpoint important trends.

## What makes life better at home: the case of IKEA

Ever looked at a Brimnes bed? Or considered a Malm chest of drawers? Or even bought an Oumbärlig saucepan set? If you're one of the 817 million IKEA customers or 2.1 billion visitors to IKEA.com, then you just might have done. You might also be one of the people that love IKEA, but for many the relationship with the brand is quite functional. People shop there (especially the young) when moving into their first apartment, when they need something basic or when they want to save money. The challenge that IKEA has been working on is how to keep people as customers as they age and how to build a more emotional relationship with those customers. That means getting close to customers and unearthing their feelings towards home; it means digging deep to find out more about their hopes, fears, needs and dreams. It's something IKEA has been doing since 2014, with ever more creative approaches to building insights.

## IKEA's 2017 Life at Home report

For IKEA to realise its vision 'to create a better everyday life for the many people', it has to know as much as it can about how people feel about their homes. From their research during the three years preceding 2017, IKEA had identified four key dimensions of the home: relationships (the people you live with), place (the neighbourhood you live in), space and things. The goal for 2017 was to explore the interplay between these four dimensions by taking a journey into the lifestyles of people. As with many adventures there was a goal and some expectations, but also a willingness to learn and to adapt along the way. Rather than opting for the obvious method of research, IKEA chose a multi-layered, immersive approach that provided breadth and depth, but also created the possibility for surprise. The research process featured:

- social media listening;
- 36 in-home interviews in Chengdu, Austin, Osaka, Copenhagen, Mumbai and Munich;
- twelve weeks collaboration with 18 people, living in unusual or creative places, via text chats and video diaries plus a one-day workshop with them to understand what better homes feel like;
- four interviews with experts from such fields as ethnography, psychology and anthropology;
- engaging with online communities in seven core countries (the US, China, India, Denmark, Germany, Japan and Russia) with 650 people over 12 weeks;
- a quantitative study of 21,419 people in 22 countries.

So, what's different here from a traditional research process? First, it combines elements of ethnography and netnography in the way that it uses online and offline mechanisms in an overall research quest. While there are four dimensions that give the research some focus, the process is iterative-inductive. It doesn't start with a theory or a position; rather through exploration and repetition, the process seeks to build insight into what truly matters to people and for them to tell their own stories in their own words. Also true to an ethnographic stance, much of the research takes place in context, in peoples' homes, rather than in an office. The benefit of this is that rather than seating people around a conference table and getting them to talk about home life, they can talk about the environment they are in, which makes the experience far more tangible. Second, the process subverts the idea that you research and then reach a conclusion. Again, taking a cue from ethnography, the research process here recognises that you learn as you go along. So, for example, the activities in the online communities were designed in four-week cycles, so that the direction could be adapted based on what had been learned. As the insights unfolded, so IKEA worked to develop global and local narratives of what they were learning in what they called writers' rooms. About two-thirds of the way through the research, the key plot lines about what people wanted to achieve in their homes, and the barriers that stop them from realising those aspirations, became apparent. Third, there is a belief that while you can generate insights from consumers, they are not creative or knowledgeable enough to generate solutions. However, here, the 18 home pioneers and the online community members were not only commentators, but also creators. This was particularly noteworthy in the one-day workshop in Copenhagen, where the pioneers worked cohesively to help frame the tensions of the investigation and to suggest how they could be tackled.

## The core themes that emerged from the research

Amidst the ethnographic and netnographic approach there was a quite standard piece of research, which was the quantitative study across 22 countries. For IKEA this was important both to validate what they had learned and to give some statistical meat to the consumer insights, which could be used in the Life at Home report. The five tensions that emerged were:

1) The importance of meaningful objects versus the pressure to declutter. Forty-nine per cent of people say that the main cause of domestic arguments is due to different feelings about clutter. Part of the solution is to buy things that honour experiences and help us to view possessions more objectively.

2) The need for our personal space and things versus the struggle to ask for this. Within homes there is my space, your space and our space. Forty per cent of people say that they live with things they hate which belong to others and 19 per cent say they have thrown away something that belongs to someone else without telling them. The solution here is to create a shared value for belongings.

3) The feeling of home starting within us versus the outside creeping in to distract us. Fifty-seven per cent of people say they are mentally present in the home; the rest are distracted by work and technology. The way to create presence is to purposefully design homes with consideration to things, spaces and nature.

4) The endless possibilities of technology versus its downsides for home unity. People are excited by the possibilities of technology in the home while at the same time recognising that it can be disruptive – a tension they are still learning how to balance.

5) The constantly evolving home versus the desire for it to be 'finished'. People do want to feel they have finished working with their home, but then they also know it is a never-ending project. Feeling comfortable with one's home is best achieved when a home reflects present needs, rather than previous or anticipated needs.

You might think that it is all very well to identify such tensions, but also want to ask what IKEA did with them? It told people's stories in the Life at Home report, so that other consumers could empathise with them. The company explored the tensions with experts and the Home Pioneers, and with them found inspirational ideas and adaptations to better meet people's needs and dreams, while IKEA's product designers and developers used the scenarios to inform the designing of new products and environments. Underpinning the whole project is the belief that creating an everyday better life for the many is not something that IKEA does alone. Instead, the idea comes to life through the insights, creativity and actions of consumers as they co-create it.

## Summary

Brands can shape their future if they are aware of their special (historical or current) abilities, if they listen to customers and non-customers and identify their unconscious needs, if they recognise market developments and trends and interpret them – and if they know how to use all of this information to position themselves to stand out from the competition. To shape the future, brands need to carry out a comprehensive self-analysis to uncover their authentic selves, using such methods (among others) as ethnography and netnography. Second, competitors must be analysed to identify differentiation potentials. And third, customers and non-customers must be researched and central industry trends and so-called 'mega-trends' identified and evaluated with regard to their own brands, in order to assess the relevance of different positioning options.

## Reflections/questions

1) What are the central questions of self-analysis in the context of strategic brand analysis?
2) Why is it important for brand managers to have knowledge about their own and external perceptions of a brand?
3) What methods can be used to analyse competitive brands?

4) How do functional, emotional and social customer needs differ? Within each market, cite an example of such an analysis and think about which brand aims to meet that need as a matter of priority.

5) Which mega-trends do you know and why are they of great relevance for brand management?

6) How does ethnography and netnography work? What are the main differences from classical market research approaches?

7) What reasons for brand valuation come to your mind?

## We recommend the following reading to expand your learning experience:

Balmer, J.M. & Burghausen, M. (2018). 'Marketing, the past and corporate heritage', Marketing Theory, https://doi.org/10.1177/1470593118790636.

Cuomo, M.T., Tortora, D., Festa, G., Giordano, A. & Metallo, G. (2016). 'Exploring consumer insights in wine marketing: An ethnographic research on# Winelovers', Psychology & Marketing, 33(12), 1082–1090.

Florin, D., Callen, B., Mullen, S. & Kropp, J. (2007). 'Profiting from mega-trends', Journal of Product & Brand Management, 16(4), 220–225.

Heinonen, K. & Medberg, G. (2018). 'Netnography as a tool for understanding customers: implications for service research and practice', Journal of Services Marketing, 32(6), 657–679.

Keller, K.L. & Brexendorf, T.O. (2017). 'Measuring brand equity', In: Esch, F.-R. (ed.), Handbuch Markenführung, Wiesbaden: Springer, 1–32.

Stewart D.W. (2019). 'Creating and Measuring Brand Value. In: Financial Dimensions of Marketing Decisions', Palgrave Studies in Marketing, Organizations and Society. Cham: Palgrave Macmillan.

# CHAPTER SEVEN

# Defining and adjusting brand strategy

## In this chapter...

A brand strategy should be closely inter-connected with the organisational strategy. The two should be mutually supportive, so that the organisational strategy sets the context for the brand strategy and it, in turn, enables the organisational strategy to be realised. The brand strategy indicates what a brand stands for today and in what direction brand managers want to develop the brand in the future. The brand's identity and its positioning are part of the brand strategy. A brand identity is a summary of the most important connotations associated with the brand and addresses what a brand stands for in the eyes of internal stakeholders. It also asks how it is understood in terms of its image in the eyes of external stakeholders. Under the co-creative perspective, brand identity is not a fixed asset that gets written down once and then remains untouched – a brand's identity is subject to constant mediation and re-interpretation as the brand's meaning is co-created by its employees, customers and by others. Nevertheless, brand managers are well advised to clearly define their brand's identity, because a profound understanding of the brand is needed internally as a starting point from which to stimulate and facilitate the co-creation of brand meaning within certain limits.

For the purpose of clarity and for internal purposes (teaching new employees about the brand or briefing an advertising agency, for example), various models exist that show and explain how a brand identity can be formulated in a practical manner. Some of the models are concrete and some more abstract, but they are widely used by practitioners. A brand's positioning is based on its identity, but also follows a more tactical approach. A positioning aims to provide continuity of brand experience, adapted to various target groups throughout all brand touch points. It is the art of brand management to meet the need for consistency and, at the same time, continuous change.

## Learning Objectives

After reading this chapter you should

- understand which elements must be considered when defining a brand's strategy;
- realise that to take full advantage of co-creative brand management, managers need a clear idea of what their brand stands for;
- know what the term brand identity means and be aware of the difference between a brand's identity and its positioning;
- be able to specify a brand's identity in a practical way;
- understand the important requirements in brand positioning and know selected elements of a positioning strategy;
- be aware of the difficulties in managing a brand consistently while adapting to change.

## Brand Strategy

Imagine a warm and sunny day. You are hiking in the Alps. You didn't take a map, the power of your iPhone is low, and your goal is to reach a mountain shelter on the other side of the valley by dawn. You can already see the hostel, which is still quite far away, but there is no road that can lead you directly towards it. You're going to have to walk across the landscape. In this situation, you probably will take some basic decisions and make a plan, such as which direction to go in, the mountain path to follow and where to cross the river. You cannot be sure about the best and shortest way, but even if you have some doubts you have to use the information available to you and set off towards your destination. On your way, you may realise that the trail you followed was heading somewhere else, or that the hill that you chose to climb was too steep for you, and you may turn back and adjust your path. And you will be doing so until you reach your final destination. At the start of your trip, your plan was created in your mind based on previous experience of such walks and your imperfect knowledge of the area and the conditions. You imagined yourself walking confidently, the sun beating down on your head (it's why you're wearing a cap) and the possibility of blisters on your feet, but as the reality of bodily engagement with the terrain bites, you start to adapt your plan. As the phenomenologist Maurice Merleau-Ponty points out, we often believe that we think our way into action, but in reality, we act our way into thought.[246] And as Nietzsche (who was very keen on Alpine hikes) suggests, walking is a good way of thinking: 'Only ideas *won by walking* have any value.'[247]

This Alpine expedition is similar to a strategic process. The word 'strategy' is a synonym for a plan. When the word came into general use at the start of the nineteenth century it reflected a growing confidence in empirical science and the application of reason by 'inserting, deliberate calculating thought' into planning an activity.[248] A strategy uses insight from the past to connect the present to a desired future. It establishes explicit and implicit norms and guidelines that focus all possible activities on achieving one's goals. Though a strategic plan does not consist of concrete actions, the practice of strategy does. Without a sense of strategic direction, actions can lead you into places you probably shouldn't go. What is true for strategy generally is also true for a brand strategy – without which, the risk of taking decisions that move you further and further away from your brand-related goals is high. A brand strategy answers the questions of what the brand stands for today and where managers see it going. It defines the authentic identity of a brand and its ambitions. It covers the unique positioning of a brand and inspires ideas for the future. This might sound very prescriptive and authoritarian – but it is not, as our Alpine hike suggests and the following paragraphs will show.

## What is brand identity?

A brand strategy builds on the identity of a brand. But how can we define the term brand identity? Definitions have traditionally taken an aspirational perspective, describing what managers wanted the brand to be and emphasising the need for stability over time (some authors still adhere to this definition today).[249] Additionally, the concept of identity has often been defined as distinct from image – which, broadly, can be defined as the set of associations linked to the brand that consumers hold in memory.[250] Let's take a look at some of the corresponding definitions of brand identity:

Table 7.1  Definitions of brand identity

| Source | Definition |
|---|---|
| Kapferer, 1992 (p.37) | 'Image is on the receiver's side…Identity is on the sender's side. The sender's duty is to specify the meaning, intention, vocation of the brand. Image is the result thereof, a decoding.'[251] |
| Aaker, 1996 (p.68) | Brand identity is 'a unique set of brand associations that the brand strategist aspires to create or maintain.'[252] |
| De Chernatony, 1999 (p.165) | 'Identity is about the ethos, aims and values that present a sense of individuality differentiating the brand, i.e. firm centred, while image is a holistic impression of the relative position of a brand among its perceived competitors…i.e. customer centred.'[253] |
| Nandan, 2005 (p.265) | 'Brand identity originates from the company, i.e. a company is responsible for creating a differentiated product with unique features.'[254] |
| Veloutsou & Delgado-Ballester, 2018 (p.256) | Brand identity is defined as 'the symbols and the set of the brand associations that represent the core character of the brand that the team supporting the brand aspire to create or maintain as identifiers of the brand to other people.'[255] |

From a co-creative perspective, identity is seen as the result of a social process in which multiple stakeholders are involved.[256] This shifts the idea of brand identity from stable and enduring to fluid and adaptive. Iglesias et al. describe the change in perspective as follows: 'Firstly, the traditional paradigm of brand management is based on control; yet…brands are organic entities that emerge and develop in a space where multiple interactions occur and multiple conversations among different stakeholders take place.'[257] The authors conclude: 'Therefore managers need to recognise that although they have responsibility for shaping a brand's identity, the process will evolve with the participation of many other stakeholders.' This indicates that a brand could have multiple identities within various conversational spaces where organisations and individual consumers meet.[258] What managers intend with an identity and the way it is enacted or experienced by others can be quite different.[259] Adopting a fluid and adaptive view, we define brand identity as follows:

*A brand's identity is an ever-evolving connotation, rooted in a brand's history, philosophy, practices and ambitions but subject to constant mediation and re-interpretation as its meaning is co-created by a brand's stakeholders.*

This view of identity is circular in that the identity is established by managers, then mediated and re-interpreted by stakeholders, absorbed again by the organisation and then re-presented. Following the circle, what we can see is the virtual converting into the actual. For example, managers' description of the brand identity only becomes actualised when it is acted upon, just as stakeholders' expectations only become actualised through experience. The philosopher Gilles Deleuze talks about this sense of continual becoming in terms of what he calls territorialisation, whereby organisations, in their search for stability and continuity, try to embed that which is vital to their existence. However, through actualisation and also innovation, things get de-territorialised. Then, if the organisation is receptive, some of the changes are learned as they are re-territorialised to become part of a new territory.[260]

## The elements of a brand identity

These arguments demonstrate that a brand's management cannot create a brand identity alone. Brand identity management is a dynamic process, which brand managers, consumers and other stakeholders contribute to.[261] However, even if brand identity is open to the influence of consumers and other stakeholders, it is necessary to preserve a stable sense of self.[262] The more fluid brand management is and the more brand managers are forced to give up control, the more important it is to define the platform from which all brand-related activities start. If brand managers don't have a clear view of the brand identity, they will lose the ability to influence its direction. The implication is that managers need to understand and maintain the core of the brand identity, while allowing stakeholders to elaborate and enrich it.

Authors have different opinions about the elements that constitute a brand's identity. Table 7.2 provides an overview of various conceptualisations of brand identity that have led to the best-known models.[263]

### Brand leadership model from Aaker and Joachimsthaler

The brand leadership model of Aaker and Joachimsthaler, which is rooted in Aaker's work (see Table 7.2 and over portrayal of the Brand Identity Planning Model in Chapter 5), is valuable because it distinguishes between three levels of brand identity and reminds us that there are more stable and more transient elements involved in establishing the reputation of a brand.[264] At the innermost model level, the so-called brand essence describes a single thought that reflects the soul of the brand. This level in particular communicates with employees in order to sensitise them to the brand and increase their motivation. The brand essence should be enduring and therefore timeless

Table 7.2   Overview of brand identity models (adapted from
Burmann et al., 2009; extended by us).

| Source | Conceptualisations of brand identity |
|---|---|
| Kapferer, 1992 | Brand identity is represented in a hexagonal prism reflecting the brand's physique, personality, culture, relationship, reflection and self-image. The six edges of the prism can be clustered into two dimensions: are they perceived by the sender or the receiver? And are they determined internally or externally?[265] |
| Aaker, 1996 | Brand identity consists of a core and an extended identity and is informed by four dimensions: the brand as a product reflects the product-related associations; the brand as an organisation focusses on organisational associations; the brand as a person includes the brand personality; the brand as a symbol includes the visual imagery, metaphors and brand heritage. A further development of Aaker's model is described in this section. [266] |
| De Chernatony, 1999 | The identity of a brand consists of the following dimensions: brand personality, culture and relationship, vision, brand positioning and the brand presentation. [267] |
| Burmann et al., 2017 | The identity of a brand consists of the following six dimensions: heritage, organisational capabilities, values, personality, vision and core offering. [268] |
| Greyser & Urde, 2019 | The identity of a (corporate) brand consists of a brand core that describes the brand's promise and core values and eight additional dimensions that define the mission and vision of the company, the culture (attitudes and 'how we work'), the competencies ('what makes us better than the competition?'), the personality (human characteristics or qualities), the unique or special way of communication (expression), the key offerings (value proposition), the nature of the relationships with stakeholders and the intended positioning. [269] |

in its formulation. This distinguishes it from the evanescence of a slogan (with which it can be confused) that is often tactical and targeted at customers and the public. The brand essence is also sometimes defined as the driving force behind the brand.

For example, Nivea's brand essence might be 'care', Volvo's 'safety', Coca-Cola's 'refreshment' and Virgin's, with its strong customer service focus, 'Challenge the establishment'. While this innermost level is almost philosophical in character, the second level of the model is more tangible: the authors call it the core identity. This comprises two to four associations – the most important elements of the identity – that are strongly linked to the brand and also remain largely constant when the brand opens up new markets with new products. The individual elements of the core identity, which are often referred to in the literature as brand values, should reflect the strategy of the organisation, differentiate the brand from competitors and resonate with consumers. Disney is often associated with a core identity of 'family, fun and entertainment', while Apple stands for 'simplicity, style, innovation, rebellion'.

Finally, the third level is referred to as extended identity. According to Aaker and Joachimsthaler, it should contain all other elements of the brand system that are necessary to create a convincing image of the brand. The elements can include the typical users of the brand (maybe young and successful Americans in the case of Polo Ralph Lauren), well-known and successful products (in the case of Air Jordan by Nike), visual elements of the brand appearance (such as logo, corporate colour or design at point-of-sale) as well as other important brand characteristics (such as Tony the Tiger for Kellogg's). The decisive factor in distinguishing between core identity and extended identity is the degree to which the individual elements are connected to the brand: the more explicit the connection to the brand, the more important it is for the brand system. The components of the core identity need to have longer-term validity than those of the extended identity and consequently, brand managers need to be careful when adapting them to different contexts.

## How is a brand's identity elaborated and enriched?

It is one thing to create a brand model, but how can it be filled with life? This is where the insights that we described in Chapter 6 come into play. Brand managers need to bring all the relevant information and insights together – about the brand itself, and about competitors, customers and central trends in the market. But particularly about the brand itself – its history, philosophy, practices and ambitions. To do this in practice, a good starting point is to share and discuss those brand-related connotations that are common to internal and external stakeholders. If an identity is only based on the internal perspective, the risk is high that brand characteristics are emphasised that are important from an internal view but cannot be experienced externally. Or that blind spots – a brand's characteristics that are not known about internally – are missed. Whereas if the brand identity is only based on the assessments and opinions of external stakeholders, there is a danger that essential aspects that are culturally vital inside the organisation will be overlooked.

However a brand's identity is formulated, whether through highly detailed and multi-layered information or via a more open and free structure, one thing is important to note: a brand identity should be designed to inform and to guide decision-making. It is not a corset. On the contrary, it should set a frame within which a free development of creative ideas is possible and desired, and where all stakeholders can participate in the co-creation of brand meaning. Take the example of the outdoor brand Patagonia, whose brand identity includes the ambition 'to use business to inspire and implement solutions to the environmental crisis.'[270] This statement self-evidently sets clear rules for Patagonia's management of what is right and wrong and makes a strong call for the participation of others in the co-creation of the Patagonia brand. Similarly, the brand core of Tomra, a Norwegian company that manufactures machinery and robots for collecting and sorting raw materials, is 'rethinking how we obtain, use, reuse and optimise the world's resources.'[271] This is another example of a brand statement that gives clear direction and invites others to participate in co-creation.

## Defining a brand co-creatively: the case of Hakkasan

Hakkasan started out as an upscale Chinese restaurant in London in 2001. Its appeal lay in its high-quality modern interpretation of Cantonese cuisine (it acquired its first Michelin star in 2003), its architectural elegance and the dark, luscious materials used by the French designer Christian Liaigre in its interior. By 2018, the Hakkasan brand had expanded to 12 restaurants across the world and a nightclub in Las Vegas. Additionally, it had built, both through start-ups and acquisitions, a whole series of targeted brands under distinct names in nightlife, daylife and dining in more than 60 different locations. During the expansion, the Hakkasan brand retained some points of continuity in terms of its cuisine and environment, but growth also led to a loss of clarity about the brand. What did it stand for in the eyes of employees, customers and partners? And could a restaurant brand be successfully extended into other areas, such as nightclubs and hotels? In 2013, Hakkasan management decided that understanding its brand and then integrating it into decision-making was vital, not least because of the ambition to develop a brand portfolio. Without real insight into the Hakkasan brand itself there might be too much overlap in the positioning and presentation of other group brands, such as dim sum specialist Yauatcha (London, Mumbai, Bengaluru, Kolkata, Houston and Riyadh) and the authentic Japanese cuisine of Sake No Hana (London and Bali).

Recalling the schools of thinking in Chapter 1, Hakkasan could have adopted an identity-based approach. The emphasis then would have been internal and would have concentrated on finding the unique attributes of the brand as seen by managers and employees. One of the difficulties with the identity approach is that it easily becomes a cage that constrains. People chafe at the brand and see it as a barrier that limits initiative and opportunity. Alternatively, adopting an image-based approach would have put the emphasis on the way the brand is seen by customers and other external stakeholders. This is valuable in ensuring relevance, but also stokes the idea that the brand is only about external communications and how it is projected through advertising and public relations. It's why many at Hakkasan were sceptical about the relevance of the brand. The value of the co-creative approach was that it connected the inside with the outside to define a brand whose meaning could evolve in tune with the needs and desires of employees and consumers.

In practice a co-creative approach to brand definition suggests an immersive method that aims for depth and encourages the active participation of consultants, managers, employees and external stakeholders. The approach requires an understanding of the value exchange (see Nick Coates in Chapter 3) – in other words, of ensuring that all participants realise their extrinsic and intrinsic aims within a fair process. At Hakkasan, defining the brand was an odyssey: a final destination was envisaged, but the getting there was a voyage of learning; a willingness to be open to new adventures. The consultants began by conducting internal discussion sessions with employees, talking to the heads of areas such as Pastry and Wine, and then interviewing senior managers about the strategic direction of Hakkasan. There were discussions with the kitchen staff in Chinese, observing a kitchen shift and working front of house, and finally, workshops with managers and customers. The process involved looking back to where the brand had come from and towards the future in order to understand the potential of the brand to expand and extend into new areas. This first part of the journey led to the creation of four alternative brand routes. To test the relevance and the implications of the routes, Hakkasan chose to conduct large-scale, two-day events in Los Angeles, London and Dubai. For each event there were approximately 30 customers and

15 managers, who were charged with working collaboratively as equals, to determine how the brand should be defined and to explore how it could be used in brand extensions. Typically for events of this scale, there was a high level of facilitation and a mixture of projective techniques (for example, writing a love letter to Hakkasan) and idea development and prototyping (for example, what would a Hakkasan brand hotel look like?).

One of the brand routes that people liked concerned the idea of a dark, urban energy and there was also language in the love letters that talked about energy and theatricality and a film-like quality to the Hakkasan experience – people said it was like being in a James Bond movie. It was clear that 'energy' was a key attribute, while the cinematic experience added a dash of sophistication. The brand idea – what Hakkasan calls brand essence – that was discovered through this co-creative process was called 'Cinematic Energy'. It builds on the input from customers and links to Hakkasan's dark, rich interiors, which are reminiscent of a cinema. It offers intimacy and mystery, and creates a sense of being part of a production, by curating four elements: the guests, the experience, the product and people. Nick Coates, who worked on the project, says: 'The whole thing expressed an experience that was an elevation of the previous food positioning and also capable of spanning multiple categories. Coming out of the essence was a consumer benefit, "Make me feel like I'm in a movie". So it didn't come out of nowhere. Consumer testimony inspired it, co-creation honed and sifted it out from other potential routes, and we shaped it and stress tested it.'

'Cinematic Energy' is designed to inspire and to guide decision-making, but it is not a cage – more a touchstone against which ideas can be tested. It is also sufficiently open to enable customers to contribute to its meaning. Of course, the acid test with a brand is whether the words become meaningful through usage. Are they grounded in practice? To help think through the implications of the brand, activation sessions were run with 140 employees in three markets that enabled them to take part in bringing the brand to life in specific contexts and a brand book that looked like a film story was put together for all staff. At a managerial level, Hakkasan argues that it is now a brand-first culture, by which it means that the brand leads the organisation strategically. The brand is integrated into the development of HR strategy, culture and training, and into the delivery of the brand experience and the way relationships are built with investors, developers and partners. The brand essence also helps Hakkasan determine what is not within the brand's scope. Rather than bend Hakkasan so that it worked for a younger audience as well as its established clientele, management decided not to use the brand and instead create a specifically targeted sub-brand (that came to be called Ling Ling) with its own co-created brand proposition that could be scaled in relevant international markets with lively scenes, such as Oslo, Mykonos and Marrakech.

Overall, the advantage of the highly participative, co-creative approach was to overcome the scepticism about the brand. Restaurant managers and head office staff discovered through working together with customers the importance of the brand for them, and the value they placed on being given the opportunity to contribute to its meaning.

## Positioning

The second element of brand strategy is the brand's positioning. The positioning is based on a brand's identity and derived from it, but it is also tactical and can be defined as the active communication of the brand identity at all brand touch points and towards different target groups.[272] Therefore, the positioning expresses what the brand says about itself and how it acts towards others in order to achieve its goals. Take the example of a brand like Virgin, whose identity – entrepreneurship, being the underdog and challenging the market leader – reflects the personality of its founder, Richard Branson. The Virgin Group comprises sub-companies in very different areas – for example, in the music business, mobile communications, banking, hotels and aviation. Of course, the expectations of clients – and the threats of competitors – within those very different market segments vary tremendously. Therefore, under the umbrella of the corporate brand, the different units position themselves slightly differently within their different markets – though they share the same brand identity.

When defining a brand's positioning, brand managers must look at their brand from three different perspectives. First, the history of the brand endows authenticity. If a brand, in its communications, can build on historic achievements and peak performances from the past, its corresponding arguments will be perceived as more credible by its audiences. Think of the German car brand BMW, which builds its communication on the performance of the legendary BMW engines that in the early twentieth century were developed for airplanes. Or take Starbucks. The world's largest coffee chain brought the European coffee house atmosphere to the US – it is credible when the brand claims in its mission statement that they strive to inspire and nurture the human spirit. Second, a look at the positioning of competing brands will allow a brand's management to follow a distinctive path. Differentiation is key for brand building, but in order to differentiate a brand from its competitors, one must know who the competitors are and how they position themselves in the market. A brand such as Unilever's Ben & Jerry's offers high-quality ice cream made from natural ingredients and has a commitment towards social activism and environmental responsibility. It is a good example of a brand that positions itself in a very distinctive way relative to its competitors. The unusual, comic-style design of the ice cream's packaging contributes to the otherness of the brand. The German beer brand

Astra also demonstrates its otherness by often using social outsiders in their advertisements and by employing politically incorrect headlines. Third, the positioning of a brand must be in line with the expectations and desires of its customers and should build on future trends to stay relevant. Think of the example of GLOSSYBOX in the previous chapter.

The following case of the German napkin and lifestyle brand Paperproducts Design illustrates very nicely how a brand, based on the knowledge of its identity, can develop a strong positioning.

## Brand identity and positioning: The case of ppd

Paperproducts Design (ppd), based in Meckenheim, near the German city of Cologne, and with sister companies in the Netherlands and in California, is one of the leading producers of high-quality printed and embossed napkins. The company produces around 15 million napkin packs annually at two production sites. With 130 employees working for the organisation worldwide and a turnover of around €25 million, ppd is a hidden champion – one of those typically rather unknown but highly successful companies. The ppd brand surprises its customers time and again with new, creative designs. In addition to napkins, ppd sells everything that links to the laid table, including colourfully designed, high-quality porcelain in gift boxes, glass articles and other accessories. The starting point for all products is always the decor of the paper napkin. Based on the design of the napkin, other suitable design suggestions are then developed for the supplementary articles.

Basically, ppd works like a fashion company. It has its own trend scouts and buys trend reports to inspire its employees. The in-house creative department translates these trends into designs for the napkins and for the other articles. External designers are also recruited to contribute new ideas. The ideas are implemented in two collections (autumn/winter and spring/summer) and in special editions for birthdays and summer barbecues. The sales department sells the products at trade fairs such as the Atlanta Gift Show, Maison & Objet in Paris and Ambiente in Frankfurt, and directly to retail customers such as furniture stores, household goods stores and supermarkets. The end customer is predominantly female, 25 to 60 years old, middle class, with a strong need for a 'stylish' home and a beautifully laid table. However, some customers are just looking for an uncomplicated gift or a souvenir.

In 2014, ppd was on the threshold of a new stage of development. The medium-sized company had grown strongly over the years and management was faced with the challenge of realising the potential of the ppd brand, which had previously been managed very successfully, but rather intuitively. Essentially, the company asked itself two questions. What are we? A design company, a napkin producer or a lifestyle company? And what should we do to shape our future while still retaining focus? Management was seeking a compass that could steer them in the right direction. Therefore, a project was defined to work out both what the brand stood for (the brand identity) and how it should be positioned. The company put together a project team of 12 people, representing all departments and hierarchical levels, and the objectives and timetable were agreed. To keep all employees informed, management communicated the project's purpose and process.

In the following weeks, all communication materials were reviewed, and interviews were conducted with employees and customers with the support of external consultants. The analysis focussed on questions such as: What made ppd successful? How does ppd differ from the competition? What is unique about ppd? The answers to these and similar questions were recorded and then grouped together before being condensed into five clusters. The clusters inspired the brand values: creativity, modern design, extraordinary, committed, in partnership. In addition, a brand core was identified, which described the central drive of the brand and defined ppd's overriding goal – ppd: courage for creative change.[273]

Following the definition of the brand identity, the task was to develop a sustainable brand positioning. In contrast to the brand identity, which describes what makes a brand tick, the positioning determines how the brand presents itself to its stakeholders: how it communicates or appears at the brand contact points. On the basis of an analysis of the most important competitors and customer needs, as well as of key market developments, a set of possible characteristics and benefits were determined which could form the basis of the positioning of ppd. These so-called positioning criteria were then checked to see whether they matched with ppd's identity (authenticity), whether they were important for customers and potential customers (relevance) and whether they were distinct from those of direct competitors (differentiation). As a result, it was agreed that creativity should play a central communication role and should be presented more clearly at brand contact points. The positioning statement became: 'Having emerged from a traditional family business in the paper industry, we were the first to have a modern design on our napkins. Today, we develop products for a beautiful home for our predominantly female target group. We work with a desire for creative change and modern design and act like a fashion company. As an attractive brand, we are a strong partner to retailers.'

Both the brand identity and the positioning were presented and the meaning of the ideas was discussed with all employees in a one-day event. The results of the discussion process influenced the way the brand was expressed and together the project team and employees co-created strategic programmes under the slogan of 'always creative' in communications, service offering, sales, employee development and pricing. Exhibition stands were re-designed, as were all forms and communication materials. Social media policy was changed, sales people were given brand-specific training and the new product development process was optimised.

## Adjusting a brand's strategy

We argued before that brands should be open to the influence of their stakeholders[274] – and of course, this also implies that customers, employees and suppliers may force a brand's management to rethink its identity and positioning. If we encourage others to contribute to the formation of brand meaning via social media, brand communities, participative events, workshops, market research and other instruments, we must be alert to the necessary strategic changes and adjustments that this entails. At Intuit, for example, employees can use 10 per cent of their time to develop ideas of their choice and LEGO uses suggestions from its AFOL (Adult Friends of Lego) communities to develop better products. Both organisations create the opportunity to de-territorialise the brand and change the way the brand owner and other stakeholders think about it.

A brand's strategy is therefore fluid. As with our hike across the Alps, there will be a need, and also sometimes an opportunity, to revise and adjust the journey. There have been plenty of brands that have stayed on their brand path too long and failed to adapt to changing circumstances. And there are brands such as Leica, the high-end German camera brand that had a legendary reputation among photographers, but lost its way. Leica was too swayed by its past in analogue photography and for a long time failed to adapt to developments in digital technology, before eventually realising change was needed. Looking back, this always seems obvious, but there is also virtue in consistency of positioning – it helps to build trust and a feeling of authenticity. So, what is the right mix between consistency and change? Maybe the following parable, taken from a book on the topic of personal branding, helps to explain and understand the tension.[275]

There is a girl who grows up in her loving parents' house in the country. After school, she moves to the city, goes to university and looks for new role models. She begins to become aware of her strengths and to cultivate them. She meets interesting people who have a lot of influence on her. Then she goes abroad and gets to know different cultures. All this can be a real boost to her identity. It shapes her way of thinking and her behaviour. And her experiences are reflected in her changing value system. One thing is clear, though: she will always be the girl from the country. And yet she will develop her own style and character. She can emancipate herself from her past, but she will somehow stay the same.

Brands can learn from this story. Brands should stay true to themselves, but at the same time, they have to change constantly as meaning is co-created together with stakeholders. Elements of positioning are more flexible and open for modification than elements of the brand's identity – especially, the core or essence of a brand is only likely to evolve slowly over time. By finding the right balance between consistency and transformation, brand managers create brand equity. How brand equity is co-created will be discussed in the next chapter. But before we do this, have a look at the case below of the Austrian telecommunications company A1. It will help you to understand how a company can develop the positioning and meaning of its brand in times of disruptive change and still stay true to its values.

## A1 eSports League Austria: How a brand stays young

*Author: Matthias Lorenz*

eSports is digital sport in which video game players compete with each other in athletic contests. As with other sports, team members train together, analyse their opponents and then compete against other teams. Taking part in eSports is a fast-growing trend that is highly popular with millions of (mostly young) people. But what does it have to do with brand management?

The eSports league of the Austrian telecommunications service provider A1 is a good example of why a company in our digital world can only develop the positioning and meaning of its brand in exchange with its target groups. A1 is the leading communications and network provider in Austria, with more than 5 million mobile and 2 million fixed-line customers. But despite A1's market success, as a brand it struggled to connect with the attractive target group of millennials using classic media channels – mainly because millennials no longer watch linear television and use new media instead of magazines. So A1 had to come up with something different to recharge the brand with new content and engage emotionally with its young audience. The idea A1 came up with was to communicate in a completely new way: out with one-way communication from the brand to the target group and in with dialogue and mutual exchange. The solution: build your own national league for eSports!

At first sight it might seem that eSports has little to do with telecommunications – other than a need for fast data connection via digital bandwidth. But the league is helping A1 to extend its brand meaning in new and relevant directions. A1 built up the league themselves and thus developed the idea from the ground up, together with the community. And this was perceived as highly authentic. The feeling of authenticity is central and derives from the way the project was co-created internally by employees, especially by those who had an interest in gaming, who developed and championed it. Consequently, A1 are not the sponsors or contractors of the league, but its operators.

The result: the creation of the most professional and largest platform for eSports in Austria, which is open to around 38,000 registered players in the country and has resulted in about 300,000 personal encounters that players and spectators had at events with the A1 brand within 12 months. The corresponding social media activities achieved a gross reach of 13 million contacts at the same time. And countless PR articles documented the public interest in the league. But despite those numbers, perhaps the following is the most important thing: the A1 brand is now perceived quite differently today by the young target group. This could only be achieved because A1 developed the basis for a platform where people talk to each other. This means they experience the brand in a completely new way.

## Summary

A brand's strategy is fluid, and as a brand develops and grows, there will be a need to revise and adjust it. This indicates what a brand stands for today and in what direction brand managers want to develop the brand in the future. The brand's identity and its positioning are part of the brand strategy. We defined a brand's identity as an ever-evolving phenomenon, rooted in a brand's history, philosophy, practices and ambitions but subject to constant mediation and re-interpretation as its meaning is co-created by a brand's stakeholders. Various models exist that can help managers to define the identity of their brand. The brand's positioning is based on a brand's identity and derived from it, but it is more tactical and can be defined as the active communication of the brand identity at all brand touch points and towards different target groups. Perhaps the most difficult tasks within brand management are adjusting a brand's strategy and repositioning the brand. Brands should stay true to themselves, but at the same time they have to change constantly as meaning is co-created together with stakeholders.

## Reflections/questions

1) Have a look at the brand identity model of Aaker and Joachimsthaler. Then select a brand and describe the brand's identity using the model.

2) Could you explain to someone the differences between brand identity and brand positioning?

3) Which brands appear to you as a) very authentic, b) very different from competing brands and c) very relevant and well prepared for the future?

4) Name brands that have repositioned themselves successfully and others that did not succeed with their repositioning. Do you have any explanation for the differences in success?

## We recommend the following reading to expand your learning experience:

Burmann, C., Jost-Benz, M. & Riley, N. (2009). 'Towards an identity-based brand equity model', *Journal of Business Research, 62*(3), 390–397.

Da Silveira, C., Lages, C. & Simões, C. (2013). 'Reconceptualizing brand identity in a dynamic environment', *Journal of Business Research, 66*(1), 28–36.

Greyser, S.A. & Urde, M. (2019). 'What Does Your Corporate Brand Stand For?', *Harvard Business Review*, January-February 2019, 80–89.

Urde, M. & Koch, C. (2014). 'Market and brand-oriented schools of positioning', *Journal of Product & Brand Management, 23*(7), 478–490.

# CHAPTER EIGHT

# Co-creating brand equity

## In this chapter ...

Here, we look at the third element in our co-creative brand management system, which is concerned with how stakeholders help to develop brand equity and enrich (and sometimes change) brand meaning. Having built insights into the lives of stakeholders and constructed the brand strategy, we now come to the point where choices will be made and decisions implemented – the consequences of which will impact back on insights and strategy. This third stage is vital, because it is where the meaning of the brand is realised; where we move from listening and thinking to action.

Of course, as brand equity is co-created, what managers and employees say and do is not the same as what customers and other stakeholders experience. This means that whereas the organisation sets out to establish a brand identity, the identity that actually exists and evolves is somewhat different. These two forms of brand identity are known as 'intended' and 'enacted'. The interplay between them can enrich the brand and help build brand equity, or it can sow confusion about the brand and what it stands for. As always in the co-creative perspective, this is a fluid process where intended and enacted brand identities are always in flux.

In the chapter we explain the difference between intended and enacted identities and look at the importance of authenticity within the brand management process. We also look at how managers try to shape the building blocks of brand equity through crowdsourcing, storytelling, brand communities, social media influencers and employee behaviour. And we show the limits of that influence and how managers need to let go of their brands.

## Learning Objectives

After reading this chapter you should

- understand that the intended and enacted identities of strong brands are usually pretty congruent though not completely identical;
- be aware that the concept of 'authenticity' is central in building brand equity;
- recognise how stories can contribute to a brand's meaning and how the co-creation of stories works;
- know the importance of brand communities and social media influencers in modern brand building;
- understand the tremendous contribution a brand's own employees can make within the brand building process.

## Brand equity and brand meaning

Francisco Guzmán and colleagues argue that co-creation takes place when two or more actors collaboratively interact to create value.[276] From a brand management perspective, the co-created value results in brand equity. But what is brand equity? In Chapter 5, we offered the simple but telling answer that brand equity is about the difference between the perception of a product or a service with and without a brand name attached. Imagine a pair of plain unbranded sneakers versus a pair of adidas Gazelles with their three stripes and association with supermodel Kate Moss. It might be that the functional performance of the sneakers is pretty similar, but the judgement of value and feelings towards them will probably be quite different. This is brand equity. It takes time to develop and predisposes a consumer to buying a particular brand. A variety of factors can influence the positive associations that emerge, including the product and service experience, the brand's communications and the network of interactions between different stakeholders. In the past a lot of the emphasis in building brand equity focussed on marketing communications, but as you will now know from this book, marketing departments can no longer control the flow of brand communication in the way they used to. This doesn't negate the value of strategically planned and purposefully managed brand communication, but rather recognises that multiple stakeholders are involved – intentionally or unintentionally – in co-creating brand meaning.[277] Therefore, the implementation of a brand's strategy, together with multiple stakeholders, is crucial to brand success. This is the focus of this chapter. The following sections will explore the most relevant themes connected to building brand equity.

In focussing on some specific themes, we will not dwell on some areas that are strongly linked to brand equity, but are covered in detail in other books. For example, marketing communications activity (TV, radio, billboards, print advertisements) is important in promoting a product category, building a brand's profile, linking it to specific attributes, creating desire for the product, selling the brand and developing brand satisfaction and loyalty.[278] This activity, alongside other interactions such as events, sponsorship, public relations, direct marketing, trade fairs, electronic marketing and other instruments,[279] helps to provide a consistent and meaningful brand experience across all brand touch points. Yet while integral to the brand building process, most of these elements are not directly co-creative, in that they inform and maybe inspire, but they do not purposefully encourage involvement and interaction. Indeed, for the most part they concentrate on communicating the intended brand identity, rather than participating in the enacted brand identity.

## Intended and enacted brand identity

One axiom of traditional brand management is that strong brands possess a clear and well-defined identity that makes them distinctive and desirable.[280] This conception of brand identity implies that there is an enduring brand essence and character that stakeholders encounter at different brand touch points.[281] This helps to provide a sense of continuity and a framework for brand innovation for both employees and customers. However, a well-defined identity, even when persuasive, does not imply a fixed meaning. As the semiotician Roland Barthes argued in a famous 1968 essay, 'The Death of the Author', what authors intend and what readers read are two very different things.[282] A brand identity can be well-articulated by an organisation, and yet provide room for different interpretations of the brand meaning by a brand's stakeholders (customers, employees, management and the general public).[283] A campaign from Anheuser-Busch that aired during the 2017 Super Bowl about the German immigrant founders of the company could be read as the story of the American Dream (an ideal rooted in the Declaration of Independence, which advocates the potential for success and prosperity for all) or as a political statement. In the politicised landscape of the time, and following US President Trump's executive order banning travel from certain Muslim countries, the advertisement was seen by many people as a pro-immigration message, which affronted the President's supporters. Rather than passively accept this, they took to social media, swearing not to drink the beer again and asking their peer group to boycott the brand.[284]

What Barthes illustrates is the challenge of the fluidity of meaning. Brand identity develops, often from the beliefs of founders, inside the organisation and is influenced by employees through their actions and communications (note Lucy Gill-Simmen's section below), but it is also subject to adaptation through the interactions of others: 'by consumers who create relations, emotions and communities around brands' independent of the organisation.[285] The fashion brand Lonsdale, for example, never intended to stand for right-wing beliefs, but some of its customers saw that the 'nsda' in the middle of the name could be linked to the German acronym of the Nazi Party. This subverted the intended brand meaning and made it popular with young right-wingers. Lonsdale then fought to reclaim its meaning by sponsoring anti-racist events. Similarly, the fashion brand Burberry lost control over its intended identity when the brand became popular with some English football supporters. These examples suggest that there can be a considerable gap between intention and enactment, but it should be noted that for most successful brands the core meaning of an identity does not alter significantly.[286] Nike's brand identity, which can be described as being passionate to perform;[287] the British retailer John Lewis' conscious business model, which centres on fairness and trust;[288] and LEGO's identity, which is rooted in creativity and imagination,[289] are all largely consistent over time. These brands and others like them do stand for something specific, which is determined both by brand management (intended brand identity) and social interaction processes among stakeholders (enacted brand identity).[290]

Take the example of Deutsche Telekom (DT), which is the largest telecommunications operator in Europe. In 2017, they decided to dedicate time and money to better understand the needs of German municipalities with respect to digital solutions. The problem was that they were not well positioned in this market. In the past they would probably have briefed an agency, developed a campaign and claimed to be the experts in digitalisation for public authorities. However, they were aware that this one-way approach of communicating at public authorities would no longer work. Their innovative approach was to invite city representatives to work together with DT's employees to co-create solutions to the municipalities' most important problems. They wrote to the mayors of all cities in Germany with more than 20,000 inhabitants and invited them to take part in a co-creation project. Fifty cities agreed to participate in the three-month process, which started with an event to decide the most important areas of action (traffic and transportation, citizen's self-service, clean energy). At this stage, the participants also determined the topic on which each city would work. DT supported each topic design team with experts. The teams met regularly and worked on concrete solutions. Then, some weeks later, there was a workshop that gave the participants the opportunity to see what the other teams were doing and to share common ideas. This led to a prototyping workshop where ideas could be made more concrete. After three months, a major workshop took place, where all the prototypes that had been developed by the design teams were presented and tested. What were the benefits of this co-creative approach? First, numerous product and service prototypes were developed that were relevant to the needs of the municipalities and also helped to complement the company's product portfolio. Second, the process itself enabled DT and the participants to learn about ways of working together that could be used with new audiences and new challenges. Third (and this was perhaps the most important benefit), DT could position itself as an open and transparent partner who wants to listen and work with its clients. The DT example shows stakeholder expectations have changed to encourage participation. It also shows how a co-creative approach, which was designed to enhance the relevance of the DT brand, can help to align the intended and enacted brand identity.

## The importance of authenticity

That certain brands manage to achieve a good alignment between the intended and enacted identity is also an issue of authenticity. Brands achieve authenticity both by ensuring that they link their future strategies to their past and by delivering on the identity claims they make.[291] In his study of cultural branding, Douglas Holt notes that iconic brands are willing to take risks to realise 'populist authenticity'.[292] In other words, they adhere to their beliefs come what may and are courageous enough to sacrifice broader popularity for a 'committed philosophy'. In describing the fidelity of such brands, Holt writes: 'This willingness to defend a particular set of ideas, even when they offend a substantial fraction of the buying public, is a consistent thread among iconic brands.'[293] He further notes that brands fail if they think they can do this in a superficial way by simply attaching their brand to a populist cause. Two examples, those of Pepsi-Cola and Nike, may be of use to illustrate this thought further. In 2017, Pepsi aired a commercial featuring the celebrity endorser Kendall Jenner. The scenario was a street protest with marchers and police confronting each other. The cause of the protest was not-specified, but it tapped into a time when confrontations between protestors and the police had become more frequent. To diffuse the tension, up marches Kendall Jenner, who offers an ice-cold Pepsi to a policeman. Perhaps not surprisingly, the commercial was strongly criticised, both for mis-reading the mood of the times and for its superficiality. The pressure from social media led Pepsi to pull the campaign. Just over a year later, Nike launched a campaign with fallen American football star Colin Kaepernick, an American political activist and quarterback who had played for the San Francisco 49ers and had protested against police violence by kneeling when the American national anthem was played at games. Nike created a commercial and a poster featuring a close-up of Kaepernick together with the line 'Believe in something. Even if it means sacrificing everything'.

Both Nike and Pepsi represent examples of attempts to develop the intended brand identity. However, Nike works much more effectively because it aligns with previous experience of the brand. Nike has consistently created advertising based on political and social issues, as when portraying a female athlete wearing a Hijab or when launching the 'Juntas Imparables' (Together Unstoppable) campaign in Mexico (a country known for its machismo) featuring only female athletes. The consistency of approach makes the Kaepernick campaign credible and authentic (even if some who disagreed with Kaepernick attacked Nike on social media). By contrast Pepsi, with the Kendall Jenner campaign, failed both for its lack of credibility and its tone-deafness.

# The formation of brand equity

When it comes to implementing a brand strategy the goal should be to help develop brand equity. Brand equity has long been written about, but the focus has tended to be on one-way communication rather than the network of interactions that we find in co-creation. The potential influence of more participative processes on a brand's meaning varies, as does the degree of collaboration between the brand and its stakeholders. However, one thing that is common to different co-creative approaches is that participation makes people feel closer to a brand; it helps fuel the sort of relationship that can lead to attitudinal and behavioural loyalty. In the sections that follow, we will not try to provide a scientifically relevant systematisation of consumer brand equity co-creation – this has already been done elsewhere.[294] Rather, here we will concentrate on the most relevant means available to the co-creative brand manager in building brand equity: the use of crowdsourcing as a means of generating ideas, the power of storytelling, the use of brand communities, the role of social media influencers and the interactions between a brand's employees and its external stakeholders.

# Crowdsourcing

The term crowdsourcing has been defined as 'the act of a company or institution taking a function once performed by employees and outsourcing it to an undefined (and generally large) network of people in the form of an open call.'[295] The open call can be more or less 'open', which means that the rules of how to respond to the call may vary and may effect a more intense interaction between a brand and its stakeholders or a one-time communication, as when consumers share product ideas via platforms such as 'MyStarbucksIdea'.[296] With crowdsourcing, the level of interaction between participants, and between the participants and the brand, may not always be very high, which reduces the co-creativity of the process, but co-creation does occur when externally generated ideas lead to changes in the brand's content or communications.

Strong brands can create their own crowdsourcing platforms, but there are also a number of public platforms that connect brands with consumers and professionals. For example, eYeka is a popular crowdsourcing platform[297] where brands can set competitive challenges for creative individuals and small organisations to solve. The scope and rules of the competitions vary considerably, but the motivation for participants is both extrinsic (peer recognition and financial reward) and intrinsic (the enjoyment of dedicating time and resources to solving an interesting challenge). The advantage for brands is that they gain quick and rather cheap access to the know-how of potentially hundreds of creative people and can choose the solution that might best fit the brand's strategy. Procter & Gamble, for example, developed an electronic toothbrush (Oral-B SmartSeries 7000) that could be connected to an app. To speed up the development process and access more creative resources, P&G used the eYeka community to crowdsource ideas as to how to develop and position the concept. The company received 67 ideas that 'uncovered strong needs for more personalised dental regimens, eagerness to learn proper techniques and a strong desire to turn a chore into enjoyment, often through ramification of the brushing experience'[298] and helped to build equity for the brand.

The example of Simba, a South-African crisps brand (presented in the next section), provides another instance of a crowdsourcing activity that supported a brand's ambition to grow. However, it should also be noted that crowdsourcing is not without its problems: there have been instances of brands that have lost trust through crowdsourcing processes. The US retailer Gap, the Italian stationery brand Moleskine and even New Zealand tried to crowdsource new symbols, but ended up being ridiculed on social media. New Zealand tried to crowdsource a new flag, but after a long-winded process ended up retaining the flag it had, while Gap suffered such social media criticism for a new logo design that it too opted out of change. Both of these attempts seemingly failed because the quality of crowdsourced input wasn't strong enough. For Moleskine, the challenge came from the process they followed, which was seen to be unfair. Moleskine's virtual fan base, which was enjoined to design a new logo, turned on the brand when people started to feel exploited by the brand requiring the winning design to assign their intellectual property rights in return for a €7,000 prize.[299] These various examples illustrate that crowdsourcing should be approached with care. Like other co-creation techniques, it requires a well-thought-through and managed process that is clear, transparent and fair.

## How co-creation can strengthen positioning: Simba crisps flavour case

*Author: Pieter Steenkamp*

Germany, 1955. Leon Greyvensteyn visits a food fair in search of ideas to diversify the product range of his family business. Since 1939 the Greyvensteyn family has been selling their Ouma Rusks in South Africa (Ouma is an Afrikaans word for grandmother). At the fair Leon meets one of the founders of the Frito-Lay company and after extending his trip to the US to learn more, he returns to South Africa. In 1957, he founds a potato crisps and snacks brand that is now known as Simba.[300]

Simba the lion, wearing a crown as any king should, is the prominent brand element on all packaging and related material of Simba crisps. In Swahili, an east/south-eastern African language, Simba means lion. The brand is centred on the concept of 'Mapha', meaning the joy of sharing.[301] The slogan 'Roarrrs with Flavour' positions the brand and links the lion mascot (that roarrrs) to one of the key differentiators of the brand (its flavour). To innovate new flavours, Simba collaborates with other well-loved South African flavour brands, like the flame-grilled burger brand Steers and Mrs H.S Ball's Chutney. To extend its flavour strategy and to strengthen its positioning, Simba has also invited customers to co-create flavours. The company held a competition that asked, 'What's your lekker flavour?' (*lekker* is Afrikaans for nice). Simba promoted the competition by going out and discussing the question with people. Some 187,000 entries were received via SMS and a microsite, suggesting flavours such as bobotie and bunny chow. The public voted and judges initially reduced the submissions to 20. 'The criteria used to judge the flavours considered whether the flavour is original and creative; simple, straightforward and fun; whether it fits with the rest of the Simba range; whether it is easily produced; and whether it is truly South African.' The 20 flavours were reduced further and the final four flavours were: snoek and atchar, walkie talkie, masala steak Gatsby and vetkoek and polony.

The person that entered the masala steak Gatsby described it as 'the bunny chow of Cape Town – a fresh footlong bread roll is stacked with delicious fillings like cheese, onions, polony and chips and then smothered in a delicious sauce. Every fishery or take-away joint that one finds in Cape Town will have Gatsbys on the menu. It is the perfect meal to have when you have a big appetite as it is a huge portion of food and is very affordable.'[302]

Because the proof of the flavour is in the tasting, the four flavours were introduced to supermarket shelves so that consumers could select their favourite. The campaign was supported by advertising and prizes. In the end 'the choice of the winner was based on sales (60%) and the remaining 40% came from public votes. A staggering 15-million packets of chips were sold during the final phase of the competition.'[303]

Ultimately, there could only be one winner of the R200,000 prize and a 1 per cent share of sales value of the winning flavour – estimated at up to R500,000 per annum, for as long as the flavour remained on the market. And the winner was Aletta Crofton's Walkie Talkie Chicken. Aletta explained that 'her inspiration for the flavour came from a photograph her brother took of a little girl enjoying a chicken potjie in the Eastern Cape: It caught my eye because she looked so happy and was sitting with a "walkie" (chicken foot) in one hand and "talkie" (chicken head) in the other.'[304]

Simba could have decided to continue with the safe and familiar by simply observing their customers to identify their flavour preferences (as with the Steers and Mrs Ball's examples), or it could have developed new flavours itself and narrowed these down through taste tests, but the brand went a step further by co-creating flavours with its customers. This brave decision allowed customers access to the heart and soul of Simba. This strengthened the brand's positioning by providing it with flavours that were not commercially available, but were highly relevant to and part of the daily lives of its customers.

## Storytelling

In the co-creative era brand identity cannot be defined solely by the aspirations and perceptions of brand managers – and neither can identity be implemented in one-way communication. Instead, 'the line separating consumers and brands continues to blur.'[305] However, this doesn't mean managers can just put their feet up. Managers need to be active in nurturing the brand identity and using it as a compass to guide direction. Indeed, the more fluid the brand identity becomes, the more brand managers need to build relevant content for stakeholders – which brings us to the importance of storytelling. Brand stories are an effective way of communicating a brand's values and beliefs in an authentic and persuasive way, not least because authenticity is not inherent in objects but needs to be constantly claimed and asserted.[306] Rhetoric and narrative are essential to effect perceptions of authenticity by helping to establish favourable brand meanings and assist consumers in understanding branded initiatives.[307] Let's look at the example of two very different brands that use the power of storytelling to create brand equity: the city of Barcelona (yes, cities can be brands – you can read more about this in the case of Hulst in Chapter 9) and the technology brand Samsung.

Branding Barcelona is a good illustration of how many people can contribute to the development of stories. Barcelona, like other major cities around the world, has to compete to attract tourists, talents, companies, events and residents. The city had been very successful in attracting tourists, but Barcelona's representatives felt that the city's brand meaning was too narrowly focussed and needed to reflect its other strengths and the unique qualities that characterised it. To co-create relevant insights into how the city should position itself, in 2017 Barcelona conducted a benchmarking study followed by international qualitative and quantitative research with experts and the public, as well as online interviews with local respondents. This was followed by interviews with representatives of public organisations and then by co-creation workshops with specialists (in fields such as urbanism, knowledge and education and entrepreneurship), residents and managers. The process led to a definition of the city's purpose (how it wishes to be perceived), its pillars (key strengths that legitimise the objectives of the process) and its personality (the city's way of expressing itself). All of this was written down in a brand book entitled *A Collaborative Storytelling*, with the aim 'to inspire each organisation, group or institution to activate the storytelling in its own sphere of activity, however is most convenient.'[308] In the book, Barcelona is described as 'a city for all of life's ventures', 'a model of progress which allows for both professional and personal growth while allowing people to enjoy life to the full in every respect.'[309] Of course, the co-creation of the city brand did not stop with the writing of the brand book. Rather, it was the starting point. Local organisations, city managers, businesses and residents are encouraged to communicate the story of the city in an ongoing, participative effort to evolve and refine the Barcelona brand.

The technology company Samsung also helps to illustrate the power of storytelling. It makes clear that co-creative storytelling cannot be controlled, but is rather a way to encourage participation and the re-telling of stories. During Berlin Art Week in 2018, Samsung supported a project called 're:imagine Street ARt', which involved co-operation with street artists. The project's objective was to transform everyday spaces into galleries in an imaginative, thoughtful and provocative way.[310] Thanks to augmented reality (AR), street artists could turn entire walls and even rooms into colourful worlds and works of art. To fully experience the artwork, people needed to download an App on their smartphones. For example, the street artist ELLE created a collage of fused faces and other motifs presented on a wall in a rather classical gallery style. Using Samsung's AR App, the artwork could be seen as a three-dimensional space with powerful visual effects (such as a crying eye). While the walk-in art experience was inspirational, the Samsung brand was in the background – the initiator but not the controller of proceedings. 're:imagine Street ARt' linked the topic of augmented reality to the Samsung brand and created space for a variety of stories about the personal experiences of visitors without forcing the Samsung storyline upon them. Even though Samsung was criticised by some for the commercial exploitation of art, the interesting aspect of the collaboration lay in the brand's willingness to allow meaning to emerge through the sharing of different stories. As Sjödin and Ind argue: 'Managerial attempts to shape brand meaning meld with input from critics, consumers, competitors, and others in processes of authentication.'[311] By encouraging others to tell their own narratives, brand meaning is enriched and brand equity is built.

# Co-creative brand storytelling: from persuasion to identification

*Author: Richard Gyrd-Jones*

> If you want to build a ship, don't call people together to collect wood and don't assign them tasks and work, but rather teach them to long for the endless immensity of the sea.
>
> (Antoine de Saint-Exupéry)

Branding is fundamentally about persuasion, and brands are fundamentally persuasive in nature. Brands persuade directly through their firm-controlled communication: their adverts, their postings, their products, their service interactions, their dress. They invite us in – through their stories, their colours, their logos – to become aware of them, to understand what they stand for and to ultimately persuade us to join them commercially and psychologically. But they are much more than this. They do not stand alone as a proposition that we either accept or reject, but are active in the constitution of identities: of their own and those of others. This makes it impossible to separate brands from identity. Brands persuade through communication, through their publics, communities and online and offline media. They are thus defined through continuous and multifarious rhetorical interconnections of actions and interactions. The problem is that the nature of this persuasion and knowledge – of who is doing the persuading – is less clear than at any time since brands emerged as powerful symbolic and economic tools, not least because the notion of the sender and the receiver in the branding world has been thoroughly challenged.

Let me begin with two examples. In 2009 the Canadian singer Dave Carroll posted a protest YouTube video chronicling how

United Airlines broke his guitar in transit, and the subsequent poor service he experienced. As a popular singer, Carroll was able to show the vulnerability of brands in a multi-stakeholder eco-system where social media allow brand publics to express supportive, orthogonal or contrary views of the brand.[312] His video set into play a multiple-level, multi-stakeholder set of interactions and influence, which resulted in 15 million hits and 21,000 comments.[313] While a network analysis of the interactions reveals a complex level of engagement and (purposive) outcomes, the way key stakeholders engage reveals links back to their own positions and identities in the network and their own life stories and experiences, including their feelings towards United.

The second example concerns the proliferation of social media influencers. One particular example I share with my students is that of the influencer Zoella. This fashion blogger began displaying her clothes from shopping 'hauls' from the fast fashion retailer Primark in 2009. Beginning as a hobby, her YouTube channel now has 4.8m followers. Zoella has become a major advertising channel for Primark, but one over which they have little control. She is not alone, but is reflective of the increasing number of influencers who promote brands via their YouTube channels. They represent the emergence of a new, independent phenomenon often known as the blogosphere, reflective of a new breed of human brands[314] whose authenticity is based as much on postings about their lives and passions as about the brands they promote, and who are more important than the brands they are promoting.

In each of these cases, the brand is the focus, but the brand does not participate in the blogger/follower conversation. What exactly then are these conversations? As several scholars of brands have noted, we are witnessing a paradigm shift in the relationship between the focal brand and its stakeholders. Brand meaning is increasingly (co-)created in a market-space defined by multiple stakeholders, where brand meanings are fluid, dynamic, multiple and contested and discursively constituted, and where the brand becomes de-centred. For brand scholars and brand managers, the key question is how to persuade an audience (that may not be really listening) that brands have something relevant to say.

Our ability to answer this question is hindered by two facts. First, research and practice on brand co-creation is largely either conceptual and abstract and/or managerial. Second, the literature persists in the belief that brand meaning is singular: regardless of whether brand meaning is created by the brand or co-created with stakeholders, the results are assumed to deliver a consistent, uni-dimensional whole. This essay suggests that we need to focus on the processes of persuasion and meaning creation to understand how brands persuade. In particular:

- there is a need to study the mechanisms and contexts of brand meaning co-creation as they unfold over time and in relation to single and multiple stakeholders.[315] As Fournier & Avery note: 'Brand marketers no longer controlled the reach of their messages, consumers did … As brands struggled to leverage social media, consumers learned how to leverage brands for their own purposes and ends';[316]
- we need to conceptualise brand narratives as rhetorical narratives in order to enable us to follow key brand articulations and negotiations as persuasive forces.

There is a growing focus on the ways in which brand conversations are used by different publics to articulate identities. Brand opponents – such as Dave Carroll – activate their brand identities in opposition to the brand; influencers – such as Zoella – develop their identity as human brands; and consumers communicate their identity through offline activities such as purchasing, owning and disposing, and online activities such as liking, following and posting. Brand identities provide the (necessary) backdrop to the telling of public lives, where the brand is not the focal point of the conversation and where identities are played out in the polyphony that arises through the multiple interactions in the stakeholder eco-system. 'The (brand) public resonates brand-related meanings and identities that are articulated elsewhere', note Arvidsson and Calliandro.[317] Or more succinctly: brands are identities.[318] Brands provide rich sites for the study of culture or even assemblages of culture.[319] They both challenge and reflect culture. Brands may have lost their cultural hegemony to the sovereignty of the consumer, but, at the same time, they are powerful symbolic and cultural repositories for consumer-driven identity projects. As outlined quite percipiently by Holt,[320] brands are not going away. But their existence no longer relies on a mono-centric broadcasting of brand meanings and messages to passive audiences waiting to be seduced, but to a plethora of marketplace actors, networks, structures and actions in entropy and temporary stabilisations. Brands may appeal to individuals, but these individuals cannot be seen in isolation from their social, economic and cultural context and the market and social systems within which brands' rhetorical narratives are interpreted.[321] These contexts must be seen in relation to the nested interplay of identities that are played out when brands are enacted at the individual level.[322] In this context, brands are only persuasive to the extent that they become relevant in these nested layers of identity: identities related to personal life projects, to self-conceptualisations, to friendship and kinship groups, and to other collective identities based around communities, organisations and societies.

How does the brand persuade in this environment?

In Aristotelian rhetoric, the rhetorician persuades their public through the act of speech. Rhetorical strength depends on the core attributes of the speech-act and the orator: the *logos* of the argument, the *ethos* of the speaker and the *pathos* of the message. Iglesias and Bonet note that in the contemporary brand environment, where multiple stakeholders are co-creators of the brand, the brand can only ensure alignment between intended and enacted brand meanings through using such rhetorical persuasion.[323] Rhetorical theory, however, requires the speaker to secure the audience's attention and the willingness of the audience to be persuaded. In brand co-creation literature there tends to be an implicit or explicit assumption that brand publics are interested in the brand and interested in co-creating with the brand. But ask most stakeholders whether this is true and it appears to be far from the case. It says little about the context within which the speech-act takes place, or the impact of context on the persuasive strength of these arguments. Burke provides another view of rhetoric that moves rhetoric from simply an act of persuasion to one of identification.[324]

By evoking identification rather than persuasion as the key element of rhetoric, Burke recognised the essential role of social context within which orators and audiences exist and the fundamental role of human relations in assessing rhetorical acts. For Burke, the act of persuasion is an act of identification and for persuasion to take place there must be an implicit or explicit identification between the rhetoric and the audience. In this way his ideas open up the rhetorical act to include social identity, because, he argues, the individual is not free to be persuaded, but interprets messages from within their identification of their own social identity. For Burke, the forces of social cohesion are stronger than those of liberation and individuals are not free *per se* to be persuaded unless and until they embody the persuasive discourse. Thus, for Burke, identification is rhetorical. And, importantly, it is not the conscious act of persuasion that unites the sender with the receiver, but identification between them. In much the same way, identity is in a constant, rhetorical dialectic between the subject and its surroundings.

This brings us back to the role of identity and identification in understanding how brands persuade. If we follow Burke's line of thought, brand publics are constituted through the rhetoric of the brand. A theory of constitutive rhetoric, based on the principle of identification, suggests that persuasion occurs when individuals are 'interpellated' or called into being through rhetorical narratives of, and around, the brand.[325] In this case, the brand becomes part of the assemblage of individual identities.

## A rhetorical theory of brands

This approach allows us to think about the role of the context of brands and to develop a rhetorical theory of brands (not branding) and of brands and individuals. Brands can be viewed as rhetorical devices, or even as existing rhetorically – not just as persuasive devices, but in their very existence. Brands exist in relation to others: other brands, but also other people, towns, places, times. Brands move from defining the symbolism around their product universe to encompassing narratives about consumers' (and other stakeholders') lives. Brands are a relational construct: they exist because of their relations to others. In this respect brands are action: they are in motion, which might be described as a state of dynamic stability. They exist in this state, just as they are constantly being created and reaffirmed.

A rhetorical theory of branding suggests three things about brand co-creation. First, publics may have little agency or interest to change and thus to directly co-create with the brand. We cannot assume stakeholders are going to engage in co-creation activities and, when they do, we need to understand on what basis they engage with the brand. Second, brands do not persuade in an Aristotelian sense, but rather they become relevant and 'powerful' as they form rhetorical identification with their publics. This rhetorical link between the brand and its publics creates a powerful basis for co-creation. However, brands need to understand that persuasion is as much achieved in the conversational space between the brand and consumers as it is by intended brand enactments. Last, brands cannot be divorced from their context (and the context of the context); brands persuade because they are culturally situated.[326] If we reflect on the quotation at the beginning of this essay, it is clear that the persuasive brand is one that evokes identification rather than one that tries to persuade.

## Brand communities

As long as brands have existed, so have brand communities. These are the physical and online social spaces where we exchange opinions, ideas and sometimes disappointments about the brands we buy and use. According to the researchers Muniz & O'Guinn, a brand community can be defined as 'a specialised, non-geographically bound community, based on a structured set of social relations among admirers of a brand'.[327] Brand communities can be founded and managed by the admirers of a brand, or set up by a brand's management, as a way to build insight and to co-create new ideas. In the case of the former, the rules of the community and its agenda are defined largely by the participants. Due to the passion of the community members, these communities can have high levels of participation, but because they are generally not managed, discussions tend to be organic. Brands can learn much about the enacted brand meaning from listening to this type of brand community, and also by providing commentary and support, but they also have to exercise a degree of caution in that fans, while loyal, do not necessarily reflect the broader base of current and potential customers. In the case of the latter, company-sponsored communities tend to be more directed by the sponsoring organisation, and membership can be tailored to specific needs. An important attribute of these communities, which tend to be closed to non-members, is the high level of interaction between the organisation and members. Here, there is a real opportunity for community members to influence brand meaning. Within these communities there is a complex interplay between different identity levels: individual, collective community and intended – with each influencing the other. Individual identities evolve through dialogue and action, the collective community identity develops through the emergence of a shared perspective, while the intended brand identities provide the context. When communities are effective they improve brand awareness, identification, loyalty and trust, positive word-of-mouth and willingness to pay.[328]

An illustration of a fan community is 'Porsche rennlist' – a discussion forum of Porsche enthusiasts with more than 10,000 registered users. This is a valuable resource for enthusiasts to share experiences and, on a practical level, buy and sell parts. The connectivity between the participants helps to create a bond between the brand and its customers. However, as an illustration of the challenge posed by enthusiasts, when Porsche introduced the Cayenne, the fan base was strongly against it, because it undermined their sense of what the brand was about. In a business-to-business environment, SAP has a long-established online community with some 2.5 million community users and over 100,000 blog posts. SAP's community is a valuable resource for allowing the company to connect with its customers (both small and large); to share knowledge and to connect customers to each other.[329]

Brand communities provide multiple benefits, including a sense of closeness to a brand and a feeling of creativity in influencing its direction[330] – which can be seen in some of the quotations from online community participants:[331]

- 'I've bought the product more, read more of its contents and nutritional values, and enjoyed giving my opinion on future development of the product and its marketing.'
- 'My perceptions really haven't changed other than I'm more positive mainly because now I realise that they really care about what consumers think and welcome their ideas and opinions.'
- 'Well, I have spent so much time on the Activia site that the brand is etched on my eyeballs – I love it – and recommend it whenever the occasion arises. It's MY brand!!'
- 'It is all about new ideas, different ways of doing things so creativity always plays a big part in the community.'
- 'I had projects, with the use of videos and photographs to participate in and this allowed me, and others, to experiment and use what creative skills we had.'

Whereas brand equity was once seen as something that organisations built, increasingly, it can be seen as something that is co-created in the social context of brand communities.

## Social Media Influencers

As an illustration of the commercialisation of social media influencers, the researchers Alison Hearn and Stephanie Schoenhoff narrate the following story:[332] 'In January 2013, Canadian blogger Zach Bussey began a year-long effort to live an entirely sponsored life. He cleared all his belongings out of his apartment and attempted to live solely off the perks he generated by his social media influence alone. Bussey offered different promotional services, such as special dedicated blog posts, twitter mentions, Tumblr images and YouTube videos to those brands and companies who would provide him with products or perks.' They conclude: 'Bussey appears to be the first person to offer his entire life as a platform for marketers.'

We do not know if Bussey really can be called the first social media influencer, but influencer marketing has grown rapidly in importance.[333] In itself, influencer marketing is not new – marketers have long used celebrities and market mavens to influence others in their purchasing decisions.[334] However, with the proliferation of digital social media platforms like YouTube, Instagram, Snapchat and TikTok, more and more people have established their own audiences and become a useful means to promote products and services and to co-create brand equity.[335] Statistics show that two out of three millennials block traditional advertising. If you want to reach this audience, you have to tap into the power of influencers.[336] Influencers are an integral part of the marketing process,[337] and help co-create brand meaning by stimulating dialogue with their followers about brands and products. This not only enhances the influencer's own value co-creation experience, but through the creation of original and brand-related content sets the stage for consumers to interact with the brand, to explore its meaning and potentially deepen their relationship.[338] Influencers can build up and facilitate their own communities and give the brand access to social interaction processes. This, of course, only works if there is a relationship of trust between influencers and followers and a belief in the authenticity of influencers.

The danger for brands in passing power over to influencers is that they lose further control over the intended brand identity, but most marketers recognise that it is better to be part of the game than a bystander. In the next section, Stefan Markovic and Ranim Helwani show how brands and social media influencers can co-create effectively.

## Co-creation and Social Media Influencers

*Authors: Stefan Markovic & Ranim Helwani*

While co-creation has become an established part of brand management thinking, and researched in the context of product, service and corporate brands,[339] it is also now connected to the idea of human brands.[340] In the traditional perspective of brand management, human brands were seen as commercially valuable entities, professionally created and managed through marketing and communication activities.[341] In the era of co-creation, however, attention has shifted towards the idea that human brands are not unilaterally created and managed, but socially and dynamically constructed and orchestrated by multiple stakeholders.[342] Human brands, such as celebrities, movie stars, athletes and politicians, are co-created by the celebrity him/herself and by multiple stakeholders, which can be human (other celebrities, fans, spectators) or non-human (advertisers, talent agencies, commercial organisations).[343] Celebrities form their brands through the everyday actions they perform in public, which include appearances in TV shows, films and/or commercials; postings on social media platforms; and online or face-to-face interactions with stakeholders. In turn, stakeholders share their experiences with, and perceptions of, the celebrity brand among themselves and with the celebrity.

The diversity of social media platforms has enabled celebrities to have a greater social influence and attract more brand collaborators through a more direct and personal relationship that builds and boosts the relevance and the reach of their brands.[344] Many consumers or fans see celebrity brands as integral parts of their lives and develop feelings of relatedness and emotional bonds with them.[345] Consumers or fans often believe it is legitimate to take part in the social discourse around the celebrity brand and express their opinions on social media platforms.[346] On these platforms, consumers or fans imbue the celebrity brand with their own media flows, using likes, shares and comments. In parallel, an increasing number of product, service and corporate brands seek endorsements from celebrities to boost their awareness and to generate positive consumer attitudes, purchase intentions and word-of-mouth recommendations.[347]

However, consumer perceptions of celebrity brands not only influence the endorsed brand. The interaction can also function the other way around.[348]

Although most research on human brands focusses on celebrities, human brands are not limited to them. Driven by the endless content producing and sharing possibilities of social media platforms (such as Facebook, Snapchat, YouTube, Instagram), anyone can become a human brand. This is the case for social media influencers (SMIs) – think YouTubers and Instagrammers – who represent the latest generation of human brands. Some SMIs have been able to develop a distinct personal brand and boost their social prominence and influence by sharing insights from their everyday lives on diverse social media platforms with a wide audience.[349] The audience that follows SMIs often perceives them as authentic and trustworthy sources of inspiration, ideas and information. This audience even actively seeks SMIs' personal opinions and recommendations within their fields of expertise, which can be (among others) fashion, beauty, food, technology, health or travel. Unlike mainstream celebrities, SMIs are believed to be accessible, credible and relatable,[350] as they tend to interact with their followers directly and on a more ongoing basis.[351] Therefore, SMIs have the potential to create engagement, drive conversation and influence the attitudes, decisions and the behaviours of their audience.[352] As a result of this, many product, service and corporate brands have started to collaborate with SMIs to promote their offerings. For example, the recently established watches brand Daniel Wellington has placed SMIs at the core of its marketing strategy.[353] In addition, even some traditional luxury brands, such as Tiffany & Co. or Dolce & Gabbana, have recognised the potential of SMIs in reaching younger target groups.[354]

The development of SMI brands provides another example of how co-creation processes increasingly permeate branding.

An SMI brand is co-created in a social discourse between the SMI and his/her stakeholders (audience, brand collaborators, media) and among stakeholders themselves. These stakeholders attach their own meanings to the SMI brand by sharing content with the SMI and with each other.[355] Thus, the interactions between the SMI brand and its stakeholders, and the interactions among stakeholders themselves, represent the basis of SMI brand co-creation. When thinking about SMI brands, a number of important issues need to be addressed:

- Which stakeholders take part in SMI brand co-creation and what are their motivations?
- Which type of stakeholder has the strongest influence over SMI brand co-creation processes?
- Which type of engagement with the SMI (in the form of likes, comments, shares) has the strongest influence on the SMI brand-building processes?
- Which are the key performance indicators that SMIs should take care of in order to boost the strength of their brand and attract more brand collaborators?
- On which criteria should the SMI brand choose its collaborators, and vice versa?
- How can the choice of brand collaborators, the focus on a certain target audience, and/or the type of content posted help SMIs boost their brand equity?
- How and to what extent should the SMI align the expectations of the sponsoring brand and his/her followers?
- What degree of control should the SMI have over the co-creation process of his/her brand? What can the SMI do to retain some control over his/her brand?
- What are the main drivers and outcomes of the perceived authenticity of an SMI brand?

- How does the co-creation process of an SMI brand differ across the different fields of expertise of the SMI (fashion, beauty, food, technology, health, travel)? Who are the relevant stakeholders in each field, and how and where do they interact and influence SMI brand-building processes?

Brands are increasingly recognising the commercial value of SMIs, as they can help them to promote their offerings more effectively than traditional advertising methods.[356] In fact, SMIs have opened up a new way to connect with increasingly elusive audiences that seek authenticity and relatability. Understanding how SMI brands are co-created, and the sponsoring brand's role in this co-creation process, will help brands find an SMI that is closely aligned with their strategies and objectives, and thereby ensure successful influencer marketing campaigns.

## Internal stakeholders

In building brand equity, much emphasis has been given to the idea of integrated marketing communications (ensuring that the various means of communicating with audiences align), and a lot of time and money has been invested in activities aiming to directly influence external stakeholders' (customers, general public and so on) perceptions. What has tended to be underplayed is the important role employees play in building brand equity through what they say and do. A brand can only develop its full potential if the brand is internalised by the company's executives and employees and used in interactions with others. Therefore, involving internal stakeholders throughout the brand management process and inspiring them to 'live the brand' is a major building block of brand equity. The initiatives that aim to strengthen internal brand equity[357] are commonly known as 'Internal Branding'.[358]

The role of employees in brand building is becoming increasingly important. Employees who identify with the brand they represent and who are willing to do more than their job requires have always been valuable in brand building, but now there are more reasons to make internal branding central.[359] First, the importance of the service sector and of services within other sectors gives emphasis to relationship building. Second, the most sophisticated and critical consumers have become more sceptical towards advertising claims and more demanding of a coherent brand experience. Third, there is a greater variety of touch-points online and offline, where employees and stakeholders interact.[360] Accordingly, the question has arisen as to how employees can live the brand and, therefore, how companies can transfer their brand values and positioning to external stakeholders via employees' behaviour.

Increasingly, employees interact with customers in multiple ways (often beyond the control of the company), which means interactions must be inspired by the overall positioning of the brand, rather than by a rule book. In contrast, much of the research in the field of internal branding has focussed on instruments that lead to brand commitment and employees' brand-related behaviour. In a behaviouristic tradition, researchers have attempted to identify the 'hot buttons' that can transform established employee behaviour (for example, being friendly) into behaviour that would strengthen the brand and express its values, namely brand-driven, brand-related or brand-oriented behaviour. The general advice that has been given to practitioners includes managing carefully their internal communication activities, considering brand management within the field of human resource management and encouraging a more transformational leadership style among their managers.[361] More specifically, measures like publishing a brand handbook for internal audiences; printing brand values on t-shirts (and other internal giveaways); organising events to celebrate the brand; chatting with the CEO in an internal blog about brand-related topics; training new staff about the brand; aligning pay systems with the brand values; and generally being more inspiring to staff members, were among some of the proposals.

It is indisputable that those insights were highly relevant and quickly gained acceptance in practice. But if what we call brand is the result of a permanently ongoing bilateral negotiation between a brand's management and its stakeholders, and if brand value is more and more created through conversations between employees and external target groups, the question arises as to whether the button to push in order to influence employees' brand-related behaviour exists at all.[362] Maybe, as Henkel et al. propose, managers should focus on the creation of an organisational environment 'that enables employees to find their own individual ways of articulating a brand to customers'.[363] In this sense, the following multi-firm case-study may help us to better understand employee brand co-creation behaviour.

## Towards a model for Employee Brand Co-Creation Behaviour – a multi-firm case-study

*Author: Lucy Gill-Simmen*

What do Lush, Southwest Airlines, Ritz Carlton, Zappos and Starbucks all have in common? These are brands which are renowned for their employees delivering extraordinary brand-oriented behaviours that have become virtually synonymous with the brand and (even more importantly) have afforded it a significant competitive advantage.

As marketing scholars, a question we are often asked by managers is 'How do we get employees actively involved in brand delivery and contributing to the on-going development of the brand?' In other words, how can organisations facilitate active involvement in co-creation of the brand? Despite the increasing recognition of the changing role of the employee and the common use of terminology such as employees 'living the brand', acting as 'brand champions' and as 'brand ambassadors' and employees who transform brand vision into brand reality, exactly how employees perceive their own brand and how firms may drive co-creation behaviours on the part of employees remains poorly understood. It is a complex process and one which goes far beyond the realms of in-house training, on-boarding exercises or team-building 'away days'. This complexity sets the critical point of departure for our study considering the largely untouched area of research in employee brand co-creation.

We conducted our study in a number of different firms around the world[364] – including 3M, Mayo Clinic, Nikon, Audi and ING Bank – in order to explore the relationships employees have with their brands and to unpack that relationship to identify key mechanisms that help facilitate co-creation behaviours.

Our study points to two essential constructs as the foundations for co-creation behaviour: employee self-brand connection and employee brand identification. More specifically, our research shows that employees draw on the benefits they perceive the brand to offer them and use these benefits to form self-connections with the brand, to identify with the brand and subsequently to deliver brand co-creation behaviours (see Figure 8.1). We thus suggest

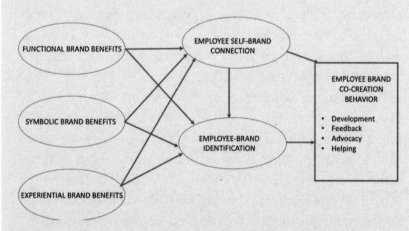

Figure 8.1 Pathway to employee brand co-creation behaviour

that employee self-brand connections and employee-brand identification serve as central constructs in the development of co-creation behaviours. What follows is greater insight into each of these particular constructs.

## Perceived brand benefit types

Brand benefits are characteristic of the value attached to the brand attributes: they represent what the brand can do for the user. Brands can deliver functional, symbolic and experiential enhancements and a single brand may offer a mixture of benefits. A functional concept is designed to solve utilitarian needs. A symbolic concept provides the user with association to a particular group, role or self-image. An experiential concept answers the needs for stimulation and variety.[365] In our grounded theory study, the expression of perceived benefits of the brand emerged from our data in all three categories.[366]

## Perceived functional benefits of the brand

The participants in our study highlighted aspects of the brand they perceived as possessing functionally beneficial characteristics. Functional benefits are primarily instrumental and utilitarian in nature, satisfying immediate and practical needs and often associated with problem-solution or avoidance. Employees saw their brand as offering them functional benefits in terms of career and life opportunities and enhancement. Participants spoke of how employment with the brand enhanced their career and improved prospects for the future. They saw an opportunity to achieve things, to obtain access where otherwise it might have been denied, and the opportunity to travel. In terms of life enhancement, informants spoke of the brand facilitating their development and growth and furthering their learning.

## Perceived symbolic benefits of the brand

A second category of benefits widely expressed by employees were symbolic benefits, which allow users to construct social identities, to assign meaning to themselves and to signal meaning to others. The symbolic nature of brands, specifically the range of distinctive images they reflect, means that they are particularly useful as a means of satisfying self-definitional needs such as social approval, self-expression and outer-directed self-esteem. Brands not only allow users to express their identities but also to reaffirm their principles or beliefs. Thus, the brand is a symbol whose meaning helps define the consumer's self-image, which leads consumers to choose brands with a desirable personality that reflects their view of their own sensibility. For several of our participants, the satisfaction of self-definitional needs was central to their account of the symbolic benefits of the brand. In this context, the brand represents a vehicle for employees to express themselves, enhance their self-esteem and self-worth, and to achieve a sense of pride and status. Several sub-categories of such self-definitional needs emerged, including prestige, self-expression and status symbolism. Prestige often related to the feeling of pride when telling others about employment with the brand, enabling employees to signal their self-image to others. Self-expression was shown to emerge as employees described certain congruences which they felt to exist between the brand and their own culture or origin. Others made reference to the fact that their brand is well-known, famous or even a status symbol, which confers status on employees.

## Perceived experiential benefits of the brand

For consumers, 'experiences' occur when they 'search for products, shop for them and receive service, and when they consume them'.[367] Experiential benefits are typically sensory, affective, social, behavioural and intellectual. Employees in our study widely described how, through their employment, particular feelings and emotions were evoked which could be broadly categorised as experiential, since they arose as a result of the employees' working experiences with the brand. Brand experiences may be short-lived or long-lived, and it is those that are long-lasting which are stored in the memory, thus affecting feelings of satisfaction and loyalty. Employees' experiences are by nature long-lived on a daily employment basis. They described sensory benefits such as excitement, fun and freedom, empowerment and feeling good and social/affective benefits which arise from the feeling of belonging to or being a part of the brand. For instance, some employees commented on how they encountered specific feelings of excitement, fun, feeling good and freedom through associations with their brands. Others spoke of a feeling of making a difference through the brand and also of how the brand is 'there for them', providing a sense of belonging.

## Employee self-brand connection (ESBC)

Our study also provided evidence for the construction of a connection between the brand and the employee's self-image. Possessions and brands can be used to satisfy psychological needs, such as actively creating one's self-image, reinforcing and expressing self-identity, and allowing one to differentiate oneself and assert one's individuality. When brand associations or meanings are used to construct one's self, or used in the communication of one's self to others, a self-brand connection is made.[368] When the brand is categorised as part of the self, a sense of oneness with the brand develops. These brand connections may reflect who one is or wants to become in terms of goals, personal concerns and life projects. A self-brand connection may thus be conceptualised as the extent to which individuals have incorporated brands into their self-image. When the self and the brand image overlap, a brand connection is formed.[369] Consistent with most employees' accounts was the notion that the brand was incorporated to some extent into the concept of self: an employee self-brand connection was formed. We defined this as 'the connection an employee forms with the brand when brand associations are used to construct the self'. The brand often appeared to satisfy an identified psychological need, from which a strong and meaningful self-brand connection stemmed. In some instances, the notion of a relationship or a connection with the brand was described directly. In other instances, employees made reference to the brand in such a way that implied that they viewed the brand and the self as being the same, or that the brand was incorporated into the self.

## Employee-brand identification (EBI)

On another level, many participants expressed their particular feelings and experiences in response to external opinions of the brand. For example, public criticisms of the brand are taken personally and employees then express how they would defend the brand. This suggests a deep relationship between the employee and the brand at a level that may be likened to brand identification. In other words, the employee defines him or herself with the same attributes that he or she believes define the brand. Indeed, the brand serves as 'a concrete actualisation' of the firm and represents a social category with which employees are able to identify, enabling the transfer of meaning between the brand and the self. Employee-brand identification appeared in our study to encapsulate a process whereby the brand identity became integrated with self-identity, and where brand identity was characterised by the set of brand associations from which the employee derived functional, emotional and self-expressive benefits.[370]

## Employee brand co-creation behaviours

Our participants referred to a number of different brand-related behaviours that they enacted. Such behaviours are categorised as co-creation behaviours and fall under the categories of development, feedback, advocacy and helping.[371] It is worth noting that these behaviours are largely extra-role behaviours, in that they may be described as 'employee actions that go beyond the prescribed roles for the good of the corporate brand and are discretionary'.[372] In terms of development of the brand, employees spoke of a number of different activities, including writing online content about the brand in their spare time and developing and thinking up new ideas for the brand. Advocacy behaviours included positive word-of-mouth and encouraging others to work for the brand. Some participants described how they talk about and 'talk up' the brand outside of work. Such personal advocacy of the brand outside of the work context is particularly discretionary, since this is not behaviour required of employees in the workplace.

Beneficial behaviours were described in terms of telling others new things about the brand and giving advice to other employees (such as suppliers) about the brand. Others explained how they provided useful ideas to improve the brand and relayed their ideas to improve the brand to others within the organisation.

Such feedback behaviours are connected to a desire for the brand to be successful.

Our multi-firm case demonstrates a specific means by which employees of the brand track a particular path towards co-creation behaviour. More specifically, employees were found to draw on the perceived benefit of the brand to form employee self-brand connections, engage in employee-brand identification and, as a result, display brand co-creation behaviours.

## Summary

This chapter has emphasised that brand equity is co-created, rather than solely the result of the actions of brand managers. Managers need to know what their brand stands for (the intended brand identity) and take responsibility for presenting the brand coherently to stakeholders. But what matters is how stakeholders receive and interpret messages and experiences (the enacted brand identity).[373] This may lead to a situation where the intended brand identity is different from the enacted brand identity. But one characteristic of strong and authentic brands is that intended and enacted brand identity are largely overlapping. The implication for brand managers is that while they should aim to provide intense brand experiences, they should also involve stakeholders in the co-creation of brand equity. This can be best done by offering opportunities to participate in brand building activities (like product development); by providing room for the joint development of brand-related stories; by co-operating with stakeholders in brand communities; by using the power of social media and influencer marketing; and by inspiring the brand's employees to live the brand.

## Reflections/questions

1) Explain the differences between intended and enacted brand identity. What is the difference between the latter and the concept of brand image?

2) Think of three examples of brands where the intended and the enacted brand identity do not match.

3) Name two brands that you perceive as rather authentic and two brands that you perceive as rather inauthentic. What are the reasons for your opinion?

4) Think of a brand story and tell it to someone else. Does the story help you to understand what the brand stands for?

5) Which influencers do you know? How can they be described? Would you say they have developed into human brands?

6) Think about an outstanding experience you encountered with an employee of a brand. What made this encounter outstanding? How did it contribute to the creation of brand equity?

## We recommend the following reading to expand your learning experience:

Delgado-Ballester, E. & Fernández-Sabiote, E. (2016). '"Once upon a brand": Storytelling practices by Spanish brands', *Spanish Journal of Marketing – ESIC, 20*(2), 115–131.

Iglesias, O. & Bonet, E. (2012). 'Persuasive brand management: How managers can influence brand meaning when they are losing control over it', *Journal of Organizational Change Management, 25*(2), 251–264.

Kornum, N., Gyrd-Jones, R., Al Zagir, N. & Brandis, K.A. (2017). 'Interplay between intended brand identity and identities in a Nike related brand community: Coexisting synergies and tensions in a nested system', *Journal of Business Research, 70*, 432–440.

Saleem, F.Z. & Iglesias, O. (2016). 'Mapping the domain of the fragmented field of internal branding', *Journal of Product & Brand Management, 25*(1), 43–57.

Schmidt, H.J. (2017). 'Living brand orientation: how a brand-oriented culture supports employees to live the brand', In: Ind, N. (ed.). *Branding Inside Out: Internal Branding in Theory and Practice*, London: Kogan Page, 13–32.

BRAND
COMPASS

N
W · E
S

BRANDS IN
DIFFERENT
CONTEXTS FACE
DIFFERENT
CHALLENGES

$

**ottobock.**

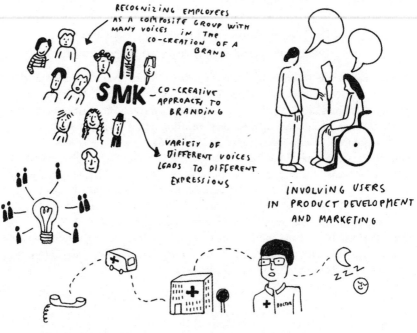

RECOGNIZING EMPLOYEES
AS A COMPOSITE GROUP WITH
MANY VOICES IN THE
CO-CREATION OF A
BRAND

**SMK** — CO-CREATIVE
APPROACH TO
BRANDING

VARIETY OF
DIFFERENT VOICES
LEADS TO DIFFERENT
EXPRESSIONS

INVOLVING USERS
IN PRODUCT DEVELOPMENT
AND MARKETING

DOCTOR

ZZZ

**MAYFAIR**
DIAGNOSTICS

OBSERVING PATIENT JOURNEYS TO
UNDERSTAND FUNCTIONAL AND EMOTIONAL
EXPERIENCE

# CHAPTER NINE

# Co-creation in different contexts

In this chapter …

Those readers who are still with us in this penultimate chapter will probably share our view that meaningful brands are co-created in an ongoing process: The Co-Creative Brand Management System. But we all know that one size rarely fits all. This is also true in the context of brands. Even if the co-creative perspective is becoming more and more widely used and discussed throughout the brand management discipline, not all brands are created equal and the context in which brands operate creates different requirements. Therefore, the role of brands can differ across industries and the way brands from different sectors use elements of co-creation within their approaches to brand management can differ, too. However, a book like ours is not the right medium to discuss those differences in detail. But it would also be wrong to simply skip over them. Therefore, in this chapter, we will first briefly discuss the different nature of brands in consumer, business-to-business (B2B), service and not-for-profit markets. Then we will point at some of the major disparities between those sectors by offering examples of the co-creation activities of relevant market players. In this more practical part of the chapter, we introduce our readers to business-to-business brands, service brands, not-for-profit brands and city brands, and provide relevant cases that are illustrative of their methods. Some of the cases are written by our guest co-creators, who have researched or worked with organisations in these sectors, while others are built on interviews we have conducted with practitioners. Overall, this chapter offers valuable insights into the challenges and opportunities of brand co-creation in different sectors.

## Learning Objectives

After reading this chapter you should

- understand that brands working in distinct social and business contexts face quite different challenges;
- know some examples of brands outside the fast-moving consumer goods sector that have used co-creative methods to successfully position their brands;
- be inspired to take a deeper look into the various contexts that are not always in the forefront of people's minds when talking about brands.

## Institutional perspectives on brands

The traditional focus of brand management has been on consumer goods – the sort of products, everything from Coca-Cola to Dove soap to Uncle Ben's rice, that one might buy in a supermarket. Much of the literature reflects this bias and therefore concentrates on the strategies and techniques required to capture shelf space and influence consumers to buy products. However, look at the economic structure of economies and it is services that dominate. In 1997, services' contribution to Worldwide Gross Domestic Product was 63 per cent, and in 2015, it was 68.9 per cent. In high-income countries, the 2015 figure was 74.0 per cent. Services are also where most people work. In the UK, 95.7 per cent of people work in services and the figures are 87.4 per cent in France and 86.3 per cent in the USA.[374] Consequently, in this book, we have given emphasis to businesses where the service element is important, which in turn brings the people and the nature of relationships to the fore. The principles of good brand management still apply in non-consumer goods areas, but there are also important points of difference connected to the diversity of audiences, the way relationships develop, the motivations of employees and the attitudes of stakeholders. Just imagine the task of building a brand in a business-to-business sector in the aviation industry for Airbus or Boeing, versus doing so for an airline such as Delta or Virgin, or for an arts brand such as MOMA or Tate Modern.[375] Even if each area requires an insight into the psychology of buyer behaviour, each area also requires a radically different approach in terms of the way the brand engages and communicates with its stakeholders.

In the following sections, we zero-in on the basic principles of brand management practice and how they apply in different areas such as consumer brands, B2B brands, service brands and not-for-profit brands. There are plenty of excellent books that cover these (and other) areas in detail, but our purpose here is to demonstrate the implications of a co-creative approach to building brands.[376] Building on existing theory and using cases to illustrate the points, here we will concentrate on three questions:

- what is the key role a brand plays when it comes to co-creation within consumer, business-to-business, service and not-for-profit markets;
- how important is it to involve your employees in co-creating the brand;
- how relevant is co-creation within different areas?

We will start our analysis by a look at consumer markets.

## Consumer brands

Researchers and writers have paid considerable attention to consumer brands and various models have been developed to explain consumer behaviour – including one by David Aaker. His model argues that brands deliver three types of benefits: functional, emotional and self-expressive. Building on Aaker's model, in an article on co-creation, we argued that co-creation delivered an additional benefit of participation.[377] The essence of the argument is that we expect brands to deliver at a functional level in terms of performance, but we also expect them to create some sort of emotional connection when we buy and use them. We don't, for example, buy a Hermès handbag for €6,500 just for its functionality. We buy it for its look and feel, for its heritage, its hand-madeness, and for the emotional cues it provides. And we probably also buy it for what it says to others about us – its self-expressive quality. The reason we added participative benefits to the list is that when consumers become involved in helping to co-create the brand, they also begin to realise some of the intrinsic benefits we referred to in Chapter 3. Brands, though, do not all deliver these benefits in the same way, because they can choose to orient themselves around specific benefits and underplay others. Marketing Professor Jan-Benedict Steenkamp notes that what distinguishes brands from each other is whether they have a more functional or emotional value for the consumer and their relative market price.[378] From the functional and emotional dimensions, Steenkamp builds a system from which five types of brands can be derived, which are described below according to their function for the consumer, the role of employees in creating brand meaning and the importance of co-creation:

- **value brands** are usually brands with a strong functional use, whose price is far below the market average. Typical examples would be the airline Ryanair or the retail discounter Lidl. Both these brands have low-priced offers with functional service. If an emotional connection exists, it is the emotion of the successful bargain hunter. The brand function, which seems to be particularly relevant here, is to help guide consumer choice. The brand provides orientation and helps provide us with an overview, which is valuable in confusing markets where competition is high and differences in quality are low between different providers. Employees do not play an important role in delivering the brand promise, which is primarily concerned with function. Co-creation, if used at all, is tactical. It is seen as a marketing tool to bring people's attention to a new product, a new positioning or a sales initiative;

- **mass brands** are brands with a functional benefit complemented by emotional aspects. Their market price is set at the level of the market average or slightly above. Typical examples are Volkswagen or Samsung. The most important function of mass brands is to reduce customers' perceived risk of buying. Their customers know and appreciate their content and trust them. They are confident in the brand offer, and even if there is a price-premium to pay, customers believe there is a good price-quality relationship. For mass brands, employees can be important in creating a positive brand experience, but are usually not key to the brand's positioning. Service is a brand support and not a differentiator. Co-creation is particularly important for mass brands in order to generate innovations at a reasonable cost and to maintain customer relationships;

- **premium brands** are high-quality brands that offer a highly emotional range of benefits to consumers. They are significantly more expensive than other brands in their industry. Typical premium brands are BMW and Apple. Risk reduction is an important brand function for premium brands, but they also fulfil strong social and experiential needs and the behaviour of employees must be strongly aligned with the brand's positioning in order to bring the more emotional side of the brand to life. Co-creation is also very important for premium brands, as it ties the customer very closely to the brand, so that the brand becomes more tangible from the customer's point of view. Here, co-creation is used to help build an innovative edge together with stakeholders;

- **prestige brands** are brands that consumers buy for their emotional value, which in this model includes the value of self-expression. The emotional value they provide results above all from the extremely high price, which makes these brands desirable, and the status they confer on the buyer. An example of this category comes in the form of fashion brands such as Alexander McQueen, or Gucci or Vertú (a supplier of luxury mobile phones). In delivering a prestige experience, these brands need employees with a strong passion for what they do. Co-creation is rarely used in these cases because luxury normally excludes customer participation. It is the skill and creativity of the designer, and sometimes the craft of the product, that sets a prestige brand apart. Customer involvement tends to dilute this;

- **fun brands** are brands that go beyond the typical relationship between price and type of use expressed in the first four brand types, where the higher the price, the more emotions play a role. Fun brands are emotional, although they are more likely to be priced like value brands. Typical representatives of this category are the airline Virgin and the car brand Smart. As brands, they provide orientation and at the same time meet social and experimental needs. Internal Branding can be important, but is usually not seen as the key to success, whereas co-creative activities can be a central success factor for these brands in order to stand out from comparable offers in their markets.

## B2B brands

Stakeholders in B2B markets can be diverse, ranging from suppliers of materials and services, intermediaries (such as wholesalers), distributors in the supply chain and professional users and buyers who typically use the acquired products within their own production processes (what is called derived demand). The network of stakeholders employed in the car or food industry, for example, is both extensive and complex. And typically co-creative, in that B2B brands are rooted in relationships and long-term interactions.[379] The B2B sector is inevitably very heterogeneous and covers such diverse areas as office supplies, standard and individualised software, vehicles, ingredients, machinery, building materials and spare parts. With such diversity, the brand building process is also variable, but there are some common traits. The buying process has been described as:

- highly formalised;
- more rational (although often not as rational as people think);
- and more collective (see the concept of so-called 'buying centres').[380]

Much brand research has been devoted to consumer goods markets and in relative terms, brand management within B2B markets has been neglected by research. This has resulted in a lack of systematic theory development.[381] Also, B2B brand managers have languished in the shade, too often relegated to being communication managers rather than brand builders. As a result, the value of developing a strong B2B brand has not always been recognised.[382] Nevertheless, the research and case studies from practice that do exist show that brands, and specifically corporate brands, can be highly significant in the B2B sector and have contributed to the success of brands in industries such as mechanical engineering (General Electric), IT (Cisco) and chemistry (BASF).[383] In such industries, brands serve as signs of quality in sometimes opaque markets and make the life of the purchaser easier by aiding decision-making and reducing perceived risk. A study by the consultants McKinsey shows that in the US, on average, the brand makes up 18 per cent of the purchasing decision of industrial buyers. Respondents attribute the prime reason for brand influence on their decisions as concerned with risk reduction. A legendary adage about IBM from the 1970s played on that concern when it stated: 'Nobody ever got fired for buying IBM.'[384] The McKinsey survey also points out that B2B brands are perceived as particularly relevant in tangible goods sectors, such as those involving machines and components, and somewhat less so in intangible sectors.[385]

Within the brand management discipline of B2B brands, it has often been argued that it is important that the whole organisation has understood that the brand and employees can support the brand and brand management through what they say and do.[386] This is due to the fact that B2B brands are almost always corporate brands that have many touch points between employees and customers. If employee behaviour is not driven by identification with and internalisation of the brand values, a customer's brand experience could be negatively influenced. The concept of brand orientation and the tools of internal branding therefore have the potential to play a major role within B2B brand management.[387]

In managing B2B brands, co-creation offers opportunities to develop insights into, and to strengthen, a brand's reputation.[388] Co-creation can be used to identify and implement customer-centric innovations, improve customer loyalty and build a strong bond with employees. Co-creation is often a natural way of working for B2B brands, because there are existing co-operative relationships between such brands and their network partners. In the Ottobock case below, you can see how a co-creation perspective can transform a once product-focussed B2B brand into an open company that successfully offers and implements solutions, instead of products. The interview with a Siemens manager, which follows the Ottobock case, explains the rationale behind co-creation in B2B markets in more detail.

## Ottobock – Transformation from a high-tech product to a co-created technology brand

*Authors: Carsten Baumgarth, Christin Franzel & Samuel Kristal*

### Ottobock – History and company overview

In 1919, the orthopaedic mechanic Otto Bock founded a company in Berlin designed to supply people disabled during the First World War with prostheses and orthopaedic aids. However, traditional methods of craftsmanship could not keep up with demand, so Bock started mass-producing prosthetic components and supplying them direct to orthopaedic mechanics. This marked the beginning of the orthopaedic industry. The company grew steadily and was employing 600 people by the Second World War. After the war, though, the family's entire private assets and the factory in Königsee were expropriated without compensation. The company began again in Duderstadt in Lower Saxony and Bock's son-in-law, Dr-Ing. Max Näder E.h., became managing director of the newly founded Otto Bock Orthopädische Industrie KG.

In 1958, the first foreign Ottobock company was founded in Minneapolis (in the US) and in 1969, the company's modular leg prosthesis set a worldwide standard (its patent making a valuable contribution to the company's market position). Another milestone during the 1960s was the development of the myoelectric arm prosthesis, which is controlled by muscle signals. With the use of such complex technologies, Ottobock changed from a manufacturer of individual components to a supplier of complete prosthesis systems. In 1990, Professor Hans Georg Näder took over the management of the family business. In 1992, the Näder family bought back the expropriated headquarters in Königsee and set up wheelchair production there. Initially, 200 wheelchairs were manufactured per year. By 2019, the production capacity was over 45,000 units. In 1997, Ottobock introduced the C-Leg, the world's first completely micro-processor-controlled leg prosthesis system, which opened up new dimensions in walking. Innovation remains the most important source of company growth: for example, the Genium leg prosthesis system, the Michelangelo Hand and the mechatronic C-Brace orthosis system. In 2016, Näder announced the sale of shares and the formation of a new company, Ottobock SE & Co. KGaA. This was the first time in 98 years that there was a non-family shareholder as a partner.

Today, the family-run company has turned into a global player with more than 8,000 employees, operations in more than 50 countries and sales of over €1 billion. In addition to medical technology which is offered by the company Ottobock SE & Co. KGaA (the entity discussed in this article), the Ottobock Group also includes other companies, such as Technogel (producing polyurethane products especially for medical technology), Sycor (an IT service provider) and Baltic Yachts (specialising in carbon-fibre based yachts).

### Phases of the brand transformation
The transformation of the Ottobock brand can be divided into four overlapping phases.

### Marketing for high-techproducts (1988–2008)
The first phase – 1988 to 2008 – was characterised by a classic B2B approach for technology brands. A so-called Info Department was responsible for advertisements and brochures and Product Management managed sales and marketing activities. However, there wasn't an integrated brand department. Brand-related activities were more or less the result of luck and the communication approach was characterised by: 1) a concentration on only professional target groups (orthopaedic technicians, physicians and health insurance companies); 2) a lack of integrated communications; and 3) a focus on technology as well as product features. The use of 'dark blue' – a typical choice for B2B companies – symbolised the brand. The result of this brand approach is visualised in Figure 9.1.

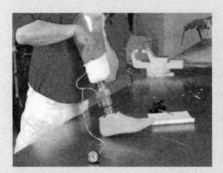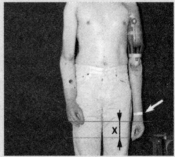

Figure 9.1 Examples of early advertisements and brochures

However, in this phase the first tentative moves to transform the brand emerged. In 1992, Hans Georg Näder met the Canadian engineer Kelly James, who presented a prototype of the C-Leg at the World Congress of the International Society for Prosthetics & Orthotics (ISPO) in Chicago. During the congress, Näder recognised the enormous potential of this groundbreaking development and concluded an exclusive agreement. Five years later, Ottobock engineers brought the innovative product to market. The so-called C-Leg is still a success story today.

From 1988 onwards, Ottobock started supporting the Winter and Summer Paralympic Games. In 2004, the Paralympics became an explicit part of PR and CSR work and soon an official partnership agreement was signed with the International Paralympic Committee. At the 2016 Paralympic Games in Rio, the technical team comprised around 100 technicians and service personnel from 29 countries, who carried out around 2,400 repairs for over 1,000 athletes in around 14,500 hours (see Figure 9.2).

Figure 9.2 Ottobock technicians at the Paralympics

Before 2003, Ottobock had no formal marketing department, but in that year, the first corporate communication department was established and a first Corporate Identity guideline was released. One of the first activities of this new department was the creation of advertising targeted at B2C and B2B customers. These advertisements showed for the first time users of products, instead of focussing solely on products and technical attributes. The new communication style showed the people behind the product (see Figure 9.3).

Figure 9.3  Photo examples of the first user campaign (2003)

In 2005 Ottobock started to use external brand ambassadors in communications. For example, Heinrich Popow, a German sports star who won two gold, one silver and five bronze medals at the Paralympics in long jump and sprint, has been a brand ambassador since 2007 (see Figure 9.4). At the beginning, Ottobock supported Popow through technology and funding. But over time the relationship has deepened and Popow has become the most important face of the brand and a co-developer of new products and an initiator of several CSR-related activities (see phase 2).

Figure 9.4  Heinrich Popow as a brand ambassador for Ottobock

As a sign of its growing openness, in 2007 Ottobock held an open house, which around 25,000 visitors attended.

## Professionalisation of brand management and user-focus (2009–12)

Based on the vision and initiative of Professor Näder, in 2009 Ottobock opened a public Science Center in Berlin, located between Potsdamer Platz and the Reichstag (see Figure 9.5). The idea was to connect visitors and the general public with the topics of prosthetics, orthoses and mobility. The exhibition covers

Figure 9.5  Ottobock Science Center Berlin

three floors and focusses on interactive elements to acquaint visitors with the complexity of the human body, the history of the company and the functionality of its products. The idea of the Science Center is twofold: to provide information and fascination.

A 2010/2011 customer survey showed that the brand was well-known for its high-quality products, but was also seen as arrogant and product-focussed. This led the company to a) change the existing brand organisation and b) to intensify and professionalise brand management activities. As a consequence, the well-known creative agency Edenspiekermann was asked to create a new corporate design for the brand. The aim was to align the brand for the future and to step away from being positioned as an engineering brand (dark blue) focussed solely on technical product features in its positioning. The mission was to create a brand in a brand-free environment and to shift the focus from product to user, from pure B2B to B2B and B2C. In 2011, the brand logo was changed (see Figure 9.6). A new brand platform was created that bears the most important corporate design guidelines, internal brand ambassadors were assigned and a new clear and easy-to-understand brand language was established. Also, a management team came up with 15 brand values that were codified in a brand book. These values were verified by customer research and internal workshops involving all employees from all over the world. Responsibility for Global Brand Management, which was assigned to the newly defined CMO position, held by Christin Franzel, focusses on marketing and brand communications and has a strong voice on the management board.

Figure 9.6 Old and new brand logo of Ottobock

Inspired by a group of Swiss runners (who approached Heinrich Popow to learn how to jog properly with a prosthesis), Popow – in co-operation with Ottobock – founded Running Clinics. In the Running Clinics participants learn how to run, sprint and do sports while using a prosthesis. The clinics are conducted all around the world by Popow and the number of available places is strictly limited to 15 participants to ensure the provision of individual, intensive support. Besides the idea of supporting amputees in their wish to live an active life, the Running Clinics also help the brand to promote its corporate social responsibility. Also, with the help of Running Clinics, Ottobock reaches target groups that would otherwise not be approachable. Feedback from the clinics is used to further develop and optimise products and services. The Running Clinics and other activities should overcome the 'market leader trap'. Ottobock was the preferred brand in the market, but there was a lack of emotional connection and as stated earlier, it was seen as a bit arrogant.

Popow and other brand ambassadors are also important partners in product development. An example is the knee joint 3S80 for sports that was co-created with Popow and that has become world market leader in this category of product (see Figure 9.7).

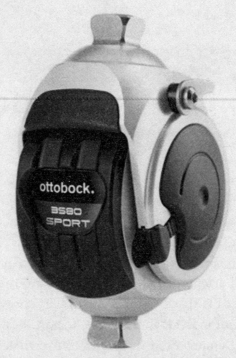

Figure 9.7  Co-created knee joint 3S80 (PR11)

Heinrich Popow describes his role as follows: 'Since 2007, I have repeatedly integrated my experience from sports into the company…Ottobock equipped me with a technician and the know-how and a product was developed that is meanwhile used by the whole world.'

The existing brand platform was extended in 2012 and a new communications approach developed, based on the emotional stories of users. Posters follow a black and white design (see Figure 9.8).

Figure 9.8 Current user and sports campaign

As well as external communication, internal communication has also changed. In 2012/13, internal bottom-up workshops with various groups of employees were conducted to narrow down the 15 brand values to the main core values that make up the brand: human, reliable, inventive.

An additional aspect of the re-branding process was the introduction of design-thinking. Product users were invited to participate in workshops together with various groups of employees, such as product managers, engineers, designers, marketing managers and senior managers. After some initial resistance, Ottobock product managers have started to accept the importance of a) design-thinking and b) external sources, especially in the form of users, when it comes to developing and designing new products. An example here is an actual project for developing a new design for the mechatronic knee joint C-Leg, Genium and Genium X3, where designers and users have been integrated from the very beginning.

In the process of opening up the brand, the Ottobock presentation at fairs has been changed (see Figure 9.9). Employees have been trained to focus on the brand's core values and to ensure that their behaviour is in line with those values when communicating with visitors and other external groups. Instead of brochures and other paper-based info-material, testimonials in the form of users have been used.

Figure 9.9 Ottobock 'brandworld' at a fair in Germany (Source: conhIT Berlin, 2017)

## Living the brand (2013–15)

In this phase a so-called brand compass was introduced (2013), to remind all employees of the three core values and to enable them to check that their behaviour aligns with those values. The brand compass also helps to further embed the brand and its values into the culture and language of employees and to make clear that the brand is much more than just a question of design. Every employee can check if their behaviour is in line with the values. Figure 9.10 shows the general brand compass.

**Differentiating brand values**
The differentiating values make us unique when compared to the competition. Human, inventive, reliable – this triad shapes Ottobock and the direction for all of our communications.

**Brand essence**
The essence of our brand is the promise that matters the most for the use of our products and for our target groups: Independence and Quality for life .

**Cultural values**
Our cultural values define the qualities of our company culture. They describe the way we behave and determine our positive relations with customers and colleagues.

**Substantial values**
Substantial values also concern our competitors and are market standard – under no circumstances are they to be damaged.

Figure 9.10  Brand compass

The brand compass is depicted in a second brand book, *Living the Brand*, which emphasises the three main brand values and the increasing importance of a brand-oriented organisation. Additionally, an internal campaign called 'I am Ottobock because ...' helps employees to express why they are part of the brand and why they are a brand ambassador. The topic of 'brand' has become more important and more embedded in the minds of employees (see Figure 9.11).

Since 2014, the use of social media channels for purposes of communication and listening has intensified. Ottobock does not lead the dialogue, but rather interacts with, and supports, followers. The insight and feedback are used to develop ideas for new products and optimise existing ones. The focus of social media marketing is Facebook, Instagram and YouTube. An example of the use of YouTube is a recent series of videos where

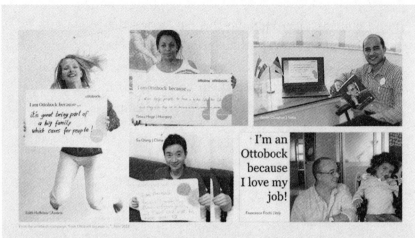

Figure 9.11  Internal campaign 'I am Ottobock because ...'

Heinrich Popow interviews users of Ottobock products (see Figure 9.12). A further example of the increased activity in social media is the campaign 'Passion for Paralympics', which achieved nearly 20,000 likes on Facebook (September 2018). Furthermore, Ottobock supports the establishment of brand communities on social media, such as the Running Clinics.

Figure 9.12  Heinrich Popow interviewing a user (Christian Neureuther – former alpine ski racer) at the OTWorld 2018

## Co-created brand (2016–today)

Since 2016, co-creation in innovation, particularly open innovation processes, has expanded. This has involved establishing an open innovation space in Berlin called FabLab, which opens up the product development and innovation process to external groups beyond brand ambassadors or (lead) users. With the help of new technologies, such as 3D-printing, Ottobock has started to use rapid prototyping. Berlin is good for attracting external talents and links to the vibrant start-up scene. The FabLab integrates the co-creation of new medical technical products, such as the C-Leg and the Genium prosthesis, and digital apps. To build on the success of FabLab in 2017, Ottobock opened a CreativeLab in its headquarters in Duderstadt. This collaboration has since been expanded to external partners. For example, Ottobock is currently involved in a project together with Allianz, where the question is: can you actually think of sports equipment in a completely different way? Now, Allianz is an insurance company that has no idea about medical technology. But they do have different knowledge and skills, exemplified by a discussion with Toyota on the subject of future mobility.

## Brand co-creation is nothing without classical brand management

The Ottobock case shows that brand co-creation is not a single event or instrument, but a new way of thinking and implementing brand management. Brand co-creation is also not characterised by a single measure, but rather by multiple initiatives at the management level, in the corporate culture, in employee behaviour and in internal as well as external communications. The case also illustrates that brand co-creation is neither static nor stable but develops continuously over time with different levels of intensity and reach.

Finally, the case emphasises that brand co-creation is not an alternative to classic approaches to brand management, but rather builds on them. To achieve generalisations from one case study is impossible. However, our depicted case raises the thesis that successful brand co-creation requires some preconditions: superior products and services, a professional brand management and an internal anchoring of the brand within the company.

## Co-creation at Siemens Gas & Power

*INTERVIEW WITH OLIVER HIRSCHFELDER*

**Mr Hirschfelder, you work in the Innovation & Business Development department at Siemens Gas & Power (GP). What is the task of innovation management at Siemens GP and what significance does it have for the company?**

Innovation management is of outstanding importance for every technology company: it ensures long-term competitiveness by developing new products and solutions. This is also true for Siemens. As a leading supplier of systems for power generation and transmission, innovation is at the core of our business. In addition to technical innovations, the department that I work for also promotes innovative business models that are implemented in established and new business areas.

**Siemens GP is a company with a very broad scope of products and services. To what extent does a strong brand help?**

In the business-to-business sector, generally, a brand may be regarded as an important intangible asset. Stakeholders like customers, suppliers, regulators, users and investors have a certain and hopefully strong and positive association with a brand that can be a door-opener for future business. And a strong brand can help to bring new products to the market faster, because people believe in their superiority and trust the vendor.

The Siemens brand is often associated with technological leadership and innovativeness. We are seen to be playing a pioneering role in advancing new topics and creating social benefits. The positive perception of our brand helps us to market our core competencies across a wide-ranging competence portfolio. We are top-of-mind and a preferred partner for many organisations that are searching for innovative technical solutions. The reputation of our brand is therefore an asset that contributes to value creation. Our brand is of the highest importance for us and is an integral part of our business strategy. This is why our positioning is embodied in our slogan 'Ingenuity for Life'. This is more than an advertising claim, it serves as our guiding principle.

**In this book we have defined 'co-creation' in the context of brand management as an 'active, dynamic and social process based on interactions between the brand and its stakeholder(s)'. Now I understand that the permanent development of new ideas is extremely important for Siemens in order not to lose the reputation of technology leadership. But why do you need external input for this? Can't Siemens engineers create good products themselves?**

Social dynamics and technological advancements lead to the fact that conventional market paradigms quickly lose their validity. For example, in the energy sector, we see the mega-trend of decarbonisation, which has a considerable impact on our markets. While power plant performance and security of supply used to be at the forefront of all energy-related discussions, today, green energy, the decentralisation of supply, flexibility and stable transmission and distribution networks are getting more and more important. These complex contexts require a holistic view of the energy market involving all stakeholders. For example, the process of collaboratively and interactively creating solutions together with customers and regulators enables rapid adaptation to market needs. The process of co-creation is therefore a promising way to drive innovation to market.

**What kind of resistance do you encounter if, in such a large and technologically oriented company as Siemens, external groups – for example, customers – are participating in innovation processes? Is there something like a 'not invented here'-syndrome?**

The described disruptions in our markets must be accompanied by changes in corporate culture and structures: the principle 'we can do it alone' is largely replaced by a collaborative process. But of course, it takes a while until everybody within a global company like Siemens has internalised this. It requires not only new processes, but also a change in the mindset of people. Siemens GP has roughly 65,000 employees. Change is taking place, but of course this needs time.

**How do you see the role of co-creation in the business-to-business sector?**

Fast-changing market conditions, new technologies like artificial intelligence or robotics and mega-trends such as globalisation, sustainability and the growth of the earth's population require more complex solutions. Due to such disruptive change, you have to look at the entire value chain, together with all stakeholders. Nobody has the know-how required for this alone. Co-creation in the business-to-business sector is therefore an important component for solving complex problems. At the forefront of all this is the creation of value for the customer. Thus, close customer involvement in the technical-economic solution concept is a key success factor.

**And at Siemens? What experiences do you have with co-creation? And what results do you expect?**

For us, when markets were relatively stable, co-creation was not an area of real interest. This has now completely changed! We are now intensively working on several pilot projects across different business units, especially in the field of business development. In these pilot projects, we collaborate with a wide range of business partners, including customers, regulators and providers, but non-disclosure agreements prohibit me to tell you more about it.

Most of the projects are just starting. Thus, it is difficult to make an estimate of the success rate. But we expect that co-creation will help us to bring products to the markets faster, to develop solutions that are strongly aligned with customer expectations, and to strengthen our brand reputation.

**Finally, your assessment: how will co-creation develop at Siemens GP?**
My opinion is that co-creation will become an increasingly important building block of our innovation strategy. The topic will become more important, especially for business development, in order to enable a closer connection between the innovation department and sales in a fast, customer-oriented and focussed way. This is of value for both Siemens and the customer.

## Service brands

In the service industry, we find consumptive and investive services. Consumptive services are those that are directed to the private sector (an airline flying tourists to their holiday destinations, or a hairdresser), while investive services are directed at other companies (business consulting, cleaning of buildings, leasing of company vehicles, industry services) and are therefore related to B2B brands. Also, the paradigm shift in marketing brought about by the perspective of Service-Dominant Logic (which was mentioned in Chapter 2) places service at the centre of the considerations of all exchange processes. In this view, everything is a service because it is what a product or service does that creates value, not the product or service as such. One consequence of this new way of thinking is that the idea of service and how it links to brands has received more and more attention from both researchers and practitioners.[389] Key elements of service brands include:

- integration of the external audience (i.e. the client) into the brand process – interactions between individuals leads to variability in performance;

- dependence on the attitude and behaviour of employees, which can enrich the service experience, but is also variable;
- the immateriality of the product, which is not transportable or storable.

The lack of constancy in the delivery of the brand creates the potential for increased uncertainty. We may enjoy the experience of staying at a hotel or flying with an airline, but we cannot be certain that it will be the same next time because the nature of the interactions will vary. The immateriality of a service experience also means that the service cannot be tested before it is consumed. Therefore, choices are made on past experience and perceptions as to the reliability and performance of the brand. This again puts emphasis on the role of the brand as a risk reducer.

In the service context, concrete measures of co-creation are often used to improve the service design – that means the way the client experiences the service process during use. The case of Mayfair Diagnostics discussed below illustrates the power of using co-creation (in this case with medical imaging patients) for this objective. It is also important to note that services are provided and consumed by people and the perceived attitude and behaviour of an employee is a powerful contributor to the overall service experience. This shows that internal branding is of undisputed importance in service branding.

## Using co-creation to define a new experience: The case of Mayfair Diagnostics

If you've ever needed an X-ray to check for a broken bone, or magnetic resonance imaging (MRI) for a detailed look inside the body, you'll know the sense of dread and anxiety that accompanies a visit to a clinic, the investigative process and the waiting for the results. The experience can be even more unsettling if you are in pain. It's an emotional and vulnerable time, which is further complicated by an environment and systems that have historically been designed around operational efficiency and functionality rather than the needs of the patient – think cold interiors, service based on necessity, handwritten signs and long waits on hard chairs. This stereotypical experience is what led to the use of co-creation by Mayfair Diagnostics, a Canadian medical imaging company based in Calgary. Mayfair Diagnostics has more than 400 employees across numerous community-based medical imaging clinics. They had a long history and good reputation as a provider of screening and diagnostic imaging services, but wanted to find a way to continue to deliver results while also providing a more comfortable experience for patients.

In 2016, the medical imaging environment was changing with new companies emerging in the same space and a growing need for more patient-centric services. Mayfair wanted to build their brand and its relevance among referring physicians to generate more patient referrals, as well as to anticipate potential regulatory environment changes that would mean greater scrutiny of the value provided by private medical clinics.

Mayfair faced an important question – how to build its profile while enhancing the experience for patients and delivering value. Should the new strategy be evolutionary or radical? At an initial scoping workshop, the divergence between the incrementalists and the revolutionaries became evident. Rather than argue the case based on received wisdom, they elected to ask the consultancy CSpace to diagnose the current situation and explore the options that could then be applied to existing clinics and a new one that was planned.

The first stage in the process was to build insight into the way the existing clinics functioned through ethnographic research. This involved observation of the patient's journey and an assessment of their functional and emotional experience. To do this, the consultants observed behaviour and discussions between employees and patients and then interviewed them to better understand their perceptions and feelings. David Franke, who worked on the project, says, 'We started by sitting in the waiting area, just watching as patients walked into the clinic . . . They're like in pain and they're a little bit vulnerable because they're going to a medical clinic, and the first thing they see is all this signage yelling at them, and then the people on the other side of the reception desk, who are busy, furiously typing away, doing data entry.' When the consultants asked patients about the arrival experience, they described feeling confused, in the way and awkward interrupting the receptionists. For their part, the receptionists said they saw people come in and they felt guilty about ignoring them, but they had so much pressure to get data entered into the system that they couldn't always stop what they were doing.

Across the patient journey, many challenges were identified, such as difficulty finding parking, an unfriendly welcome, feeling lost in the clinic, undressing in small closets with a shower-type curtain for privacy, limited contact with the radiologists and lacking a sense of clarity over the process. Some of the pain-points and the emotions they generated were obvious through observation, but others became evident as patients and staff talked about the experience of dealing with one another.

With insight into the key issues and a commitment to put the patient at the centre of everything, Mayfair now needed to decide what this meant in practice. They chose to co-create the future of medical imaging. To do this, they hosted a large workshop comprised of about 35 patients and various Mayfair employees, including senior managers from Mayfair administration, receptionists, technologists and radiologists. Together, this group explored the key issues that affected the organisation and discussed potential opportunities for improvement. Franke says the session had a very different atmosphere from traditional consumer sessions because they had to adjust some of the exercises to accommodate some physical challenges: 'We had people who had, you know, torn ligaments, like people who were in serious pain, and we had lots of people breaking down crying about their overall situation. There was a sense of vulnerability.'

The involvement of the patients in the process helped to ensure that there was a human focus to the strategy. The workshop generated six patient-inspired moments in the customer journey that began before the visit to the clinic and ended after the exam was completed. This led to more transparency in the process and such initiatives as an appointment confirmation and reminder process, parking attendants, a more welcoming and redesigned reception experience and a more comfortable patient lounge featuring refreshments.

One of the virtues of the workshop was that it created advocates for change both at a senior management level and in the clinics. By spending time listening to, and working together with, patients, Mayfair now had real insights into the issues from the patients' point of view. These insights were reiterated in an edited video featuring highlights of the co-creation process and a booklet outlining Mayfair's new patient-focussed vision, which were shared across the organisation. This vision was also showcased in the development of a new clinic with a new approach to design and language, while the existing clinics were re-worked within the constraints of the existing spaces.

Mayfair Diagnostics is an apt illustration of the co-creation brand management system at work. It illustrates how an organisation can generate brand insights, design and adjust its brand strategy and co-create brand meaning. Most importantly, from Mayfair's point of view, a co-creative process involving employees and patients worked. It improved the functional performance of the clinics and customer satisfaction scores and enhanced the brand in the eyes of patients and physicians.

## Not-for-profit brands

Brand building is also becoming more important for not-for-profit companies (even if they don't always like the commercially tainted word 'brand'), because competition has similarly increased among charities, NGOs and in the public sector. Here, brands like the Red Cross, Médicins sans Frontières, World Vision, The Guggenheim Museums and Foundation, The City of Barcelona and Greenpeace International stand out from the crowd and work as a compass for clients and supporters in often confusing and opaque markets. In the case of a social organisation, a strong brand is especially helpful in reducing the uncertainty for donors about the use of their money. A strong brand reassures contributors that money is being used in the right way. Sometimes, not-for-profit brands also provide participative benefits to their supporters. For example, the much-discussed 'ALS Ice Bucket Challenge', which raised money to fight the disease Amyotrophic Lateral Sclerosis, was very popular on social networks in the summer of 2014. On Facebook, people could nominate their friends to participate in the challenge. If you were nominated, you could donate €10 to the ALS society or pour a bucket of ice water over your head – the latter of course documented in a video which one had to upload on to the social network. Most participants donated and uploaded videos, which showed them experiencing a very cold shower of ice water. The ALS Ice Bucket Challenge became a huge success, with countless people nominated and significant sums raised. It was cool to get nominated – and the participants were probably just as eager about publicly presenting how coolly they could deal with the challenge as they were to donate the €10. Many people even got nominated various times and were proud of it.

In general, in the context of not-for-profit brands, the behaviour of the organisation's representatives is highly relevant for their audiences. People don't trust a manager of a not-for-profit brand if he or she doesn't 'walk the talk'. Internal branding is therefore a major building block within the brand strategy of such organisations. And co-creation is widely used because participation offers the potential to connect audiences emotionally to the brand. How important this is can be seen in the cases of the Danish National Gallery and the city of Hulst, which are provided below – and which also show some of the complexity involved in building and managing brands.

## The case of SMK – Co-creation in the context of The Danish National Gallery

*Authors: Line Schmeltz & Anna Karina Kjeldsen*

In 2011 the Danish National Gallery, today called SMK (an acronym for 'Statens Museum for Kunst/National Gallery of Denmark'), decided to initiate a branding process under the working title 'From institution to brand'.[390] The Gallery felt a need to change its brand image among visitors – and particularly non-visitors – because they had an image of being fusty and old-fashioned, inapproachable and very formal – a place for the select few. As a public organisation and with an obligation to be a place for everybody, they needed to do something. Heavily inspired by the latest developments within corporate branding, the Gallery decided to work with a co-constructive approach to branding as a way to open up the brand to all its different stakeholders. The head of communications explained that they wanted 'a more holistic approach to communication that places users (or recipients) at the center of things.'[391]

The mission succeeded. SMK experienced great success with their first step in the co-creation process – a campaign called 'What is SMK to you?', where they invited people to co-create the brand. The campaign targeted both existing and potential visitors and was highly successful in engaging external audiences. A communications consultant involved in the process explained:

> In order to overcome the preconceived notions of what the museum
> is – especially among the younger target groups – we needed to
> engage them. We created an opportunity for involvement by

inviting them to co-create the story of the acronym SMK and to contribute their experience of, and feelings about, the SMK.[392]

Since 2012, the gallery has continuously and successfully worked on its branding process. SMK used the outcomes of the 'What is SMK to you?' campaign as the point of departure for co-creating with external (potential) audiences.

On the face of it, the Gallery is a perfect example of what working with brand co-creation can do for an organisation in terms of reinventing itself, empowering stakeholders, democratising the brand, creating trust and, consequently, building a stronger brand. However, the Gallery recently entered into what they themselves describe as the more difficult phases of the process. When initiating the internal dialogue about what the Gallery is and should be, disagreement among the diverse groups of employees soon became very obvious. So, working with brand co-creation internally is actually where SMK has met the most serious challenges – and this is where our study begins.

## The special challenges for public organisations

Public sector organisations, like SMK, are often characterised by great diversity in employee groups and departments. Public organisations encompass very complex power relations, and sometimes even power struggles, and several studies have found that branding processes within this sector often meet more resistance than in private corporations. At the same time, many different actors in the organisation communicate SMK's brand, not just the communication department and management. The curators communicate through the exhibitions, research publications and networks; the educators through tours, catalogues and exhibition texts; and the artists through their shows. So, this type of public organisation embraces a range of actors who all potentially communicate the brand simultaneously.

In this way, co-creating the brand is not only a matter of the organisation engaging external stakeholders in the dialogue, but also how all the internal employee groups react to a co-creation branding process; how they respond to being asked to change their work processes, and ways of seeing their own profession, in relation to the whole organisation and to share their power and control.

## SMK's touchpoints in focus

A considerable challenge for any organisation taking a brand co-creation approach is to get all employees on board and make them aware of their role as co-creators. This is important because the organisation's different touchpoints[393] (i.e. brand expressions), where the co-creational dialogue with stakeholders takes place, need to be coherent. This doesn't mean the touchpoints controlled by the organisation and handled by a range of different groups of employees must be consistent. Rather, touchpoints should express an internally shared understanding and support of the brand, while allowing the individual employee to voice her own interpretation of the brand – what van Ruler refers to as communicating *compatible zones of meaning*.[394] In practice, this means that the brand is presented across diverse touchpoints in rhetorically and stylistically diverse yet compatible ways – as Belova et al. suggest: this means embracing and encouraging diverse voices that still support each other and coexist in harmonious polyphony.[395]

In our study, we looked at SMK's many different touch-points (in the form of websites, outdoor marketing posters, exhibition texts, posts on Instagram, Facebook and Wikipedia). It was easy to identify rhetorical diversity and when we clustered these touch-points according to what rhetorically characterises them, it was clear the Gallery spoke in various voices. The figure below illustrates the six voices we found and their relative size. We have placed them in a matrix consisting of two continuums spanning from *formal* to *informal* and *lay/simple* to *expert/complex*, respectively:

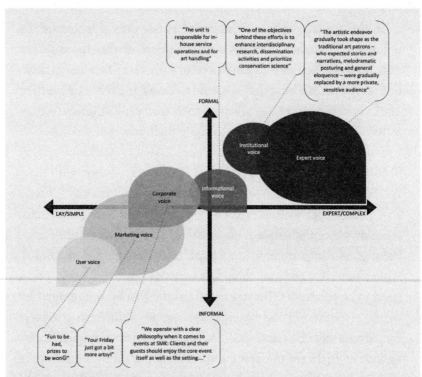

Figure 9.13 Illustration of the six voices. From Schmelz, L., Kjeldsen, A.K. (2019)

## Competing or compatible zones of meaning?

The six different voices of the Gallery have a very wide range, spanning from the very informal, layman-oriented user and marketing voices to the very formal, expert-oriented institutional voice. While the institutional voice clearly addresses governmental stakeholders with its focus on the legal requirements of the Gallery, the corporate voice expresses SMK as a business brand that reflects the market-oriented expectations of corporate stakeholders. This in itself is not problematic. Many companies will have a marketing voice communicating with new and existing customers, a corporate voice communicating with employees and an expert voice communicating with other experts such as colleagues and business partners. Theoretically, we refer to this as *brand ambidexterity*[396] – where organisations simultaneously pursuing multiple strategic goals through communication use different voices to address and adapt to different groups of stakeholders. The very idea of co-creation is to embrace the diverse meanings that various stakeholder groups may attach to the brand and therefore it does not make sense to strive for stringent alignment (which the traditional approach to branding would have us do). However, a certain level of compatibility, or compatible zones of meaning between brand expressions, needs to exist so as to avoid conflicting perceptions about the brand, especially when addressing the same stakeholder group.

In the case of SMK, it is particularly interesting to note that the different SMK voices actually often speak to the same group of stakeholders: the visitors. Thus, potential visitors are greeted by the user and marketing voices prior to or in between visits to the Gallery, but once they enter the building, visitors are primarily, almost exclusively, met by the expert voice. This means that the Gallery operates with two large clusters of zones of meaning that come across as not entirely compatible – actually, seen from the outside, they seem conflicting or clashing.

## Power struggles and territorialising

SMK's range of professional areas of (communication) practice shows the existence of the six different voices. Trying to understand this through the concepts of polyphony, and further adopting what Ind and Bjerke (2007) term *territorialising*,[397] may also explain the disharmony and conflict between the six voices: the curators (the main senders of institutional and expert voices) have traditionally held a high status, a position of power, as the true professional experts of the Gallery. However, with the gradual introduction of other professional experts, such as the communication professionals and the educators (the main senders of the corporate and marketing voices), and particularly with the decision to open up the creation of the brand to other stakeholders, the curators' superior position is challenged. The internal dialogue about the brand has actually resulted in growing concerns and heated discussions among the different groups of employees about how the Gallery can and should communicate (as expert, layman, populist and so on). So, the process of co-creating the SMK brand has brought about a potential renegotiation of power and the disharmony between the six voices could then be seen as indicative of competing zones of meaning among internal stakeholders who are fighting for their particular areas of practice – such as territorialising – through their individual brand touchpoints. The Gallery's head of communication also addresses this challenge, stating that for the employees: 'it was a huge change, and that was closely related to this shift of power and hierarchy in the communication. People had been used to making *their* exhibitions, projects, etc…now it all belonged to the brand and by that, you lose a lot of control, a lot of say.'

## Polyphony or cacophony?

The immediate consequence of this unresolved internal discussion is that the Gallery brand seems to be initiating a co-creational dialogue with external stakeholders with an extremely polyphonic brand expression – to the extent that it seems cacophonic.[398] This leads to the insight that we need to recognise employees not as one homogeneous unit entering into the dialogue, but as a composite group with many, potentially competing, voices in the co-creation of a brand; and that we also need to acknowledge and embrace all internal stakeholders as potential communicators of the brand.

This case illustrates how important, yet challenging, it is for internal stakeholders to let go of control when co-creating the brand. This is not only relevant to the communications department, but also for other employee groups in the organisation who create and maintain the branding touchpoints that external stakeholders encounter. Consequently, our case suggests that co-creation as co-controlling can challenge the power balance in the organisation. And therefore, at least a certain level of compatibility between internal brand expressions is called for – not least in relation to the choice of rhetorical style and invitations to co-create. Or seen through the metaphor of polyphony, there needs to be a common acceptance of a shared chord to create productive polyphony rather than destructive cacophony.

## The case of Hulst: co-creating a future-proof place brand

*Author: Rinske Brand*

The idea of promoting cities with distinctive positionings has a long history. For example, in the Netherlands, the cities of Amsterdam, The Hague and Rotterdam have for nearly 100 years positioned themselves as capital city, royal city and port city, respectively. In the quest to attract new visitors, investment, business and residents, each city has tried to differentiate itself from its rivals. What is new is the attachment of the word 'brand' to places and the emergence of the concept of place branding. Place branding is a strategic instrument employed to enable a town, city, region or country to stand out from the competition in an enduring manner and remain relevant for particular groups. This form of branding is, in essence, co-creational, because it involves intensive interaction among a range of stakeholders – not only to define the identity of the place and develop the brand, but also to promote it. This case describes the town of Hulst and how it launched a place branding process in 2018.

## Hulst

Hulst is a medieval fortified town with a population of 11,000 in the south-west of the Netherlands, on the border with Belgium. The town council wanted to put the town on the map as an attractive place for visitors, businesses and residents. They discovered that the average age of visitors and residents had increased in recent years. The main focus therefore was on targeting young people (without alienating the current target groups), so that they would find Hulst relevant and appealing as a place to visit and live.

## Place branding

Researchers offer various definitions of place branding. Govers and Go do justice to the multi-dimensional nature of place branding by describing it as 'the process of discovering, creating, developing and realising ideas and concepts for (re)constructing place identities, their defining traits and "genius loci" and subsequently building the sense of place.'[399] This unique identity, the DNA of the place, forms the basis for a brand, which then determines the direction of all sorts of tools and activities designed to strengthen that brand.

Zenker and Braun add that a place brand is 'a network of associations in the place consumers' mind based on the visual, verbal, and behavioral expression of a place and its stakeholders.'[400] Unlike products, places are multi-faceted, an amalgam of buildings, programme, events, surroundings and the behaviour of local people. As a result, those charged with creating a brand have limited control of the total brand experience. To create and then promote a shared identity, and hence a place brand, all stakeholders need to be involved. That was also the case in Hulst, where the municipality, local organisations, residents and business community worked together intensively, and still do so today.

## Widespread support through ownership

One of the biggest challenges in place branding is managing the involvement of stakeholders. Hulst had made previous attempts to develop a brand and accompanying marketing strategy, though with limited success, in part owing to the limited involvement of stakeholders. As a result, the shared sense of ownership was not what it could have been and neither residents nor the local business community felt sufficiently responsible for promoting the brand. Consequently, the aim of the place branding process was to define the brand and marketing strategy together with locals. Promoting it will therefore be a joint effort involving everybody and that will increase the chances of success.

## Starting with a shared ambition

When a variety of parties start working together, it is important for all of them to have one clear goal in mind. The first phase of the place branding process should therefore concentrate on defining a shared vision. Conversations with local organisations, residents and members of the business community revealed that the town council's initial focus on visitors could be broadened. Local stakeholders also expressed their desire to attract new residents and a new generation of entrepreneurs, and to develop a place brand that was both relevant and appealing for those groups.

## Distilling the identity of Hulst

An important aspect in place branding is the 'sense of place'. The identity of the place must be deeply felt by, and shared among, residents and visitors. The DNA of Hulst was defined through dialogue with people from the town. This happened in various ways. The annual Wall Town Festival – for which not only the whole town turns out, but also many faithful visitors pay a visit – proved to be a good reference moment. From the almost 100 personal stories and anecdotes about Hulst that were collected, a picture emerged of people who enjoyed the good things in life, who were very modest, and who had a strong sense of the past. Hulst has a rich history. During the Siege of Hulst in 1596, for example, the troops led by Prince Maurits of Nassau, who later became Prince of Orange, held out against Spanish forces for a long time. Today's residents expressed great pride in the resolve shown by their ancestors and interpret that today in what they describe as their 'individualism'. Further research was then conducted through one-to-one interviews with dozens of residents and members of the business community, enriching the identity with values such as entrepreneurship, a sense of community and 'ambience'.

## Co-creation at various levels

The place brand was developed in various co-creation sessions with dozens of 'trendsetters' from Hulst, among them entrepreneurs, policy-makers and residents in a range of age categories and from various backgrounds. In various sessions they jointly defined the core values of the town, the brand promise of Hulst and the points of differentiation in focus markets on the basis of information already gathered from local people. This led to a preliminary place brand, including the core values, brand essence, target groups and ambitions. This preliminary brand was then presented to a wider group of local residents and entrepreneurs before it was revised further and finalised in consultation with the Mayor and aldermen.

Five core values were formulated to describe Hulst. Three of them represent the current core. These values are: 'characteristic', 'simply good' (also a local expression) and 'ambience'. 'Characteristic' refers to the fact that Hulst and its residents always tend to do things slightly differently. 'Simply good' refers to Hulst being a pleasant and reliable place to live, which has led to a great sense of community among residents. 'Ambience' stands for the fact that Hulst is picturesque and atmospheric and boasts a rich history. Two core values were formulated with a future perspective in mind: 'contemporary' and 'entrepreneurial'. These refer to the fact that, besides its rich history, Hulst is also from the here and now and bustling with initiatives. The brand promise of Hulst reads: a paradise for entrepreneurial and active people, young and old(er), loving the good life.[401]

## Building together

Places are very different from products when it comes to building and promoting a brand. As mentioned earlier, the brand experience of a place is multifaceted. It is informed by many things, among them the physical environment, the behaviour of visitors and residents, and the stories told about the city.

While the name, logo and slogan play a crucial role when it comes to product brands, they are of lesser influence on the total experience of a place brand. All stakeholders are involved in promoting a place brand, consciously or otherwise. The role of the marketer is mainly to inform, stimulate and direct them and their activities. In Hulst, it was decided to build upon the already existing informal #INULST campaign ('In Ulst' is local slang for 'in Hulst'.) The life-size INULST letters in the city centre are being used as a base for the new visual identity.

In addition, making a place attractive for new target groups requires more than a marketing campaign. It requires changes to infrastructure, housing stock, retail mix and local amenities. In the case of Hulst, what was also needed were suitable homes, affordable rents and facilities that met the needs of young people.

This means that building the brand requires intensive collaboration between the marketer and the various parties in the town, from local council to property developer, and from property owner to retailer. All parties need to be committed to strengthening and promoting the brand. In Hulst, the coming together of different groups in the process sparked new collaborative ventures. The development strategy drawn up together consists not only of a marketing plan and changes in programme events and retail offerings, but also of ways of working together. Although the process in Hulst started with the local council, there is also a 'brand team' in place. The core group includes representatives of the various stakeholder groups and they initiate, coordinate and direct where necessary on the basis of the place brand.

The place branding strategy of Hulst consists of three pillars: the first being one central location for all information, on- and offline. This means not only a comprehensive website, but also a physical 'inspiration house' with a coffee shop, a store with merchandise and a local tourist centre. Second, there is a strong focus on storytelling, both through social media as well as via events and volunteering town guides. And third, the strategy focusses on fuelling pride by giving residents and local entrepreneurs a more active role in policy and implementation.

To summarise, creating a place brand is in essence a co-creational process, involving not only the development but also the promotion of the brand. It is important to give the various stakeholder groups an active role right from the earliest phases to help establish a solid foundation for everybody involved. If everybody operates on the basis of an identity that has been determined together, and with a shared goal in mind, the place can be successfully put on the map (again).

## Six success factors for place branding

1) Attention to diversity
   In bringing together relevant stakeholders, you should consider the diversity of a place. The group does not by definition have to be big, but it should be diverse. One of the most powerful instruments

for achieving this turned out to be informal local networks. In other words, people who propose other people or invite others for a follow-up meeting.

2) Bringing together levels of knowledge and interest

To ensure that everybody involved clearly understands what the goal of the process is and how they can contribute to it now, and in the future, it is vital to develop a shared level of knowledge. If the interests among stakeholders vary, it is important to find shared goals – at the risk that shared goals might be less challenging and more abstract.

3) Right scope for the brand

To achieve real results, a place brand should be the point of departure for much more than just a marketing strategy. A strong place brand can determine the course of the entire future development of a place: from events to infrastructure, and from consultation structures to campaigns.

4) Continuous involvement

People who play a role in the process should remain involved and informed throughout. This applies to both internal and external stakeholders. In this regard, clear feedback moments and lines of communication are crucial.

5) Leadership

Even if a place brand is in essence co-creational, experience has taught us that it is still good to have an undisputed leader, certainly at the start. This 'owner' inspires and motivates all stakeholders.

6) Budget and patience

Building up a successful place brand costs time, years, decades maybe, and money. This is not the responsibility of the local council alone. All stakeholders can contribute actively by providing people and tools on the basis of shared ambitions and approaches.

# Summary

In the introduction to this chapter, we stated that not all brands are created equal. We made our point by briefly discussing the different roles that brands can play and looked at the main differences between consumer, B2B, service and not-for-profit brands. We also showed that employees from different segments can influence the brand experience to varying degrees and that the importance of co-creation may vary across industries as well. Table 9.1 below provides an overview of our reasoning and can serve as a starting point for deeper discussions on the differences between different types of brands. The table lists the diverse kinds of brands that we analysed in this chapter and discusses from a consumer viewpoint how important the various functions of brands (to provide orientation in confusing markets, to reduce the perceived risk of buying, to provide experiential benefits) are, how strong the influence of employees on the brand experience usually is and how important activities of co-creation are. The reasoning for our rating (high/medium/low importance) is given within the previous paragraphs in the corresponding text passages.

Table 9.1 Brand roles, importance of internal branding and need for co-creation within various business sectors (● high importance; ◉ medium importance; ○ low importance)

| Criteria<br>Kind of brand | Orientation | Risk Reduction | Experiential Benefits | Role of Internal Branding | Importance of Co-Creation |
|---|---|---|---|---|---|
| **Consumer Brands** Value Brands | ● | ○ | ○ | ○ | ○ |
| Mass Brands | ● | ◉ | ◉ | ◉ | ● |
| Premium Brands | ◉ | ● | ● | ● | ● |
| Prestige Brands | ○ | ○ | ● | ● | ○ |
| Fun Brands | ● | ○ | ● | ◉ | ● |
| B2B Brands | ● | ● | ○ | ● | ● |
| Service Brands | ◉ | ● | ◉ | ● | ● |
| Not-for-Profit Brands | ● | ● | ● | ● | ● |

## Reflections/questions

1) What different functions do the following brands fulfil for their customers: Norwegian Airline, Volvo, Apple, Burberry and Fossil?

2) Can you name a brand that is not a consumer brand but that you really like? What makes this brand special to you?

3) What do you think are the major differences between consumer, B2B, service and not-for-profit-brands? What different functions do brands have within those industries?

4) Comment on the following: the more direct the interactions between the brand and its customers before, during and after purchase, the more important the role of employees in the brand building process.

5) Find and analyse a highly co-creative B2B brand – and one in the consumer sector and discuss the differences between them.

## We recommend the following reading to expand your learning experience:

Baumgarth, C. (2010). '"Living the brand": Brand orientation in the business-to-business sector', *European Journal of Marketing, 44*(5), 653–671.

Berry, L.L. & Seltman, K. D. (2007). 'Building a strong services brand: Lessons from Mayo Clinic', *Business Horizons, 50*(3), 199–209.

Brown, B.P., Bellenger, D.N. & Johnston, W.J. (2007). 'The implications of business-to-business and consumer market differences for B2B branding strategy', *Journal of Business Market Management, 1*(3), 209–230.

Khan, H. & Ede, D. (2009). 'How do not-for-profit SMEs attempt to develop a strong brand in an increasingly saturated market?', *Journal of Small Business and Enterprise Development, 16*(2), 335–354.

Steenkamp, J.B. (2014). 'How global brands create firm value: the 4V model', *International Marketing Review, 31*(1), 5–29.

# CHAPTER TEN

# The practice of co-creation

## In this chapter ...

We conclude the argument for a co-creative approach to brand management. To us, co-creation represents the reality of what a brand is and how it develops. Brands are loaded with intent by managers, but brand meaning is found by consumers and other stakeholders as they share their thoughts, ideas and experiences with each other in online and offline networks. Brand managers can be part of those networks as supporters, listeners, learners and facilitators. Together, managers and stakeholders can make brands relevant and desirable. What's not to like about co-creation?

There are some challenges, though – not the least of which is for organisations to balance freedom and order.[402] As we argued earlier, an organisation needs clarity about what a brand stands for if managers are to let it go and allow it to be re-interpreted and re-invented by others. As we will explore here in this chapter, this concerns a meaningful articulation of the brand identity, a co-creative approach that employs the most appropriate means of engagement and a management philosophy rooted in humility and empowerment. There are indeed degrees of letting go from the more controlled private communities and events – such as those typified by Hakkasan or Mayfair Diagnostics – to open communities and social media environments where exchanges can lead the brand in quite different directions. The upside of greater openness is that it connects a brand with its stakeholders, but the potential downside is the noise that can result, as stakeholders push and shove the brand around and clarity is lost.

Here, we will discuss the nuances of how to think about freedom and order and the implications for brand management, the participation of diverse interests in the brand and the ethical issues surrounding it. We will illustrate the chapter with the case of a company called Brandless, which demonstrates a new managerial approach that goes beyond insights to a more co-operative business model.

## Learning Objectives

After reading this chapter you should

- understand how to structure brand co-creation so that it balances the need for freedom and order;
- recognise how brand co-creation can best be managed to empower employees and partners while providing opportunities for participation from external stakeholders;
- understand the ethical issues surrounding co-creation and how these can best be managed;
- appreciate the potential of truly involving customers in building a brand.

## Positive and negative freedom

Strong brands are a mixture of continuity and surprise; they provide the reassurance of the familiar and the buzz of the unexpected. For example, Hakkasan restaurants have always strived to combine the familiar and the exotic in the delivery of memorable experiences for guests. To realise this, the brand works to have common standards in interiors, food and service. However, the brand also aims to be innovative; to extend the Hakkasan brand into new arenas and to re-invent the experience. Similarly, look at Porsche. Porsche's brand values of innovation and tradition, performance and everyday usability, exclusiveness and social acceptance and design and function, are not conjured out of the air. The magic of the Porsche brand lies in the tension between the values and how they are resolved by its engineers and managers. You can see the continuity and surprise in the brand if you look at the first Porsche, the 356, from 1948. It has a silhouette which is common to the versions of the Porsche 911 that followed it. You can see the line of continuity (literally in the Porsche Museum in Stuttgart, Germany, where the shapes are traced on the wall), but look at the performance, the engines and the technology and you can see how things have changed radically.[403] The difficulty of course for a manager is to know what to keep from the past and what to discard. For more than 30 years, Porsche used air-cooled engines before switching to water-cooled, and until 2002 and the arrival of the Cayenne, a Sports Utility Vehicle (SUV), the company was a producer of two-seater sports cars. These changes were significant for the company and its customers, who were particularly resistant to the impact on their brand of the introduction of the Cayenne.[404] However, reflect on the values. They provide the continuity, even if the meaning of them evolves in tune with new engine types and new product categories.

We can perhaps better understand this interplay between continuity and innovation in the context of co-creation by understanding what we mean by freedom. We tend to think of freedom as lack of constraint, but for a brand this would suggest incoherence. We would never quite know what to expect of a brand experience, which in one sense might be exciting, but would also probably be unnerving. If we take a more nuanced view of freedom, though, we can better see how we can manage freedom to provide coherent but interesting experiences. The point here is to distinguish what is called negative freedom – the degree to which individuals are free *from* man-made barriers – and positive freedom – the degree to which individuals are free to determine how they do things and their ability to self-organise.[405] In other words, a brand needs to set an appropriate degree of negative freedom to give itself a sense of unity. Freedom *from* allows employees and stakeholders to co-create the brand, but it sets some limits – rooted in the vision and values of a brand – to guide decisions and to determine also where the brand will not go. Freedom *to* might seem only subtly different, but it stresses that within the limits of freedom *from,* individuals have the opportunity to express themselves and not rely on the decisions of others. This positive freedom gives people the opportunity to decide how they will do things.

What does this mean in practice? It argues that the internal and external stakeholders who participate in the development of a brand need to understand the limits of freedom. For a customer in an online community, this means adhering to rules and guidelines that enable the community to function without trolling or too much digression. For an employee interacting on social media with stakeholders, this means understanding the protocols, listening to others and working within the frame of the brand vision and values. However, within these limits, the customer and the employee are free to decide how they conduct themselves. Negative freedom creates a frame within which stakeholders can explore and evolve the brand. Within the frame people have positive freedom to share their different interpretations, which can in turn shift the meaning of the brand through their diverse interpretations. Thus, through co-creation, the meaning of the brand moves – sometimes in ways unimagined by managers.

Different approaches to co-creation lead to variable degrees of freedom. As we saw in Chapter 2, LEGO participates in communities that run the gamut, from company managed activities and communities to independent fan-run communities and events. Whereas in the former case the company plays a more explicit role in setting the limits of negative freedom and a more active role in facilitation, in the latter the limits are agreed collectively by the community and LEGO provides support when relevant. Both extremes provide the opportunity for co-creation, but one is more purposeful and the other more passionate. While purposeful communities can become passionate, such fan-based communities as Alfa Romeo enthusiasts, lovers of Milanese opera or Liverpool football fans, start there.[406] What a brand manager needs to manage here is the balance of negative and positive freedom by adapting to context and recognising the limits of influence. It might generally be more comfortable to constrain freedom in pursuit of organisational goals, but it becomes counterproductive if it leads to resistance or decreased motivation to participate. Organisations, with their knowledge and expertise, can easily start out with a cynical perspective that allows a small space of negative freedom, but it could be argued that, if they are confident enough, they could open up the space of negative freedom so that co-creative brand building becomes the norm, not the exception. A part of the rationale for this is that consumers can be as good as, if not better, than employees at creating new ideas.[407]

## Trust, transparency and community

As we have seen in the earlier chapters (and here also), brands (whether they are human or not) can co-create, if they nurture an environment of trust and transparency. The philosopher David Hume argues that when we have sympathy for others we can develop relationships based on trust.[408] This implies making oneself vulnerable to others, which is easier to do when processes are transparent and we can be confident about those that we interact with and their likely responses. These are the antecedents of community, which enable people from diverse backgrounds to come together and to share ideas in common, without fear. We would argue that co-creative practices that fail to build social capital are just skimming the surface. Using stakeholders to provide inspiration and ideas through such mechanisms as hackathons, open idea labs and competitions, typically at the front end of processes,[409] are valuable, but they often miss out on the interactions between stakeholders and between stakeholders and the brand that allow an idea to evolve and develop. The virtue of a true co-creative approach to building brands, such as those used by companies like Mozilla and Orange, is that by treating consumers and other stakeholders as partners, they tap into new resources and ideas that can be realised together. This does not abrogate the responsibility of managers to steer processes, make choices, overcome resistance and to say 'no' sometimes. Rather, it means listening, and learning to share, and incorporating the knowledge, skills and intellectual capabilities of others into the brand.

## The example of Brandless

Trust, transparency and community is part of the mantra of online seller Brandless. Ironically, given their name, Brandless is a brand which has built its business model around co-creation. The San Francisco company is based on the vision of its founders, Tina Sharkey and Ido Leffler, who saw an opportunity to create an e-commerce offer providing good-quality food, baby products, beauty and household goods in simple but modernist packaging. That in itself doesn't sound very distinctive, or indeed novel. The Japanese brand Muji, whose full name – Mujirushi Ryohin – means no-brand quality goods, started in the early 1980s, as did the Basics range of the retailer, Habitat, with its quality goods and simple Bauhaus-inspired packaging.[410] But what was perhaps distinctive at the Brandless launch in 2017 was that everything was priced at $3. The Brandless offer is rooted in a direct from-manufacturer-to-customer offer and a focus on simplicity and word-of-mouth recommendation. Trust and transparency emerge because the company works to establish a dialogue with its customers and the presentation of products establishes the key attributes up front. In terms of dialogue, it is a requirement for Brandless staff, whatever their position, that they have contact with customers every day, while the packaging just says what it is. For example, their Bathroom Tissue product says simply and clearly on the front of the product, BATHROOM TISSUE, and then lists its key attributes: biobased product, made from sugarcane and bamboo grass, tree-free paper product, septic-safe and biodegradable.

What makes Brandless co-creative is not the choices of the founders, but the way the brand has evolved from its initial range of 115 products. Tina Sharkey says that through data monitoring and daily active engagement with consumers, Brandless generates insights into the needs and desires of consumers and then builds 'what the community is asking for.' This is an outside-in and inside-out process, because not only are consumers seen as community partners, but so too are the employees of Brandless. Together, they co-create the brand.[411]

Brandless is an apt example of an organisation that brings together managerial vision and consumer input to co-create the brand on a continuous basis. This doesn't mean that this is an uncritical relationship. When co-creation processes encourage dialogue in the development of ideas, diverse and critical points of view emerge.[412] This is an important component of co-creating brands, because it helps to ensure that the brand moves away from its organisational voice as stakeholders challenge the taken for granted. Within co-creation communities and at co-creation events, effective facilitation both stimulates a sense of togetherness and promotes openness. It tries to resist the temptation to pin things down and instead to push people to think differently. Co-creation can encourage people to attack their own convictions.[413]

## Ireland and its Citizens' Assembly

Another vivid illustration of co-creation at work is Ireland's use of a participative process, which involved citizens over an extended period of time, to make some key decisions about its values as a country and on some specific and contentious issues, such as gay marriage and the eighth amendment of the constitution that outlawed abortion. Given that these issues were polarising and emotionally charged, a participative process might have simply generated antagonistic positions with no possibility of compromise. But after a deliberative process called the Citizens' Assembly, a report was issued in 2017 that put forward its point of view on the issues and also made recommendations on the way forward. Ireland isn't the only country or community that has done this, but the success of its Citizens' Assembly is instructive and shows how a diverse group of people can coalesce around an approach.

The Citizens' Assembly was composed of 99 randomly selected people – plus the same number of reserves to cover people who dropped out – and was chaired by a Supreme Court judge. No politicians were involved and citizens were not paid, other than for their expenses. The Assembly invited opinions from medical experts, priests and advocates, while citizens submitted some 13,000 comments. The participants were not chosen for any particular skills and they included people who were pro and anti the subjects under debate. People had to prepare before the discussions, during which they worked on issues in small groups and afterwards they completed reports to check that they had understood what was going on. In all, there were five topics and it took some 18 months before all the deliberations were completed. On the particularly divisive issue of abortion, the Citizens' Assembly made a clear recommendation that the eighth amendment should be repealed and that it should be replaced by new legislation. Even though politicians had supported the Citizens' Assembly process, they could have baulked at this point and chosen to avoid taking the issue forward. Instead, the recommendation was put to a referendum of Irish citizens, who confirmed the thinking of the Assembly by voting 66 per cent in favour of its proposal.

One of the interesting aspects of the process was some of the feedback from participants. Comments from members of the Assembly suggest that the process was seen as transparent and fair and that the discussions worked to establish the facts, rather than being run aground through strong opinions. Because the Assembly came to feel like a safe place, people had the courage to attack their own convictions and to think again. They also felt that they weren't tied down in the same way as politicians, who were seen to be fearful of taking a stand, because of their need to calculate the implications of publicly endorsing a point of view.[414] By adopting a co-creative approach to such important social issues and ensuring that the process led to action, it engendered trust in the political arena and a belief that societal change was possible in areas that had long been seen as taboo. The Citizens' Assembly was a directed process and there were clear limits to freedom *from*, but within the space of negative freedom, participants had a large degree of discretion over freedom *to*.

## How co-creation can boost trust in corporate social responsibility

*Author: Oriol Iglesias*

Corporate Social Responsibility (CSR) might seem like a corporate practice that is determined by managers, but increasingly, CSR is co-created together with stakeholders. Partly this is due to the global influence of social media and technology, which is shaping a considerably more transparent world and bringing greater stakeholder influencer to bear on brands to behave in a socially responsible manner, reducing their negative impacts and contributing to society and the environment. Partly this is because research shows that CSR committed brands can achieve significant organisational advantages, including increased customer trust, customer loyalty and word-of-mouth recommendations.[415]

The rise of CSR has led to a significant shift in management attitudes and pushed many companies to embrace a more ethical approach. However, at the same time, critical voices also question whether companies are really committed to CSR or whether CSR practices are insincere and manipulative.[416] This scepticism towards CSR comes from two main sources. First, too often CSR efforts are tangential to the business rather than embedded in its core.[417] Second, too many brands implement selective disclosure strategies, which aim to emphasise the positive impacts of their actions while hiding the negative ones.

The combination of these two practices fuels the perception that CSR is simply about cosmetic and superficial marketing campaigns. As a result, a growing number of consumers see CSR as a reputation-cleaning mechanism that is an inauthentic reaction to social pressures. The different approaches to CSR – from the committed to the cosmetic – also make it difficult for consumers to judge who they should trust and raises question marks over the validity of CSR claims.

Given this situation, more and more companies (such as the Virgin Group and the leading Spanish financial company Banco de Santander) have changed their terminology regarding their investments and projects in this field and sometimes no longer use the term CSR. However, even if this is a perfectly understandable response, it does not solve the underlying issue of how to display an authentic commitment to CSR and differentiate from the opportunists. A potential solution lies with co-creation.

CSR aims at understanding the needs and challenges of a brand's different stakeholders as a way to build relevant solutions. As a collaborative practice, co-creation also attempts to develop relevant innovations based on insights into a brand's stakeholders. Overall, it seems quite natural to combine CSR and co-creation to achieve better outcomes. The benefits of this linkage have been shown in a research study that demonstrates that when a brand embraces co-creation, its CSR activities are more trusted and higher levels of customer loyalty are developed.[418] However, the benefits don't just happen. Companies have to invest in four key areas:

1) Opening up the organisation to the outside. This is concerned with listening, being empathetic and capable of understanding the needs and problems of customers, but also of other potential stakeholders. From this perspective, instead of defining the CSR

strategy and activities inside out, brands need to be open to the perspectives of their different stakeholders and their CSR-related priorities.

2) Involving multiple internal stakeholders. This is about moving the CSR strategy out of the CSR department and involving other internal departments and hierarchical levels in the co-construction of CSR priorities, together with the brand's stakeholders. Here, it is essential that the top management of the organisation is involved in order to ensure that the CSR strategy is embedded into the business strategy and supports and nurtures its core.

3) Promoting a genuine dialogue between the inside and the outside. This is similar to the first point, but indicates that there are degrees of openness. Here, the commitment to co-creation is rooted in an approach that treats a brand's stakeholders as key strategic partners. This requires a safe environment where all participants feel they can trust the brand and demands that the brand gives constant and rich feedback to all the participants so that their commitment progressively increases and creativity emerges.

4) Being transparent. The brand needs to provide co-creation participants with detailed and accurate information about what happens to their suggestions. Additionally, it is essential that the brand explains what can and cannot be done in the process. In essence, the brand needs to acknowledge that it is impossible to be perfect and that constraints and limitations will always exist, while showing that there is a clear roadmap and an authentic commitment to CSR.

An example of the link between CSR and co-creation comes from the French group L'Oréal. In 2011, it initiated a series of stakeholder forums around the globe to proactively engage consumers, NGOs, members of civil society and associations, employees and experts to share expectations and experiences on sustainability and social responsibility. This initiative was further reinforced in 2013 when the group worked together with more than 100 organisations to define and structure its commitments for 2020. This dialogue and the co-created process allowed L'Oréal to incorporate relevant suggestions in five key areas: responsible sourcing, biodiversity, diversity and equal opportunity policy, responsible communication and energy and climate change. Since then, the company has continued to embrace a collaborative approach to social responsibility.

All in all, brands should rethink their approach to CSR and make it more collaborative, open and empathetic. This is the only way to foster trusting brand-stakeholder relationships and to demonstrate an authentic commitment to helping stakeholders solve their most relevant challenges. A co-creative philosophy and relevant co-creative tools will make it a lot easier to achieve these goals.

## Is co-creation good for us?

One of the important points that Oriol Iglesias makes in his piece on corporate social responsibility is that the practice can be disingenuous; designed to improve corporate reputation without any real commitment. Yet he also notes that a committed and co-creative approach can build trust between a brand and its stakeholders and help solve relevant challenges. We can see similar evidence with Brandless and the nation of Ireland, in that they adopted co-creative processes designed to embed the contributions of participants into decision-making. Equally, organisations can make co-creation a charade – a useful way to suggest that participants can influence decisions without any real intention to respond to their points of view. In these situations, consumers are merely pawns in the game. We would argue that from an ethical point of view, this is unacceptable. Companies should be sincere in the way that they involve people and set out the range of positive and negative freedom at the outset. So, whether co-creation is good for participants depends on the intent of the organisation.

There are also other criticisms levelled at co-creation that go beyond the issue of organisational intent. Most co-creation writers see it as benefiting brand owners because it provides valuable insights into stakeholders' beliefs and behaviour. And most would argue that it benefits the participants, because they realise intrinsic benefits and some extrinsic ones as well. However, there are some dissenters.[419] It's worth paying attention to these critiques not only to think through an alternative point of view, but also to remind ourselves of the need to ensure that the practice of co-creation is as fair as it can be. The essence of the arguments offered are twofold. First, brands take advantage of the desire of consumers to be active and participatory. In this view, it is neither here nor there that participants find the process of co-creation joyful and rewarding. Tapping into their needs is seen as manipulative and based on a desire to control. Companies are in reality getting consumers to work for them for free (or almost for free) by meeting their desires for 'recognition, freedom and agency', rather than paying them a market rate for the work that they do: 'the co-creation economy is about experimenting with new possibilities for value creation that are based on the expropriation of free cultural, technological, social and affective labor of the consumer masses'.[420] Second, due to the input of consumers, the relevance and quality of brands is enhanced, which results in the ability of the brand owner to charge higher prices. Consumers thus contribute to their own downfall. They not only work for free, but they also end up paying more for the products and services that they help to co-create.

Let's start with the second argument first. While it may be true theoretically that consumers pay more for the products that they improve through co-creation, we have seen no empirical evidence to support the point. The first argument is more complex. With reference to Michel Foucault's work on 'governmentality', it is argued that

The practice of co-creation

co-creation is an attempt by capital to find new ways of enhancing productivity by co-opting the desire of people to be an entrepreneur of the self. In a previous co-creation community that we ran, one of the participants made exactly this point: 'Dear Prof Ind – I like your style! I wish I'd thought of your idea. Co-creation is a great money-spinning concept...because you can pay 300 people a few quid for coming up with ideas, developing them and showing which ones they like. The company gets good ideas cheaply that they can then implement without as much costly R&D, you get to write a book on it and we get a few quid and a sense of yay, I helped think of that when the ideas are acted on. Genius!!'[421]

Should we feel guilty, then, about being advocates for co-creation? There is certainly an issue of ambivalence in the way that brands involve consumers. Co-creation is both rewarding for individuals and exploitative. The breaking down of the boundaries between the consumer and the organisation gives consumers ever more freedom to create individual meaning through engagement, while at the same time organisations use their immaterial labour.[422] We could argue here that the choice to participate is freely taken, but it is also the case that individuals are committing themselves to exploitation, which reflects the question that the philosophers Deleuze and Guattari pose: 'Why do men fight for their servitude as stubbornly as though it were their salvation?'[423] If we accept these arguments, then we should try to ameliorate the dangers of exploitation and ensure that individuals realise the benefits they hope for. This requires a perspective that emphasises the individual.

One lesson, then, is that organisations have a responsibility to those that they involve in co-creation. They have to try and ensure that the needs of the organisation and the individual are balanced by rejecting the desire to control and instead encourage diversity and criticism: 'life requires the serial proliferation of amendments and retractions, burying dead opinions and promoting the growth of new critical needs'.[424] That means managers need to be cognisant of the objectives that have been set for the brand and to be attentive and listen and adapt to the needs of each individual in a community. This in turn suggests the need for a more empathetic and humble style of leadership and the rejection of the desire to control. It means both an understanding of freedom and how to manage it in a dynamic context so that the organisation and co-creationists benefit.

## Brand ethics and the significance of ethical values for co-creation

*INTERVIEW WITH GERHARD SCHWARZ*

**On your website, you describe yourself not only as a philosopher and psychologist, but also as a brand ethicist. Can you explain what a brand ethicist does?**

Ethics has been considered a philosophical discipline in the Western world at least since Aristotle, so it might not come as a surprise if a philosopher is also an ethicist at the same time. It is certainly unusual to find someone doing brand ethics, since brands have rarely been considered as a topic of academic ethical theory. My work as a brand ethicist can be divided into two main components. The first is fundamental scientific-philosophical research, which I undertake in my 'Forschungsbüro Markenethik' (Brand Ethics Research Office). The second is brand-ethical practice. I work in that respect as a consultant for businesses who are interested in the ethical alignment of their brands and in enhancing their ethical integrity.

**When it comes to ethics, do you see an analogy between people and brands?**

One should by no means rush to this conclusion. Instead, one should initially see a brand from a more conventional viewpoint. You can then reflect on the brand and think about how to complement or consolidate it with an ethical approach. I have tried to do this by taking a classical approach, so-called 'Markentechnik' (brand technique), which understands the brand itself and its management as complex human technology. With this in mind, you can develop brand ethics in terms of technology ethics and use a range of proven concepts and methods for the ethical optimisation of brands. However, other approaches to brand ethics still need to be developed. You can do a lot without conceptualising the brand as a person.

On the other hand, I believe you can hardly avoid acknowledging some kind of personhood in the brand itself, for the simple reason that consumers do it – particularly those with strong brand relationships. According to the latest research findings, brands are considered actors, which are assigned moral responsibility and have the obligation to show commitment to environmental-ethical and societal issues. Brand ethics is meant to clarify why and how this can be done as well as to work out the consequences for brand development. A brand manager is of course interested in gaining a better understanding of the expectations people have of a brand and what this means for brand design and brand management. Brand ethics can make a substantial contribution here.

**Your doctorate is on Kant. Kant writes that every human being 'exists as an end in itself, *not merely as a means* to be used by this or that will at its discretion.'[425] How does the way brands are managed fit with this?**

It is a trivial fact that humans use themselves and others as a means for a lot of purposes. Our public, professional and private lives clearly show that we are dependent on one another in many ways and that we need each other and make use of each other. The crucial point is that we must not use (i.e. abuse) humans solely as a means but must always respect their dignity. According to Kant, this dignity lies in the autonomy of the human being, i.e. in their free self-determination as a rational and spiritual being.

With a view to brand management, these thoughts lead to at least three valuable outcomes. First and foremost, purely strategic approaches that undermine or manipulate the power of judgement and the free, rational self-determination of humans are problematic. One ought to reflect upon what this means in the field of customer acquisition and customer retention and what a culture characterised by integral ethical brand communication and brand relationships would look like.

Second, there is an equally important question: do I foster the possibility of free, rational self-determination with my brand? Do I nurture a strong ethical understanding and ethical action? Or do I constrain them? Based on Kant's notion of man as an end in itself, the consequence for the brand – with all its products and deliverables, with all its communications and worlds of meaning – is the obligation to enhance and strengthen the ethical power of judgement, competence and conduct of consumers and other stakeholders. This implies that an ethically aligned brand not only responds to existing or emerging critical movements and directions in society but harbours socially critical potential within itself.

Third, if consumers can assign responsibility and ethical obligations to brands and so attribute the ability of practical self-determination to them, brands do exhibit something like dignity. In other words, they show characteristics of an end in itself. An idea such as brand dignity would of course sound bizarre if we could not attribute personhood to a brand. But when taking this conception seriously it would imply that we must not use (i.e. abuse) brands solely as a means for whatever purposes. To achieve ethically sensitive brand management, it is important to take into account what this means.

But at this point I would like to note that the ethical approach I favour is not Kant's – even though the notion of ethical insight and self-determination is of crucial significance for any form of ethics. In my view, it is necessary to have a wide-ranging notion of the good as the core principle of ethics. This ethical good, which is classically identified as the true good in contrast to what only appears to be good, goes far beyond just humans. Non-human beings such as animals and plants are included. They too must not be used or abused as a pure means to achieve a discretionary purpose. This is also true for non-living nature as well as culture and technology. They all contain precious and cherishable value, which needs to be respected. This implies the idea of a good world of all that is and can be (a good society, a good education, a good legal system, a good economy, a good consumer culture, a good brand culture). This idea should guide all our wishes, desires, aims and actions. The question we should ask ourselves is, do my wishes and desires, my actions, my accomplishments and achievements contribute to a truly good world? And the same is true for brands.

It is noteworthy here that brands are naturally inclined towards ethics, since a brand always stands for something good. This is also the reason people appreciate a brand and its products and performance. This natural tendency continues in brand ethics by targeting the ethical analysis and optimisation with respect to the true good in the brand, which may be a component and a driving force of a good world, a good economic life, a good brand culture, a good consumer culture, a good way of life and so on. The ideal is a truly good brand, which conveys and realises a maximum of good for everything and everyone and therefore enjoys everyone's well-deserved esteem.

**Throughout our book, we argue that the changing environment must lead to a new brand-management paradigm, which we call the 'co-creation perspective'. We build on a definition from Ind, Iglesias and Schultz, which describes co-creation as 'an active, creative and social process based on collaboration between organisations and participants that generates benefits for all and creates value for stakeholders.'[426] How is the call for co-creation in the brand-management context to be judged from an ethical perspective? And especially, what are the advantages and downsides of engaging multiple stakeholders in the brand-management process, from the viewpoint of a brand ethicist?**

Active stakeholder involvement is an important topic in ethically oriented corporate management and communication approaches, especially when they are inspired by discourse ethics. I take a more reserved stance towards discourse ethics. Of course, the main idea of a discourse between companies and stakeholders with heterogeneous and conflicting interests is not entirely useless where real conflicts need to be moderated and where rigidified self-centred interests have to be overcome.

However, economic players are never only determined by their individual purposes and self-centred interests. As rational-spiritual beings, people, enterprises and brands take interest in the good of a larger whole from within themselves and are intrinsically motivated to promote and realise it — even if this sometimes contradicts their own particular interests. Ethics is not a restrictive filter for social compatibility but a creative engine for a good world and an engine for creatively searching for, finding and realising the good in the world. The crucial thing when integrating multiple stakeholder perspectives is that it removes the constraints of particular interests by opening up a playful, imaginative conception of a larger and more comprehensive good. The important thing with co-creation is that it makes this aspect the focus of attention.

Nevertheless, I would like to mention three things. First, when I apply the tools I have developed, it occurs to me that it is not the real activation of stakeholders that is necessarily relevant but rather the overcoming of narrow and restricted views and interests. And this can be achieved without any external stakeholders being present. In a value or ethics laboratory, a team of company members from different business units and hierarchy levels is able to tap into the perspectives of all relevant stakeholders — and also of external stakeholders such as customers, partners, competitors — by simulating every single stakeholder's perspective step-by-step via active role-adoption in which implicit knowledge about the stakeholder is systematically explored and made tangible. This method overcomes narrow views and interests and opens new perspectives for the insightful analysis and innovative optimisation of products, services, communications, processes, structures, strategies and so on. So even if external stakeholder groups do not participate, their perspective will still be taken into consideration in a co-creative process.

Second, the literature on brand-related co-creation – also according to Ind, Iglesias and Schultz suggests that creative group processes, which are aimed at product and service innovations, are per se brand-development processes. My question would be whether this is an over-hasty conclusion. Of course, products and services on the one hand, and the brand itself on the other hand, are associated with one another. The question is, however, in what way? A product modification or improvement or new development cannot necessarily be perceived as a brand modification or improvement, or as a brand specification, explication or innovation, because it can also conflict with the brand – irrespective of whether consumers and corporate staff have engaged in the group work and perceive themselves as being close to or distant from the brand (brand intimacy). I can imagine that the idea of brand co-creation becomes clearer if one emphasises at this point how the brand and product are intertwined in co-creation processes and how a product, service or communicative innovation can have a positive, a negative or perhaps have no impact on the brand whatsoever.

Third, it seems to me that key aspects of co-creation that are relevant for the brand are not fully captured if one puts the emphasis of the definition too much on co-operation and sociality. It has been acknowledged that, for example, the adoption processes via which consumers find a gateway to the brand are sometimes very innovative. The brand, with its inherent product and performance components, its communications and value components, is often seen in a new light and experienced, used, interpreted in a highly creative manner. These creative processes can be related to social issues in many different ways and can have extreme social consequences. But they may initially occur in isolation without any social connection. Nor are they necessarily co-operative processes. Nevertheless, one can call them 'co-creative' since all these processes are brand-related creative activities involving many people. I believe it is important for brand understanding, but particularly for brand management, to take greater account of these aspects when talking about co-creation.

**Concerning your way of speaking about values: in your work as a consultant, you offer a service, which you call value-oriented organisational development. I assume that a first step in such a process is to discuss and define the values that frame the organisation's development. If this is correct, how should values be defined if you use co-creation?**

The redevelopment of value sets for organisations and brands is part of my core responsibility. In approximately two-thirds of cases I work with companies where their values have already been defined in one way or another. However, often they have not thought through how the values can be used effectively by employees. In most cases, the values are a conglomerate of different value types and value levels: identity-related, often also sector-generic, frequently technical-functional as well as economic values. Ethical values, specifically classic virtues, are often included. So altogether it is a colourful mix. In most cases, I can work with what we have. My approach is to develop methods and tools that will make it easier for staff and executives to make use of these values in their work, i.e. in their daily activities, decisions and solutions, as analysis and optimisation principles. To make their use routine, these methods need to be embedded into existing management concepts and instruments – in many cases as complementary or fundamental components. The result is something like a common, value-oriented performance culture from which value-oriented deliverables, products and communications arise. Such a culture – and this is my main point – is highly creative and highly co-creative through managers and employees co-operating across departmental and hierarchical boundaries. The active, methodical use of values in the analysis and refinement of specific problems proves to be – in a similar way as taking into account any external stakeholders' perspectives – a creativity booster. It is precisely the ethical values, which are likely to emerge as creative radicals with a high innovation potential when used correctly.

**Some people may argue that co-creation involves taking advantage of the creativity and engagement of others, like customers, in order**

to achieve a company's own goals, such as a need for growth. This may even be quite obvious in the context of user-driven product innovation. What does a brand ethicist think about such criticisms and how should companies act to avoid such criticisms?

If the criticisms are justified, companies would be well advised to take them seriously and not avoid them. I think this is a question of attitude and of an ethically reflected versus an unreflected self-conception and view of the world. My observation is that an openness towards criticism comes to life when an organisation and its members are ethically aligned and are interested in doing good work to make a difference and to change the world, society, industry and their customers' lives for the better. In this case, a natural attitude or a virtue is adopted, which is mindful of blind spots and narrow views and is keen to overcome them. And it entails the continuous endeavour to improve bad products, services, processes, structures and so on. Taking into account both aspects, we can – according to Kant – call this process theoretical and practical enlightenment. Only an unworldly, theory-dogmatic or selfish, narrow, un-enlightened understanding of the corporation or the brand would have the idea that corporations or brands have to pursue interests that are ethically illegitimate and harm the world or make it worse.

We see co-creation activities outside of the business world. For example, as we have shown in some of the cases in Chapter 9 of the book, co-creation is already used in urban-development processes and in arts and culture. Do you think co-creation can be a broader societal phenomenon?

I am convinced that this will happen. I am currently working on an ethics laboratory model for schools, which can be used in ethics lessons as well. I am likewise working on a model for urban housing policy. Altogether, I would generally recommend always incorporating ethical value perspectives in the methodical set of co-creative processes and instruments. On the one hand, this is because ethical values are powerful creativity tools and increase the output of co-creation. On the other hand, this is because they align the output with the idea of the true good and therefore increase the chances that this output will contribute to a good world.

## Summary

Core to this final chapter has been an emphasis on the need to manage co-creation with an effective balance of freedom and order. Part of the order comes from a clear understanding of the brand itself, but it is also determined by the approach to co-creation, which can encompass more structured processes that can be found in private, facilitated online communities, led by the organisation, to more open processes that enable widespread involvement. Freedom also varies by context in that organisations need to define the limits of negative freedom and then empower people to work with the brand. Co-creation does require the brand to let go, but organisations have to decide how much to do so.

## Reflections/questions

1) Could you explain to someone the difference between negative and positive freedom and illustrate your interpretation with an example?
2) What do you think of the ethics of co-creation?
3) Can you find other brands like Brandless that have built consumer participation into their brand decision-making?

## We recommend the following to expand your learning experience:

Listen to the podcast interview with Charles Trevail (CSpace) and Tina Sharkey (Brandless): https://cspace.com/podcast/tina-sharkey-brandless-ceo (accessed 17 June 2019).

# References

1   Klein, N. (1999). *No Logo: Taking Aim at the Brand Bullies*. New York: Picador.
2   See: https://marketing-dictionary.org/b/brand (accessed 14 June, 2019).
3   1) De Chernatony, L., & McDonald, M. (1992). *Creating Powerful Brands: The Strategic Route to Success in Consumer, Industrial, and Service Markets*. Butterworth-Heinemann. 2) Keller, K. L., Apéria, T., & Georgson, M. (2008). *Strategic Brand Management: A European Perspective*. Pearson Education.
4   Veloutsou, C., & Delgado-Ballester, E. (2018). Guest editorial. *Spanish Journal of Marketing – ESIC, 22*(3), 254–271 (p.256).
5   Aaker, D. A. (1996). *Building Strong Brands*. New York: The Free Press.
6   See: https://blogs.lse.ac.uk/impactofsocialsciences/2016/03/14/addicted-to-the-brand-the-hypocrisy-of-a-publishing-academic/?fbclid=IwAR3VpKQ_x71ha6_gH0z32Iz_5O1UhTI4nFNrnvM424GxG3kHwZ4s0Hyxw4s#author (accessed 22 May, 2019).
7   Lev, B. (2004). *Sharpening the Intangible Edge. Harvard Business Review, 82*(6), 109–116.
8   Ind N., & Iglesias O. (2016) *Brand Desire*. Bloomsbury, London.
9   See, for example, the following studies: 1) Madden, T., Fehle, F., & Fournier, S. (2006). *Brands Matter – An Empirical Demonstration of the Creation of Shareholder Value through Branding. Journal of the Academy of Marketing Science, 34*(2), 224–235. 2) Harter, G., Koster, A., Peterson, M., & Stomberg, M. (2005). *Managing Brands for Value Creation*. www.strategyand.pwc.com/media/uploads/Managing_Brands_for_Value_Creation.pdf (accessed 22 May, 2019).
10  De Chernatony, L., & Dall'Olmo Riley, F. (1998). 'Defining a "brand": beyond the literature with experts' interpretations'. *Journal of Marketing Management, 14*(5), 417–443 (p.417).
11  See, for example: Romani, S., Grappi, S., Zarantonello, L., & Bagozzi, R.P. (2015). 'The revenge of the consumer! How brand moral violations lead to consumer anti-brand activism'. *Journal of Brand Management, 22*(8), 658–672.
12  Rozin, R.S. (2002). 'The branding iron: From cowboys to corporations'. *Journal of Brand Management, 10*(1), 4–7.
13  Grzesiak, M. (2018). *Personal Brand Creation in the Digital Age*. Cham: Palgrave.
14  Ibid.
15  See: https://www.meissen.com/en/world-meissen-couture/maison-meissen-couture/300-years-heritage (accessed 5 September, 2018).
16  Low, G.S., & Fullerton, R.A. (1994). 'Brands, brand management, and the brand manager system: A critical-historical evaluation'. *Journal of Marketing Research, 31*(2), 173–190 (p.175).
17  Wu, T. (2016). *The Attention Merchants*. New York: Knopf (p51).
18  McGovern, Ch. F. (2006). *Sold American: Consumption and Citizenship, 1890–1945*. Chapel Hill: University of North Carolina Press (p.25). Advertiser Claude C. Hopkins is cited in the corresponding paragraph. Also see Wu, T. (2016). *The Attention Merchants*. New York: Knopf (p.52).

19    Wu, T. (2016). *The Attention Merchants*. New York: Knopf (p.53).

20    Moss, S (2009). 'Demythologizing the McElroy Memo'. *The Journal of the Medinge Group, 3*(1). http://medinge.org/test-post-3 (accessed 22 May, 2019).

21    Aaker, D.A., and Joachimsthaler, E. (2000). *Brand Leadership*. New York: The Free Press.

22    Pitcher, A.E. (1985). The role of branding in international advertising. International Journal of Advertising, *4*(3), 241–246.

23    Ries, A., & Trout, J. (1981). *Positioning: The Battle for the Mind*. New York: Warner.

24    The term unique selling proposition has dominated product marketing for decades. See: Knox, S., & Bickerton, D. (2003). 'The six conventions of corporate branding'. *European Journal of Marketing, 37*(7/8), 998–1016.

25    Aaker, D.A., & Joachimsthaler, E. (2000). *Brand Leadership*. New York: The Free Press.

26    Hatch, M.J., & Schultz, M. (2009). 'From corporate to enterprise branding'. *Organizational Dynamics, 38*(2), 117–130 (p.117).

27    Urde, M. (2013). 'The corporate brand identity matrix'. *Journal of Brand Management, 20*(9), 742–761.

28    1) Aaker, D.A. (2004). 'Leveraging the corporate brand'. *California Management Review, 46*(3), 6–18. (p.6). 2) Kernstock, J., Esch, F.R., Tomczak, T., Redler, J., & Langner, T. (2014). 'Bedeutung des Corporate Brand Management erkennen und Denkschulen verstehen'. In Esch, F. R., Tomczak, T., Kernstock, J., Langner, T., & Redler, J. (eds.), *Corporate Brand Management*. Wiesbaden: Springer Gabler, 3–26.

29    Vargo, S.L., & Lusch, R. F. (2004). 'Evolving to a new dominant logic for marketing'. *Journal of Marketing, 68*(1), 1–17.

30    1) Von Hippel, E. (2006). *Democratizing Innovation*. Cambridge: The MIT Press. 2) Cova, B., & and Dalli, D. (2009). 'Working Customers: The Next Step in Marketing Theory'. *Marketing Theory, 9*(3), 315–339.

31    A wonderful overview of central developments within the brand management discipline is also provided by: Merz, M.A., He, Y., & Vargo, S.L. (2009). 'The evolving brand logic: a service-dominant logic perspective'. *Journal of the Academy of Marketing Science, 37*(3), 328–344.

32    Ibid. Also see: Fournier, S.M. (1998). 'Consumers and their Brands: Developing Relationship Theory in Consumer Research'. *Journal of Consumer Research, 24*(4), 343–374.

33    Schmidt, H.J., & Redler, J. (2018): 'How diverse is corporate brand management research? Comparing schools of corporate brand management with approaches to corporate strategy'. *Journal of Product & Brand Management, 27*(2), 185–202.

34    Veloutsou, C., & Delgado-Ballester, E. (2018). Guest editorial. *Spanish Journal of Marketing – ESIC, 22*(3), 254–271 (p.256).

35    Meenaghan, T. (1995). 'The role of advertising in brand image development'. *Journal of Product & Brand Management, 4*(4), 23–34 (p.23).

36    Veloutsou, C., & Delgado-Ballester, E. (2018). Guest editorial. *Spanish Journal of Marketing – ESIC, 22*(3), 254–271 (p.256).

37    Ind, N. (1997). *The Corporate Brand*. Palgrave Macmillan, London (p.13).

38    Wiedmann, K.-P. (2015). 'The future of brand and brand management. Some provocative propositions from a more methodological perspective'. *Journal of Brand Management, 21*(9), 743–757 (p.750).

39    In contrast to a market-based view which proposes that comparative advantage can primarily be gained by fulfilling customer needs better than others, this look inside the company has been described as a resource-based view; e.g.: Balmer, J.M.T. (2007). 'A resource-based view of the British monarchy as a corporate brand'. *International Studies of Management and Organization, 37*(4), 20–44.

40  Harris, F., & de Chernatony, L. (2001), 'Corporate branding and corporate brand performance'. *European Journal of Marketing, 35*(3/4), 441–456.

41  Wiedmann, K.-P., Hennigs, N., Schmidt, S., & Wuestefeld, T. (2011). 'The importance of brand heritage as a key performance driver in marketing management'. *Journal of Brand Management, 19*(3), 182–194.

42  Saleem, F.Z., & Iglesias, O. (2016). 'Mapping the domain of the fragmented field of internal branding'. *Journal of Product & Brand Management, 25*(1), 43–57.

43  1) Punjaisri, K., & Wilson, A.M. (2007). 'The role of internal branding in the delivery of employee brand promise'. *Journal of Brand Management, 15*(1), 57–70. 2) Punjaisri, K., Evanschitzky, H., & Wilson, A. M. (2009). 'Internal branding: an enabler of employees' brand supporting behaviours'. *Journal of Service Management, 20*(2), 209–226. 3) Burmann, C., Zeplin, S., & Riley, N. (2009). 'Key determinants of internal brand management success: an exploratory empirical analysis'. *Journal of Brand Management, 16*(4), 264–284.

44  The identity school is closely related to the concept of brand orientation. A brand-oriented company is one that centres all its activities around its brand(s). For example, see: Urde, M. (1999). 'Brand orientation: A mindset for building brands into strategic resources'. *Journal of Marketing Management, 15*(1–3), 117–133. The concept of brand orientation is often demarketed from market orientation. To find out more, we suggest the following reading: Urde, M., Baumgarth, C., & Merrilees, B. (2013). 'Brand orientation and market orientation – From alternatives to synergy'. *Journal of Business Research, 66*(1), 13–20.

45  1) Veloutsou, C., & Delgado-Ballester, E. (2018). Guest editorial. *Spanish Journal of Marketing – ESIC, 22*(3), 254–271 (p.256). 2) Vallaster, C., & von Wallpach, S. (2013). 'An online discursive inquiry into the social dynamics of multi-stakeholder brand meaning co-creation'. *Journal of Business Research, 66*(9), 1505–1515.

46  1) Kornum, N., Gyrd-Jones, R., Al Zagir, N., & Brandis, K.A. (2017). 'Interplay between intended brand identity and identities in a Nike related brand community: Co-existing synergies and tensions in a nested system'. *Journal of Business Research, 70*(3), 432–440. 2) Wallpach, S.V., Hemetsberger, A., & Espersen, P. (2017). 'Performing identities. Processes of brand and stakeholder identity co-construction'. *Journal of Business Research, 70*(3) 443–452.

47  1) Hunter, G.L., & Garnefeld, I. (2008). 'When does consumer empowerment lead to satisfied customers? Some mediating and moderating effects of the empowerment-satisfaction link'. *Journal of Research for Consumers, 15*, 1–14. 2) Arora, N., Dreze, X., Ghose, A., Hess, J.D., Iyengar, R., Jing, B., Joshi, Y., Kumar, V., Lurie, N., & Neslin, S. (2008). 'Putting one-to-one marketing to work: personalization, customization, and choice'. *Marketing Letters, 19*(3/4), 305–321.

48  O'Brien, C. (2011). 'The emergence of the social media empowered consumer'. *Irish Marketing Review, 21*(1/2), 32.

49  1) Franke, N., Keinz, P., & Steger, C.J. (2009). 'Testing the value of customization: when do customers really prefer products tailored to their preferences?' *Journal of Marketing, 73*(5), 103–121. 2) Romero, D., & Molina, A. (2009). 'Value co-creation and co-innovation: linking networked organisations and customer communities'. In Camarinha-Matos, L. M., Paraskakis, I., & Afsarmanesh, H. (eds.), *Proceedings Leveraging Knowledge for Innovation in Collaborative Networks: 10th IFIP WG 5.5 Working Conference on Virtual Enterprises*, PRO-VE 2009, Thessaloniki, Greece, October 7–9, 2009, Springer, Berlin, 401–412.

50  Ihrig, M., & Macmillan, I. C. (2017). 'How to get ecosystem buy-in'. *Harvard Business Review, 95*(2), 102–107.

51   Ind, N., Iglesias, O., & Schultz, M. (2013). 'Building brands together'. *California Management Review, 55*(3), 5–26.

52   Kornberger, M. (2010). *Brand Society: How Brands Transform Management and Lifestyle*. Cambridge, UK: Cambridge University Press (p.248).

53   Janus is the Roman god of beginnings, transitions and time. He is usually depicted with two faces as he looks both to the past and the future.

54   Vallaster, C., & von Wallpach, S. (2013). 'An online discursive inquiry into the social dynamics of multi-stakeholder brand meaning co-creation'. *Journal of Business Research, 66*(9), 1505–1515.

55   Ibid (p.1513).

56   Sjödin, H., & Ind, N. (2006). *Metaphor in Brand Extension*. Paper presented at Narrative in Management Science conference, Barcelona. ESADE: Barcelona.

57   Ind, N., Iglesias, O., & Markovic, S. (2017). 'The co-creation continuum: From tactical market research tool to strategic collaborative innovation method'. *Journal of Brand Management, 24*(4), 310–321.

58   Belova, O., King, I., & Sliwa, M. (2008). 'Introduction: Polyphony and organization studies: Mikhail Bakhtin and beyond'. *Organization Studies, 29*(4), 493–500 (p.495).

59   Kane G.C. (2015). 'Interview with Martyn Etherington (Mitel): Can you really let your employees loose on social media?' *MIT Sloan Management Review, 56*(2).

60   Ind, N. (2014). 'How participation is changing the practice of managing brands'. *Journal of Brand Management, 21*(9), 734–742.

61   Iglesias, O. Ind, N., & Alfaro, M. (2013). 'The organic view of the brand: A brand value co-creation model'. *Journal of Brand Management, 20*(8), 670–688.

62   Vargo, S.L., & Lusch, R.F. (2004). 'Evolving to a new dominant logic for marketing'. *Journal of Marketing, 68*(1), 1–17.

63   Heidegger, M. (1962) *Being and Time*. (Sein und Zeit, Max Niemeyer Verlag, Tübingen). Trans. John Macquarrie and Edward Robinson. Oxford: Blackwell, 190–191.

64   Ramaswamy, V., & Ozcan, K. (2016). 'Brand value co-creation in a digitalized world: An integrative framework and research implications'. *International Journal of Research in Marketing, 33*(1), 93–106.

65   Ind, N., Iglesias, O., & Markovic, S. (2017). 'The co-creation continuum: From tactical market research tool to strategic collaborative innovation method'. *Journal of Brand Management, 24*(4), 310–321.

66   1) Aaker, D.A. (1996). *Building strong brands*. New York: Free Press. 2) Kapferer, J.-N. (2012). *The New Strategic Brand Management: Advanced Insights and Strategic Thinking*. London: Kogan Page.

67   1) Iglesias, O., Markovic, S., Bagherzadeh, M., & Singh, J.J. (2018). 'Co-creation: A key link between corporate social responsibility, customer trust, and customer loyalty'. *Journal of Business Ethics*, https://doi.org/10.1007/s10551-018-4015-y. 2) Kristal, S., Baumgarth, C., & Henseler, J. (2018). '"Brand play" versus "Brand attack": The subversion of brand meaning in non-collaborative co-creation by professional artists and consumer activists'. *Journal of Product and Brand Management, 27*(3), 334–347.

68   Hatch, M.J., & Schultz, M. (2010). 'Towards a theory of brand co-creation with implications for brand governance'. *Journal of Brand Management, 17*(8), 590–604.

69   For example, see: 1) Burmann, C., Jost-Benz, M., & Riley, N. (2009). 'Towards an identity-based brand equity model'. *Journal of Business Research, 62*(3), 390–397. 2) Urde, M., Baumgarth, C., & Merrilees, B. (2013). 'Brand orientation and market orientation: From alternatives to synergy'. *Journal of Business Research, 66*(1), 13–20.

70   Ind, N. (2014). 'How participation is changing the practice of managing brands'. *Journal of Brand Management, 21*(9), 734–742.

71   Ind, N., Fuller, C., & Trevail, C. (2012). *Brand together: How Co-creation Generates Innovation and Re-energizes Brands.* London: Kogan Page.

72   Beverland, M. (2018). *Brand Management: Co-creating Meaningful Brands.* London: Sage.

73   Iglesias, O., Ind, N., & Alfaro, M. (2013). 'The organic view of the brand: A brand value co-creation model'. *Journal of Brand Management, 20*(8), 670–688.

74   For a more extensive review, see: Baumgarth, C. & Kristal, S. (2015). 'Die Mitmachmarke – Forschungsstand und -agenda Brand Co-Creation (BCC)'. *transfer – Werbeforschung & Praxis, 61*(4), 14–20.

75   1) Galvagno, M. & Dalli, D. (2014). 'Theory of value co-creation: A systematic literature review'. *Managing Service Quality: An International Journal, 24*(6), 643–683. 2) Ind, N. & Coates, N. (2013). 'The meanings of co-creation', *European Business Review, 25*(1), 86-95. 3) Ind, N., Iglesias, O. & Schultz, M. (2013). 'Building brands together: Emergence and outcomes of co-creation'. *California Management Review, 55*(3), 5–26. 4) Payne, A., Storbacka, K., Frow, P. & Knox, S. (2009). 'Co-creating brands: Diagnosing and designing the relationship experience'. *Journal of Business Research, 62*(3), 379–389.

76   Bogers, M., Afuah, A., & Bastian, B. (2010). 'Users as innovators: A review, critique, and future research directions'. *Journal of Management, 36*(4), 857–875.

77   Von Hippel, E. (1988). *The Sources of Innovation.* New York: Oxford University Press.

78   Franke, N., & Piller, F. (2004). 'Value Creation by Toolkits for User Innovation and Design: The Case of the Watch Market'. *Journal of Product Innovation Management, 21*, 401–415.

79   Chesbrough, H. (2003). *Open Innovation: The New Imperative for Creating and Profiting from Technology.* Boston: Harvard Business School Press.

80   1) Vargo, S., & Lusch, R. (2004). 'Evolving to a new dominant logic for marketing'. *Journal of Marketing, 68*(1), 1–17. 2) Vargo, S.L., & Lusch, R.F. (2008). 'Service-dominant logic: continuing the evolution'. *Journal of the Academy of Marketing Science, 36*(1), 1–10.

81   Arnould, E., & Thompson, C. (2005). 'Consumer culture theory (CCT): Twenty years of research'. *Journal of Consumer Research, 31*(4), 868–882.

82   1) Holt, D.B. (2004). *How Brands Become Icons: The Principles of Cultural Branding.* Boston: Harvard Business Press. 2) Holt, D., & Cameron, D. (2010). *Cultural strategy: Using Innovative Ideologies to build Breakthrough Brands.* New York: Oxford University Press.

83   1) Muniz, A.M., & O'Guinn, T.C. (2001). 'Brand community'. *Journal of Consumer Research, 27*(4), 412–432. 2) McAlexander, J.H., Schouten, J.W., & Koenig, H.F. (2002). 'Building brand community'. *Journal of Marketing, 66*(1), 38–54. 3) Veloutsou, C. (2009). 'Brands as relationship facilitators in consumer markets'. *Marketing Theory, 9*(1), 127–130. 4) Dessart, L., Veloutsou, C., & Morgan-Thomas, A. (2015). 'Consumer engagement in online brand communities: a social media perspective'. *Journal of Product & Brand Management, 24*(1), 28–42.

84   Christodoulides, G. (2009). 'Branding in the post-internet era'. *Marketing Theory, 9*(1), 141–144.

85   1) Arnhold, U. (2010). *User Generated Branding: Integrating User Generated Content into Brand Management.* Wiesbaden: Springer. 2) Halliday, S.V. (2016). 'User-generated content about brands: Understanding its creators and consumers'. *Journal of Business Research, 69*(1), 137–144.

86 Kristal, S., Baumgarth, C., & Henseler, J. (2018). '"Brand play" versus "Brand attack": The subversion of brand meaning in non-collaborative co-creation by professional artists and consumer activists'. *Journal of Product and Brand Management, 27*(3), 334–347.

87 Ind, N. (2014). 'How participation is changing the practice of managing brands'. *Journal of Brand Management, 21*(9), 734–742.

88 Iglesias, O., Ind, N., & Alfaro, M. (2013). 'The organic view of the brand: A brand value co creation model'. *Journal of Brand Management, 20*(8), 670–688.

89 Kornberger, M. (2010). *Brand Society: How Brands Transform Management and Lifestyle.* Cambridge University Press (p.40).

90 Ind, N., Iglesias, O., & Schultz, M. (2013). 'Building brands together: Emergence and outcomes of co-creation'. *California Management Review, 55*(3), 5–26.

91 Ind, N., Iglesias, O., & Markovic, S. (2017). 'The co-creation continuum: From tactical market research tool to strategic collaborative innovation method'. *Journal of Brand Management, 24*(4), 310–321.

92 Cova, B., & Dalli, D. (2009). 'Working Consumers: The Next Step in Marketing Theory'. *Marketing Theory, 9*(3), 315–339 (p.319).

93 Heidegger, M. (1962) *Being and Time.* (Sein und Zeit, Max Niemeyer Verlag, Tübingen). Trans. John Macquarrie and Edward Robinson. Oxford: Blackwell, 190–191.

94 Prahalad, C.K., & Ramaswamy, V. (2000). 'Co-opting customer competence'. *Harvard Business Review, 78*(1), 79–90.

95 Da Silveira, C., Lages, C., & Simões, C. (2013). 'Reconceptualizing brand identity in a dynamic environment'. *Journal of Business Research, 66*(1), 28–36.

96 Payne, A. F., Storbacka, K., & Frow, P. (2008). 'Managing the co-creation of value'. *Journal of the Academy of Marketing Science, 36*(1), 83–96.

97 Von Wallpach, S., & Kreuzer, M. (2013). 'Multi-sensory sculpting (MSS): Eliciting embodied brand knowledge via multi-sensory metaphors'. *Journal of Business Research, 66*(9), 1325–1331.

98 Vallaster, C., & von Wallpach, S. (2013). 'An online discursive inquiry into the social dynamics of multi-stakeholder brand meaning co-creation'. *Journal of Business Research, 66*(9), 1505–1515.

99 1) Ind, N., Iglesias, O., & Markovic, S. (2017). 'The co-creation continuum: From tactical market research tool to strategic collaborative innovation method'. *Journal of Brand Management, 24*(4), 310–321. 2) Markovic, S., & Bagherzadeh, M. (2018). 'How does breadth of external stakeholder co-creation influence innovation performance? Analyzing the mediating roles of knowledge sharing and product innovation'. *Journal of Business Research, 88*, 173–186.

100 1) McAlexander, J.H., Schouten, J.W., & Koenig, H.F. (2002). 'Building brand community'. *Journal of Marketing, 66*(1), 38–54. 2) Muniz, A.M., Jr., Albert, M., & O'Guinn, T.C. (2001). Brand Community. *The Journal of Consumer Research, 27*(4), 412–432.

101 Muniz, A.M., Jr., Albert, M., & O'Guinn, T.C. (2001). 'Brand Community'. *The Journal of Consumer Research, 27*(4), 412– 432.

102 1) McAlexander, J.H., Schouten, J.W., & Koenig, H.F. (2002). 'Building brand community'. *Journal of Marketing, 66*(1), 38–54. 2) Muniz, A.M., Jr., Albert, M., & O'Guinn, T.C. (2001). 'Brand Community'. *The Journal of Consumer Research, 27*(4), 412– 432.

103 1) Harwood, T., & Garry, T. (2010). '"It's Mine!" – Participation and ownership within virtual co-creation environments'. *Journal of Marketing, 26*(3–4), 290–301. 2) Merz, M.A., He, Y., & Vargo, S.L. (2009). 'The evolving brand logic: A service-dominant logic perspective'. *Journal of the Academy of Marketing Science, 37*(3), 328–344.

104 1) Merz, M.A., He, Y., & Vargo, S.L. (2009). 'The evolving brand logic: A service-dominant logic perspective'. *Journal of the Academy of Marketing Science, 37*(3),

328–344. 2) Vallaster, C., & von Wallpach, S. (2013). 'An online discursive inquiry into the social dynamics of multi-stakeholder brand meaning co-creation'. *Journal of Business Research, 66*(9), 1505–1515.

105   1) Haarhoff, G., & Kleyn, N. (2012). 'Open source brands and their online brand personality'. *Journal of Brand Management, 20*(2), 104–114. 2) Iglesias, O., Ind, N., & Alfaro, M. (2013). 'The organic view of the brand: A brand value co-creation model'. *Journal of Brand Management, 20*(8), 670–688.

106   1) Haarhoff, G., & Kleyn, N. (2012). 'Open source brands and their online brand personality'. *Journal of Brand Management, 20*(2), 104–114. 2) Iglesias, O., & Bonet, E. (2012). 'Persuasive brand management: How managers can influence brand meaning when they are losing control over it'. *Journal of Organizational Change Management, 25*(2), 251–264.

107   Iglesias, O., Ind, N., & Alfaro, M. (2013). 'The organic view of the brand: A brand value co-creation model'. *Journal of Brand Management, 20*(8), 670–688.

108   Libert, B., Wind, Y., & Beck Fenley, M. (2015). 'What Apple, Lending Club, and AirBnB Know About Collaborating with Customers'. *Harvard Business Review.* https://hbr.org/2015/07/what-apple-lending-club-and-airbnb-know-about-collaborating-with-customers (accessed 14 June, 2019).

109   Payne, A.F., Storbacka, K., & Frow, P. (2008). 'Managing the co-creation of value'. *Journal of the Academy of Marketing Science, 36*(1), 83–96.

110   Iglesias, O., Ind, N., & Alfaro, M. (2013). 'The organic view of the brand: A brand value co-creation model'. *Journal of Brand Management, 20*(8), 670–688.

111   Ind, N., Iglesias, O., & Markovic, S. (2017). 'The co-creation continuum: From tactical market research tool to strategic collaborative innovation method'. *Journal of Brand Management, 24*(4), 310–321.

112   Matthing, J., Sandén, B., & Edvardsson, B. (2004). 'New service development: learning from and with customers'. *International Journal of Service Industry Management, 15*(5), 479–498.

113   Von Hippel, E. (2005). *Democratizing Innovation.* Cambridge, MA: The MIT Press.

114   1) Cova, B., & Dalli, D. (2009). 'Working consumers: the next step in marketing theory?' *Marketing Theory, 9*(3), 315–339. 2) von Hippel, E. (2005). *Democratizing Innovation.* Cambridge, MA: The MIT Press

115   1) Dahlsten, F. (2004). 'Hollywood wives revisited: a study of customer involvement in the XC90 project at Volvo Cars'. *European Journal of Innovation Management, 7*(2), 141–149. 2) Mascarenhas, O.A., Kesavan, R., & Bernacchi, M. (2004). 'Customer value-chain involvement for co-creating customer delight'. *Journal of Consumer Marketing, 21*(7), 486–496. 3) Payne, A.F., Storbacka, K., & Frow, P. (2008). 'Managing the co-creation of value'. *Journal of the Academy of Marketing Science, 36*(1), 83–96. 4) Prahalad, C.K., & Ramaswamy, V. (2004). 'Co-creation experiences: The next practice in value creation'. *Journal of Interactive Marketing, 18*(3), 5–14.

116   Sawyer, K. (2008). *Group Genius: The Creative Power of Collaboration.* New York: Basic Books.

117   1) Iglesias, O., Ind, N., & Alfaro, M. (2013). 'The organic view of the brand: A brand value co-creation model'. *Journal of Brand Management, 20*(8), 670–688. 2) Ind, N., Iglesias, O., & Schultz, M. (2013). 'Building brands together'. *California Management Review, 55*(3), 5–26.

118   1) Carù, A., & Cova, B. (2015). 'Co-creating the collective service experience'. *Journal of Service Management, 26*(2), 276–294. 2) Ind, N., Iglesias, O., & Markovic, S. (2017). 'The co-creation continuum: From tactical market research tool to strategic collaborative innovation method'. *Journal of Brand Management, 24*(4), 310–321.

3) Schau, H.J., Muñiz Jr, A.M., & Arnould, E.J. (2009). 'How brand community practices create value'. *Journal of Marketing, 73*(5), 30–51.

119    Nambisan, S., & Baron, R.A. (2007). 'Interactions in virtual customer environments: Implications for product support and customer relationship management'. *Journal of Interactive Marketing, 21*(2), 42–62.

120    Ind, N., Iglesias, O., & Schultz, M. (2013). 'Building brands together'. *California Management Review, 55*(3), 5–26.

121    Füller, J. (2010). 'Refining virtual co-creation from a consumer perspective'. *California Management Review, 52*(2), 98–122.

122    Ibid.

123    1) Hatch, M.J., & Schultz, M. (2010). 'Toward a theory of brand co-creation with implications for brand governance'. *Journal of Brand Management, 17*(8), 590–604. 2) Pini, F.M. (2009). 'The Role of Customers in Interactive Co-Creation Practices: The Italian Scenario'. *Knowledge, Technology & Policy, 22*(1), 61–69. 3) Ramaswamy, V., & Gouillart, F. (2010). 'Building the co-creative enterprise'. *Harvard Business Review, 88*(10), 100–109. 4) Sawhney, M., Verona, G., & Prandelli, E. (2005). 'Collaborating to create: The Internet as a platform for customer engagement in product innovation'. *Journal of Interactive Marketing, 19*(4), 4–17.

124    Jaruzelski, B., Loehr, J., & Holman, R. (2013). 'The global innovation 1000: navigating the digital future'. *Strategy+Business, 73* (Winter), 32–45.

125    1) Schwartz, M.S. (2002). 'A code of ethics for corporate code of ethics'. *Journal of Business Ethics, 41*(1–2), 27–43. 2) Stanislawski, S. (2011). 'The Service-Dominant Logic of Marketing and the Ethics of Co-Creation'. *The Bulletin of the Graduate School of Commerce – Waseda University, 73*, 109–133.

126    Meyassed, D, Peters A., & Coates N. (2010). *Sex, Lies and Chocolate: How communities can change the way you think about innovation for good.* Paper presented at Research 2010, London.

127    Shirky, C. (2010). *Cognitive Surplus: Creativity and Generosity in a Connected Age.* London: Penguin.

128    Delanda, M. (2003). *A Thousand Years of Nonlinear History.* New York: Swerve (p.274).

129    Bal, A.S., Weidner, K., Hanna, R., & Mills, A.J. (2017). 'Crowdsourcing and brand control'. *Business Horizons, 60*(2), 219–228.

130    Ramaswamy, V., & Ozcan, K. (2016). 'Brand value co-creation in a digitalized world: An integrative framework and research implications'. *International Journal of Research in Marketing, 33* (1), p.94

131    Ind, N., Iglesias, O., & Markovic, S. (2017). 'The co-creation continuum: From tactical market research tool to strategic collaborative innovation method'. *Journal of Brand Management, 24*(4), 310–321.

132    Schlack, J.W. (2011). 'The 64% Rule: What real customer engagement looks like'. Communispace Corporation.

133    Von Wallpach, S., Hemetsberger, A., & Espersen, P. (2017). 'Performing identities: Processes of brand and stakeholder identity co-construction'. *Journal of Business Research, 70*, 443–452.

134    Muniz, A. M., & O'Guinn, T. C. (2001). 'Brand community'. *Journal of Consumer Research, 27*(4), 412–432.

135    1) Skålén, P., Pace, S., & Cova, B. (2015). 'Firm-brand community value co-creation as alignment of practices'. *European Journal of Marketing, 49*(3–4), 596–620. 2) Saldanha, F.P., & Pozzebon, M. (2015). 'Fiat Mio: the project that embraced open

innovation, crowdsourcing and creative commons in the automotive sector'. *International Journal of Case Studies in Management, 13*(1).

136 Meyassed, D., Peters, A., & Coates N. (2010). *Sex, Lies and Chocolate: how communities can change the way you think about innovation for good.* Paper presented at Research 2010, London.

137 Heath, C. (1999). 'On the social psychology of agency relationships: Lay theories of motivation overemphasize extrinsic incentives'. *Organizational Behavior and Human Decision Processes, 78*(1), 25–62.

138 Kim, W.C., & Mauborgne, R. (2003). 'Fair process: Managing in the knowledge economy'. *Harvard Business Review, 81*(1), 127–136.

139 Ind, N., & Iglesias, O. (2016). *Brand Desire: How to Create Consumer Involvement and Inspiration.* London: Bloomsbury.

140 Sharp, B. (2010). *How Brands Grow: What Marketers Don't Know.* Oxford: Oxford University Press.

141 Morgan, R.M., & Hunt, S.D. (1994). 'The Commitment-Trust Theory of Relationship Marketing'. *Journal of Marketing, 58*(3), 20–38.

142 Kant, I. (1998). *Groundwork of the Metaphysics of Morals.* Translated and edited by M. Gregor. Cambridge: Cambridge University Press (p.37).

143 Chomsky, N., & Foucault, M. (2006). *The Chomsky-Foucault Debate on Human Nature.* New York: The New Press (p.60).

144 Deci, E.L., & Ryan, R.M. (1985). 'Cognitive evaluation theory'. In *Intrinsic Motivation and Self-Determination in Human Behavior* (pp. 43–85). Boston: Springer.

145 Deci, E.L., Koestner, R., & Ryan, R.M. (1999). 'A meta-analytic review of experiments examining the effects of extrinsic rewards on intrinsic motivation'. *Psychological Bulletin, 125*(6), 627–668.

146 Frey, B.S., & Götte, L. (1999). 'Does pay motivate volunteers?' *Working paper No. 7, Institute for Empirical Research in Economics,* University of Zurich.

147 Gneezy, U., & Rustichini, A. (2000). 'A fine is a price'. *The Journal of Legal Studies, 29*(1), 1–17.

148 Füller, J. (2010). 'Refining Virtual Co-Creation from a Consumer Perspective'. *California Management Review, 52*(2), 98–122

149 Ibid (p116).

150 Mauss, M. (2000). *The Gift: The Form and Reason for Exchange in Archaic Societies.* Translated by W.D. Halls (*Essai sur le don,* Presses Universitaires de France, 1950). London: Routledge.

151 The musician David Byrne notes that in the era of audio cassettes, people would often produce mixtapes of songs and gift them to others 'in a form of potlatch' that required reciprocation. The gift was both a projection of one's own musical tastes and an estimate of what the recipient would like. He argues that the reciprocation wasn't so time sensitive, but there was an expectation of a response: 'The gift of a mixtape was very personal … Other people's music – ordered and collected in infinitely imaginative ways – became a form of expression.' See: Byrne, D. (2013). *How Music Works.* Edinburgh: Canongate (p.117).

152 Dolfsma, W., Eijk. R., & Jolink., A. (2009). 'On a Source of Social Capital: Gift Exchange'. *Journal of Business Ethics, 89*(3), 315–329.

153 Hyde, L. (2012). *The Gift: How the Creative Spirit Transforms the World.* Edinburgh: Canongate.

154 Shirky, C. (2010). *Cognitive Surplus: Creativity and Generosity in a Connected Age.* London: Penguin.

155 Brookings Institute (2018). https://www.brookings.edu/research/millennials (accessed 24 June, 2019).

156 Ellyatt, H. (2015). How trillion-dollar millennials are spending their cash. http://www.cnbc.com/2015/08/17/how-trillion-dollar-millennials-are-spending-their-cash.html (accessed 24 June, 2019).

157 Verganti, R. (2009). *Design Driven Innovation: Changing the Rules of Competition by Radically Innovating What Things Mean*. Cambridge: Harvard Business Press.

158 Ind, N., Iglesias, O., & Markovic, S. (2017). 'The co-creation continuum: From tactical market research tool to strategic collaborative innovation method'. *Journal of Brand Management, 24*(4), 310–321.

159 Störk, U., Kubis, N., & Kleiner A. (2018). 'Leading a company that wants to change lives through sport'. *Strategy+Business*. 10 October, 2018.

160 Ind, N., & Schultz, M. (2010). 'Brand building, Beyond marketing'. *Strategy+Business*. 26 July, 2010.

161 Kornum, N., Gyrd-Jones, R., Al Zagir, N., & Brandis, K.A. (2017). 'Interplay between intended brand identity and identities in a Nike related brand community: Co-existing synergies and tensions in a nested system'. *Journal of Business Research, 70*, 432–440.

162 1) Hatch, M-J, & Schultz, M. (2017). 'Toward a Theory of Using History Authentically: Historicizing in the Carlsberg Group'. *Administrative Science Quarterly, 62*(4), 657–697. 2) Howard-Grenville, J., Metzger, M.L., & Meyer, A.D. (2013). 'Rekindling the flame: Processes of identity resurrection'. *Academy of Management Journal, 56*(1), 113–136. 3) Kaplan, S., & Orlikowsky, W. (2014). Beyond forecasting: Creating new strategic narratives. Sloan Management Review, *56*(1), 23–28.

163 Mead, G.H. (1913). 'The Social Self'. *The Journal of Philosophy, Psychology and Scientific Methods*, X, 374–380. In Thayer, H.S. (1982; ed.), *Pragmatism: The Classic Writings*. Indianopolis: Hackett.

164 Ind, N., Fuller, C., & Trevail, C. (2012). *Brand Together: How Co-Creation Generates Innovation and Re-Energizes Brands*. London: Kogan Page.

165 Schultz, M., & Hernes, T. (2013). 'A temporal perspective on organizational identity'. *Organization Science, 24*(1), 1–21.

166 Salter, A., Ter Wal, A.L., Criscuolo, P., & Alexy, O. (2015). 'Open for ideation: Individual-level openness and idea generation in R&D'. *Journal of Product Innovation Management, 32*(4), 488–504 (p.501).

167 Griffith, E. (2018). 'Sociologists examine Hackathons and see exploitation'. *Wired*. 20 August, 2018.

168 Lifshitz-Assaf, H. (2015). 'From Problem Solvers to Solution Seekers: Knowledge Boundaries Permeation at NASA'. In *Academy of Management Proceedings* (Vol. 2015, No. 1, p.14234). Briarcliff Manor, NY 10510: Academy of Management.

169 Dahlsten, F. (2004). 'Hollywood wives revisited: a study of customer involvement in the XC90 project at Volvo Cars'. *Journal of Innovation Management, 7*(2), 141–149.

170 Prandelli, E., Verona, G., & Raccagni, D. (2006). 'Diffusion of Web-Based Product Innovation'. *California Management Review, 48*(4), 109–135.

171 The use of this particular word is interesting, because it refers to pirates that operated on behalf of the French crown during the seventeenth and eighteenth centuries.

172 Verganti, R. (2016). 'The innovative power of criticism'. *Harvard Business Review, 94*(1), 88–95.

173 Iglesias, O., Ind, N., & Alfaro M. (2013). 'The organic view of the brand: a brand value co-creation model'. *Journal of Brand Management, 20*(8), 670–688.

174 Morhart, F. (2017). 'Unleashing the internal fan community through brand-oriented leadership'. In Ind, N. (ed.), *Branding Inside Out: Internal Branding in Theory and in Practice*. London: Kogan Page, 33–50.

175 Lindley, M., Schwartz, J., & Thompson, M. (2018). 'When cultural values lead to Groupthink, the company loses'. *Strategy+Business*. 12 November, 2018.

176 Ramaswamy, V., & Ozcan, K. (2018). 'What is co-creation? An interactional creation framework and its implications for value creation'. *Journal of Business Research, 84*(3), 196–205.

177 Gourville, J. T. (2005). 'The Curse of Innovation: A Theory of Why Innovative New Products Fail in the Marketplace'. *HBS Marketing Research Paper No. 05-06.* https:// ssrn.com/abstract=777644 (accessed 12 March, 2019).

178 See *The Times* list of the 20 most successful technology failures of all time at http:// time.com/4704250/most-successful-technology-tech-failures-gadgets-flops-bombs-fails (accessed 27 February, 2019). You may also want to have a look at the bestseller book of the eighties *In Search of Excellence* and all the excellent companies in it that then failed: Peters, T.J., & Waterman, R.H. Jr. (1982). *In Search of Excellence: Lessons from America's Best-Run Companies*. New York: Harper & Row.

179 See, for example: 1) Noble, Ch. H., Sinha, R.K., & Kumar, A. (2002). 'Market Orientation and Alternative Strategic Orientations: A Longitudinal Assessment of Performance Implications'. *Journal of Marketing, 66*(4), 25–39. 2) Deutscher, F., Zapkau, F.B., Schwens, C., Baum, M., & Kabst, R. (2016). Strategic orientations and performance: A configurational perspective. *Journal of Business Research, 69*(2), 849–861.

180 Schmidt, H.J., Baumgarth, C., Wiedmann, K.P., & Lückenbach, F. (2015). 'Strategic orientations and the performance of Social Entrepreneurial Organisations (SEOs): A conceptual model'. *Social Business, 5*(2), 131–155.

181 Ferrell, O. C., & Hartline, M. D. (2011). *Marketing Strategy*. Mason: South Western (p.398).

182 Urde, M., Baumgarth, C., & Merilees, B. (2011). 'Brand orientation and market orientation – From alternatives to synergy'. *Journal of Business Research, 66*(1), 13–20 (p.13).

183 Keller, K.L. (1993). 'Conceptualizing, Measuring, and Managing Customer-Based Brand Equity'. *Journal of Marketing, 57*(1), 1–22 (p.2).

184 See, for example: 1) Moen, R., & Norman, C. (2006). *Evolution of the PDCA Cycle.* http:// citeseerx.ist.psu.edu/viewdoc/download?doi=10.1.1.470.5465&rep=rep1&type=pdf (accessed 12 March, 2019). 2) Sokovic, M., Pavletic, D., & Pipan, K.K. (2010). 'Quality improvement methodologies – PDCA cycle, RADAR matrix, DMAIC and DFSS'. *Journal of Achievements in Materials and Manufacturing Engineering, 43*(1), 476–483.

185 For example, see: 1) Aaker's (1998) brand identity planning model, 2) Keller's (2013) strategic brand management process, or 3) the concept of identity-based brand management proposed by Burmann et al. (2017). 1) Aaker, D.A. (1996). *Building Strong Brands*. New York: Free Press. 2) Keller, K.L. (2013). *Strategic Management: Building, Measuring and Managing Brand Equity* (4th ed.). Harkow: Pearson. 3) Burmann C., Riley N.M., Halaszovich T., & Schade M. (2017). *Identity-Based Brand Management*. Wiesbaden: Springer Gabler.

186 Here and in the following paragraphs, please consider: Aaker, D.A. (1996). *Building Strong Brands*. New York: Free Press.

187 Ibid, p.68 and p.69.

188 One model of recent date overcomes the described critics: Da Silveira and her colleagues argue that a brand's identity is formed by mutual encounters, when the

brand's face meets the consumer's face, all influenced by industry and environmental conditions and competitors and partners' interactions. See: Da Silveira, C., Lages, C., & Simões, C. (2013). Reconceptualizing brand identity in a dynamic environment. *Journal of Business Research, 66*(1), 28–36.

189 The metaphor of a rubber band was originally introduced to brand management literature by researcher Carsten Baumgarth. See: Baumgarth, C. (2018). 'Elastisch ist das neue Schwarz der Markenführung – oder was ein Gummiband mit Markenführung zu tun hat'. In Steiner, H. (ed.), *Real Estate Brand Book 2018*, Berlin, 12–15.

190 The case has already been well described in various settings but serves as a good illustration of our proposed brand management cycle. See: Schmidt, H.J. (2017). 'Living brand orientation: how a brand-oriented culture supports employees to live the brand'. In Ind, N. (ed.). *Branding Inside Out: Internal Branding in Theory and Practice*. London: Kogan Page, 13–31.

191 The brand-oriented approach of the German TNT subsidiary lost speed in 2009 when, also as a result of the financial crisis, more and more decision structures were centralised within the corporate group, and came to an end when rumours began to circulate that TNT Express would merge with UPS. Today, following the involvement of the European cartel authorities, TNT Express is part of Federal Express.

192 This process will be explained in detail in chapter 7, where we will also discuss the differences between brand identity and brand image.

193 Salinas, G. (2016). Brand valuation: principles, applications and latest developments. In Dall'Olmo Riley, F., Singh, J., & Blankson, Ch. (eds.): *The Routledge Companion to Contemporary Brand Management*. London: Routledge, 80–99.

194 The latest global list and country-specific adaptations can be accessed via the following link: www.interbrand.com/best-brands (accessed 12 March, 2019).

195 See the company's explanation of their methodology here: www.interbrand.com/best-brands/best-global-brands/methodology (accessed 12 March, 2019).

196 1) Hatch, M.-J., & Schultz, M. (2017). 'Toward a Theory of Using History Authentically: Historicizing in the Carlsberg Group'. *Administrative Science Quarterly, 62*(4), 657–697. 2) Kaplan, S., & Orlikowsky, W. (2014). 'Beyond forecasting: Creating new strategic narratives'. *Sloan Management Review, 56*(1), 23–28.

197 In his model explaining perceived brand authenticity, the independent variables 'Continuity' and 'Consistency' are the most important drivers of the dependent variable 'Perceived Brand Authenticity'. See: Schallehn, M. (2012). *Marken-Authentizität – Konstrukt, Determinanten und Wirkungen aus Sicht der identitätsbasierten Markenführung* Brand authenticity – Construct, determinants and impact from the viewpoint of identity-based brand management. Wiesbaden: Springer Gabler (p.168).

198 Burmann, C., Riley, N.M., Halaszovich, T., & Schade, M. (2017). *Identity-Based Brand Management*. Wiesbaden: Springer Gabler (pp.76–77).

199 See relevant milestones of the history of A. Lange und Söhne at the company's website: https://www.alange-soehne.com/en/stories/rebirth-a-lange-soehne (accessed 12 March, 2019).

200 1) Brunninge, O. (2009). 'Using history in organizations: How managers make purposeful reference to history in strategy processes'. *Journal of Organizational Change Management, 22*(1), 8–26. 2) Ericson, M. (2006). 'Exploring the future exploiting the past'. *Journal of Management History, 12*(2), 121–136.

201 Garud, R., & Karnoe, P. (2001). *Path Dependence and Creation*. New York: Psychology Press.

202 Kaplan, S., & Orlikowsky, W. (2014). 'Beyond forecasting: Creating new strategic narratives'. *Sloan Management Review, 56*(1), 23–28 (p24).

203 Ahrendts, A. (2013). Burberry's CEO on turning an aging British icon into a global luxury brand. *Harvard Business Review, 91*(1), 39–42.

204 Feige's article with the headline 'The future of brand management' is online available at: www.brand-trust.de/en/article/2017/future-of-brand-management.php (accessed 12 March, 2019).

205 Gietl, J. (2013). Value Branding. Freiburg: Haufe.

206 See https://www.wisag.de/unternehmen/leitbild-und-marke.html (accessed: 12 March, 2019).

207 For example, see: 1) Hsieh, M.H. (2002). 'Identifying brand image dimensionality and measuring the degree of brand globalization: A cross-national study'. *Journal of International Marketing, 10*(2), 46–67. 2) Aaker, J.L. (1997). 'Dimensions of brand personality'. *Journal of Marketing* Research, 34(3), 347–356. Corresponding scales have been adopted for several sectors – see the following for various examples: Zarantonello, L., & Pauwels-Delassus, V. (2015). *The Handbook of Brand Management Scales*. London: Routledge.

208 Cambria, E., Das, D., Bandyopadhyay, S., & Feraco, A. (eds.). (2017). *A Practical Guide to Sentiment Analysis*. Cham: Springer.

209 Witell, L., Kristensson, P., Gustafsson, A., & Löfgren, M. (2011). 'Idea generation: customer co-creation versus traditional market research techniques'. *Journal of Service Management, 22*(2), 140–159.

210 Meyassed, D., Peters A., & Coates N. (2010). *Sex, Lies and Chocolate: How communities can change the way you think about innovation for good*. Paper presented at Research 2010, London.

211 Zaltman, G. (2003). *How Customers Think: Essential Insights into the Mind of the Market*. Boston: Harvard Business Press. Also see: Beverland, M. (2018). *Brand Management: Co-creating Meaningful Brands*. London: Sage. The ZMET technique is explained on p.109.

212 O'Reilly, K. (2008). *Key Concepts in Ethnography*. London: Sage (p.16).

213 Anderson, K. (2009). Ethnographic research: A key to strategy. *Harvard Business Review, 87*(3), 24.

214 Schmid, C.J. (2009). *Outlaw Motorcycle Gangs: analyzing the unlikely case of the successful organization of deviant and/or delinquent individuals as brand communities*. Paper for the 25th EGOS Colloquium in Barcelona.

215 Ind, N., Trevail, C., & Fuller, C. (2012). *Brand Together: How Co-Creation Generates Innovation and Re-Energizes Brands*. London: Kogan Page.

216 Kozinets, R.V. (2002). 'Can consumers escape the market? Emancipatory illuminations from burning man'. *Journal of Consumer Research, 29*(1), 20–38.

217 Pickover, C. A. (2001). *Dreaming the Future: The Fantastic Story of Prediction*. Amherst: Prometheus Books.

218 Kozinets, R. V. (2019). *Netnography: The Essential Guide to Qualitative Social Media Research*. London: SAGE.

219 Kozinets, R. V. (2002). 'The field behind the screen: Using netnography for marketing research in online communities'. *Journal of Marketing* Research, 39(01), 61–72 (p.66).

220 Von Hippel, E. (1986). 'Lead users: a source of novel product concepts'. *Management Science, 32*(7), 791–805 (p.791).

221 Kozinets, R. V. (2002). 'The field behind the screen: Using netnography for marketing research in online communities'. *Journal of Marketing* Research, 39(01), 61–72.

222 Ibid (p.70).

223 Belz, F.-M., & Baumbach, W. (2010). 'Netnography as a method of lead user identification'. *Creativity and Innovation Management, 19*(03), 304–313.

224   Ibid (p311).
225   Brem, A., & Bilgram, V. (2015). The search for innovative partners in co-creation: Identifying lead users in social media through netnography and crowdsourcing. *Journal of Engineering and Technology Management, 37*, 40–51.
226   Ibid (p.48).
227   Lévy, P. (1997). *Collective Intelligence: Mankind's Emerging World in Cyberspace.* New York: Perseus books.
228   Jenkins, H. (2006). *Convergence Culture: Where Old and New Media Collide.* New York: New York University Press.
229   Kozinets, R., Patterson, A., & Ashman, R. (2016). 'Networks of desire: How technology increases our passion to consume', *Journal of Consumer Research, 43*(5), 659–682.
230   Brem, A., & Bilgram, V. (2015). 'The search for innovative partners in co-creation: Identifying lead users in social media through netnography and crowdsourcing'. *Journal of Engineering and Technology Management, 37*, 40–51.
231   Zeng, M. A., Koller, H., & Jahn, R. (2019). 'Open radar groups: The integration of online communities into open foresight processes'. *Technological Forecasting and Social Change, 138*, 204–217.
232   Ibid (p.215).
233   Kozinets, R. V. (2019). *Netnography: The Essential Guide to Qualitative Social Media Research.* London: SAGE.
234   Ibid.
235   Kozinets, R. V. (2002). 'The field behind the screen: Using netnography for marketing research in online communities'. *Journal of Marketing Research, 39*(01), 61–72 (p.66).
236   Ibid.
237   Aaker, D. A. (1996). *Building Strong Brands.* New York: Free Press (p.194).
238   See: www.adweek.com/creativity/apples-get-mac-complete-campaign-130552 (accessed 12 March, 2019) for all 66 TV spots that aired during the campaign's run. In 2010, Adweek declared 'Get a Mac' to be the best advertising campaign of the first decade of the new century.
239   Aaker, D.A. (1996). *Building Strong Brands.* New York: Free Press (p191). Also compare the contribution of Lucy Gill-Simmen later in chapter 9 of this book. She identifies functional, symbolic and experiential benefits.
240   See: https://www.deutsche-startups.de/2017/08/14/glossybox-the-hut-group (accessed April 28, 2019).
241   See: https://gik.media/cms/wp-content/uploads/2018/08/b4ptrends_04_August_Influencer.pdf (accessed 28 April, 2019).
242   The term 'megatrends' goes back to the American professor, author and researcher John Naisbitt whose book of the same title was translated into 57 languages and headed the best-selling lists for months at the beginning of the eighties. See: Naisbitt, J. (1982). *Megatrends: Ten New Directions Transforming Our Lives.* New York: Warner Books.
243   See https://www.zukunftsinstitut.de/dossier/megatrends (accessed 6 March, 2019).
244   Florin, D., Callen, B., Mullen, S., & Kropp, J. (2007). 'Profiting from mega-trends'. *Journal of Product & Brand Management, 16*(4), 220–225.
245   See https://www.audi.com/de/company/research/audi-innovation-research.html (accessed 2 June, 2019).
246   Merleau-Ponty, M. (1945) (2002). *Phenomenology of Perception* (*Phénoménologie de la perception*, Gallimard, Paris). Translated by C. Smith. London: Routledge.
247   Nietzsche F. (1889/1895) (2003*). Twilight of the Idols and the Anti-Christ.* (*Götzen-Dämmerung & der Antichrist*). Translated by R. J. Hollingdale. London: Penguin (p.36).

248  Freedman, L. (2013). *Strategy: A History*. Oxford: Oxford University Press (p.72).

249  Da Silveira, C., Lages, C., & Simões, C. (2013). 'Reconceptualizing brand identity in a dynamic environment'. *Journal of Business Research, 66*(1), 28–36 (p.28).

250  Keller, K.L. (1993). 'Conceptualizing, measuring, and managing customer-based brand equity'. *Journal of Marketing, 57*(1), 1–22.

251  Kapferer, J.-N. (1992). *Strategic Brand Management: New Approaches to Creating and Evaluating Brand Equity*. London: Kogan Page.

252  Aaker, D. (1996). *Building Strong Brands*. New York: The Free Press.

253  De Chernatony, L. (1999). 'Brand management through narrowing the gap between brand identity and brand reputation'. *Journal of Marketing Management, 15*(1–3), 157–179.

254  Nandan, S. (2005). 'An exploration of the brand identity–brand image linkage: A communications perspective'. *Journal of Brand Management, 12*(4), 264–278.

255  Veloutsou, C., and Delgado-Ballester, E. (2018). Guest editorial. *Spanish Journal of Marketing – ESIC, 22*(3), 255–272.

256  Von Wallpach, S., Voyer, B., Kastanakis, M., & Mühlbacher, H. (2017). 'Co-creating stakeholder and brand identities: Introduction to the special section'. *Journal of Business Research, 70*, 395–398.

257  Iglesias, O., Ind, N., & Alfaro, M. (2017). 'The organic view of the brand: A brand value co-creation model'. *Journal of Brand Management, 20*(8), 670–688 (p.685).

258  Kornum, N., Gyrd-Jones, R., Al Zagir, N., & Brandis, K.A. (2017). 'Interplay between intended brand identity and identities in a Nike related brand community: Co-existing synergies and tensions in a nested system'. *Journal of Business Research, 70*, 432–440. The term 'conversational space' is used by: Iglesias, O., Ind, N., & Alfaro, M. (2017). The organic view of the brand: A brand value co-creation model. *Journal of Brand Management, 20*(8), 670–688 (p.673).

259  For a deeper understanding of the differences between intended and enacted identity, see: Hemetsberger, A., & Mühlbacher, H. (2009). 'Do brands have an identity? A critical reflection and extension of the brand identity construct'. In *Proceedings of the 38th EMAC Conference*, Nantes.

260  Deleuze, G. (1983). *Nietzsche and Philosophy*. Translated by H. Tomlinson. London: Athlone.

261  Da Silveira, C., Lages, C., & Simões, C. (2013). 'Reconceptualizing brand identity in a dynamic environment'. *Journal of Business Research, 66*(1), 28–36.

262  Ibid. Also see: Kennedy, E., & Guzmán, F. (2016). 'Co-creation of brand identities: consumer and industry influence and motivations'. *Journal of Consumer Marketing, 33*(5), 313–323.

263  The table is partly taken from: Burmann, C., Jost-Benz, M., & Riley, N. (2009). 'Towards an identity-based brand equity model'. *Journal of Business Research, 62*(3), 390–397 (p.391)

264  Aaker, D.A., & Joachimsthaler, E. (2012). *Brand Leadership*. New York: The Free Press.

265  Kapferer, J.-N. (1992). *Strategic Brand Management: New Approaches to Creating and Evaluating Brand Equity*. London: Kogan Page.

266  Aaker, D. (1996). *Building Strong Brands*. New York: The Free Press.

267  De Chernatony, L. (1999). 'Brand management through narrowing the gap between brand identity and brand reputation'. *Journal of Marketing Management, 15*(1–3), 157–179.

268  Burmann, C., Halaszovich, T., Schade, M., & Hemmann, F. (2017). *Identity-based Brand Management*. Wiesbaden: Springer Gabler.

269 Greyser, S.A., & Urde, M. (2019). 'What Does Your Corporate Brand Stand For?' *Harvard Business Review*, January–February 2019, 82–89.

270 See: https://www.patagonia.com/company-info.html (accessed 26 April, 2019).

271 See: https://www.tomra.com/en/about-us/our-mission (accessed 27 April, 2019).

272 Urde, M., & Koch, C. (2014). 'Market and brand-oriented schools of positioning'. *Journal of Product & Brand Management, 23*(7), 478–490.

273 In German, the following words were used to define the brand values: '*Kreativität, modernes Design, außergewöhnlich, Einsatz, partnerschaftlich*'. The brand core was defined as '*Mut zur kreativen Veränderung*'.

274 Ind, N., Fuller, C., & Trevail, C. (2012). *Brand Together. How Co-Creation Generates Innovation and Re-Energizes Brands*. London: Kogan Page.

275 Spall, Chr., & Schmidt, H.J. (2019): *Personal Branding*. Wiesbaden: Springer Gabler.

276 Guzmán, F., Paswan, A.K., & Kennedy, E. (2018). 'Consumer brand value co-creation typology'. *Journal of Creating Value, 4*(2), 1–13.

277 Remember, that in chapter 1, and building on the arguments of Veloutsou and Delgado-Ballester, we used the term 'brand meaning' to describe the reflection of 'internal and external stakeholders' mind-set about a brand'. See: Veloutsou, C., & Delgado-Ballester, E. (2018). Guest editorial. *Spanish Journal of Marketing – ESIC, 22*(3), 254–271 (p.256).

278 To better understand the various communication objectives, see: Hallahan, K. (2015). Organizational goals and communication objectives in strategic communication. In: Holtzhausen, D., & Zerfass, A. (ed.), *The Routledge Handbook of Strategic Communication*, New York: Routledge, 244–266.

279 A good overview on the marketing communication instruments is given in the following textbook: De Pelsmacker, P., Geuens, M., & van den Bergh, J. (2017). *Marketing Communications: A European Perspective*. Harlow: Pearson.

280 1) Hatch, M.J., & Schultz, M. (2008). *Taking Brand Initiative: How Companies can Align Strategy, Culture, and Identity through Corporate Branding*. New York: John Wiley & Sons. 2) Ind, N., & Iglesias, O. (2016). *Brand Desire: How to Create Consumer Involvement and Inspiration*. London: Bloomsbury.

281 Urde, M. (2003). 'Core value-based corporate brand building'. *European Journal of Marketing, 37*(7/8), 1017–1040.

282 Barthes, R. (1968). *The Death of the Author. Modern Criticism and Theory*. London: Longman.

283 1) Da Silveira, C., Lages, C., & Simões, C. (2013). 'Reconceptualizing brand identity in a dynamic environment'. *Journal of Business Research, 66*(1), 28–36. 2) Vallaster, C., & von Wallpach, S. (2013). 'An online discursive inquiry into the social dynamics of multi-stakeholder brand meaning co-creation'. *Journal of Business Research, 66*(9), 1505–1515. 3) von Wallpach, S., Hemetsberger, A., & Espersen, P. (2017). 'Performing identities. Processes of brand and stakeholder identity co-construction'. *Journal of Business Research, 70*(3), 443–452.

284 See: https://www.theguardian.com/sport/2017/feb/06/super-bowl-ad-prompts-trump-supporters-to-boycott-budweiser (accessed 13 May, 2019).

285 Kornberger, M. (2010). *Brand Society: How Brands Transform Management and Lifestyle*. Cambridge: Cambridge University Press (p.248). Also see: 1) Hemetsberger, A., & Mühlbacher, H. (2015). *The co-created, co-generated and co-constructed brand*. Paper presented at 44th EMAC Conference, 26–29 May, Leuven. 2) Iglesias, O., Ind, N., & Alfaro, M. (2013). 'The organic view of the brand. A brand value co-creation model'. *Journal of Brand Management, 20*(8), 670–688.

286 Gyrd-Jones, R.I., & Kornum, N. (2013). 'Managing the co-created brand. Value and cultural complementarity in online and offline multi-stakeholder ecosystems'. *Journal of Business Research, 66*(9), 1484–1493.

287 Kornum, N., Gyrd-Jones, R., Al Zagir, N., & Brandis, K.A. (2017). 'Interplay between intended brand identity and identities in a Nike related brand community. Co-existing synergies and tensions in a nested system'. *Journal of Business Research, 70*(3), 432–440.

288 Uffindel, E., & Paterson, S. (2016). 'Partnership for all'. In: Horlings, S., and Ind, N. (eds.), *Brands with a Conscience: How to Build a Successful and Responsible Brand*, London: Kogan Page, 31–44.

289 Von Wallpach, S., Hemetsberger, A., & Espersen, P. (2017). 'Performing identities. Processes of brand and stakeholder identity co-construction'. *Journal of Business Research, 70*(3), 443–452.

290 Hemetsberger, A., & Mühlbacher, H. (2015). *The co-created, co-generated and co-constructed brand.* Paper presented at 44th EMAC Conference, 26–29 May, Leuven.

291 Hatch, M. J., & Schultz, M. (2017). 'Toward a Theory of Using History Authentically. Historicizing in the Carlsberg Group'. *Administrative Science Quarterly*, 1–41.

292 Holt, D.B. (2004). *How Brands Become Icons: The Principles of Cultural Branding.* Boston: Harvard Business Press.

293 Ibid (p.70).

294 Guzmán, F., Paswan, A.K., & Kennedy, E. (2018). 'Consumer brand value co-creation typology'. *Journal of Creating Value, 4*(2), 1–13.

295 Howe, J. (2006). 'Crowdsourcing: a definition. Wired Blog Network: Crowdsourcing. Cited by: Whitla, P. (2009). Crowdsourcing and its application in marketing activities'. *Contemporary Management Research, 5*(1), 15–28.

296 See: https://www.starbucks.ca/coffeehouse/learn-more/my-starbucks-idea (accessed 29 May, 2019).

297 https://en.eyeka.com (accessed 29 May, 2019).

298 https://en.eyeka.com/story/oral-b (accessed 29 May, 2019).

299 Füller, J. (2012): 'Die Gefahren des Crowdsourcing'. *Harvard Business Manager* (27 June, 2012). https://www.harvardbusinessmanager.de/blogs/a-840963-2.html (accessed 29 May, 2019).

300 See: 1) https://en.wikipedia.org/wiki/Simba_Chips (accessed 20 May, 2019). 2) https://www.rclfoods.com/ouma (accessed 20 May, 2019).

301 See: 1) https://en.wikipedia.org/wiki/Simba_Chips (accessed 20 May, 2019). 2) https://www.foodstuffsa.co.za/simba-uncovers-creative-south-african-flavours (accessed 20 May, 2019).

302 See: 1) https://www.foodstuffsa.co.za/simba-flavour-winner-announced (accessed 20 May, 2019). 2) https://www.foodstuffsa.co.za/simba-uncovers-creative-south-african-flavours (accessed 20 May, 2019).

303 See: https://www.foodstuffsa.co.za/simba-and-steers-come-together-to-deliver-new-chip-flavour (accessed 20 May, 2019).

304 Ibid.

305 Guzmán, F., Paswan, A. K., & Kennedy, E. (2018). 'Consumer brand value co-creation typology'. *Journal of Creating Value, 4*(2), 1–13 (p.4).

306 Peterson, R. A. (2005). 'In Search of Authenticity'. *Journal of Management Studies, 42*(5), 1083–1098.

307 Beverland, M. B. (2005). 'Crafting Brand Authenticity: The Case of Luxury Wines'. *Journal of Management Studies, 42*(5), 1003–1029. See also: Sjödin, H., & Ind, N. (2011). 'Metaphor in brand extension'. In: Bonet, E., Czarniawska, B., McCloskey, D., & Jensen, H. (eds.), *Management and Persuasion*, Barcelona: ESADE (147–166).

308  Ajuntament de Barcelona (2019). *Identitat I posicionament de Barcelona*. Un relat coral (p.7).

309  In Catalan, the definition was the following (ibid, pp.45–50): '*La Ciutat dels projectes vitals*', '*Un model de progress que fa possible el creixement personal I professional I gaudir d'una vida plena en tots els sentits*.'

310  See: https://www.samsung.com/de/reimagine-streetart (accessed 15 May, 2019).

311  Sjödin, H., & Ind, N. (2011): 'Metaphor in brand extension'. In: Bonet, E., Czarniawska, B., McCloskey, D., & Jensen, H. (eds.), *Management and Persuasion*, Barcelona: ESADE (p.148).

312  Gyrd-Jones, R.I., & Kornum, N. (2013). 'Managing the co-created brand: Value and cultural complementarity in online and offline multi-stakeholder ecosystems'. *Journal of Business Research, 66*(9), 1484–1493

313  Li, L.P., Juric, B., & Brodie, R.J. (2017). 'Dynamic multi-actor engagement in networks: the case of United Breaks Guitars'. *Journal of Service Theory and Practice, 27*(4), 738–760.

314  Erz, A., & Christensen, A.B.H. (2018). 'Transforming consumers into brands: tracing transformation processes of the practice of blogging'. *Journal of Interactive Marketing, 43*, 69–82.

315  1) Gyrd-Jones, R.I., & Kornum, N. (2013). 'Managing the co-created brand: Value and cultural complementarity in online and offline multi-stakeholder ecosystems'. *Journal of Business Research, 66*(9), 1484–1493. 2) Vallaster, C., & von Wallpach, S. (2013). 'An online discursive inquiry into the social dynamics of multi-stakeholder brand meaning co-creation'. *Journal of Business Research, 66*(9), 1505–1515. 3) von Wallpach, S., Voyer, B., Kastanakis, M., & Mühlbacher, H. (2017). Co-creating stakeholder and brand identities: Introduction to the special section. *Journal of Business Research, 70*, 395–398.

316  Fournier, S., & Avery, J. (2011). 'The uninvited brand'. *Business Horizons, 54*(3), 193–207 (p.194).

317  Arvidsson, A., & Caliandro, A. (2015). 'Brand public'. *Journal of Consumer Research, 42*(5), 727–748.

318  Kozinets, R. (2017). 'Brand Networks as the Interplay of Identities, Selves, and Turtles: Commentary on "Interplay between intended brand identity and identities in a Nike related brand community: Co-existing synergies and tensions in a nested system"'. *Journal of Business Research, 70*, 441–442.

319  Lury, C. (2004). *Brands: The Logos of the Global Economy*. London: Routledge.

320  Holt, D. B. (2002). 'Why do brands cause trouble? A dialectical theory of consumer culture and branding'. *Journal of Consumer Research, 29*(1), 70–90.

321  Askegaard, S., & Linnet, J.T. (2011). 'Towards an epistemology of consumer culture theory: Phenomenology and the context of context'. *Marketing Theory, 11*(4), 381–404.

322  Kornum, N., Gyrd-Jones, R., Al Zagir, N. & Brandis, K.A. (2017). 'Interplay between intended brand identity and identities in a Nike related brand community: Co-existing synergies and tensions in a nested system'. *Journal of Business Research, 70*, 432–440.

323  Iglesias, O., & Bonet, E. (2012). 'Persuasive brand management: How managers can influence brand meaning when they are losing control over it'. *Journal of Organizational Change Management, 25*(2), 251–264.

324  Burke, K. (1966). *Language as Symbolic Action: Essays on Life, Literature, and Method*, Berkeley: University of California Press.

325  Charland, M. (1987). 'Constitutive rhetoric: The case of the Peuple Quebecois'. *Quarterly Journal of Speech, 73*(2), 133–150.

326  Holt, D.B. (2002). 'Why do brands cause trouble? A dialectical theory of consumer culture and branding'. *Journal of Consumer Research, 29*(1), 70–90.

327 Muñiz Jr., A.M., & O'Guinn, T.C. (2001). 'Brand Community'. *Journal of Consumer Research, 27*(4), 412–432.

328 Saak, R., & Schmidt, H.J. (2019). *Co-Creation of Brand Identities in the Context of Brand Communities: An Empirical Study.* Presentation at the 14th Global Brand Conference, May 2019, Berlin. Of course, brand communities also face the risk of negative communication about the brand (e.g., negative word-of-mouth).

329 See https://rennlist.com/forums/register.php (Porsche); https://www.sap.com/ community.html (SAP).

330 Ind, N., Iglesias, O., & Schultz, M. (2013). Building brands together: Emergence and outcomes of co-creation. *California Management Review, 55*(3), 5–26.

331 Ibid (pp.16–17).

332 Hearn, A., & Schoenhoff, S. (2016). 'From celebrity to influencer'. In Marshall, P.D., & Redmond, S. (eds.), *A Companion to Celebrity*, Wiley: London, 194–212 (p.194).

333 Key findings of the Influencer Marketing Benchmark Report 2019 show that the outlook for influencer marketing is still extremely positive. See: https://influencermarketinghub. com/influencer-marketing-2019-benchmark-report (accessed 20 May, 2019).

334 Feick, L.F., & Price, L.L. (1987). The market maven: A diffuser of marketplace information. *Journal of Marketing, 51*(1), 83–97.

335 Gross, J., & Wangenheim, F.V. (2018). 'The Big Four of Influencer Marketing. A Typology of Influencers'. *Marketing Review St. Gallen, 2*, 30–38.

336 Business of Fashion (2019). *Special Report: How to Maximise Your Influencer Strategy.* https://www.businessoffashion.com/articles/education/how-to-maximise-your-influencer-strategy (accessed 30 May, 2019).

337 Vinerean, S. (2017). 'Importance of strategic social media marketing'. *Expert Journal of Marketing, 5*(1), 28–35. See also: Morrison, K., 2017. *Influencer Marketing Is Becoming an Essential Business Strategy* (Survey). http://www.adweek.com/digital/ influencer-marketing-is-becoming-an-essential-business-strategy-survey (accessed 20 May, 2019).

338 Morteo, I. (2018). 'Influencers as Enhancers of the Value Co-Creation Experience'. *Global Journal of Business Research, 12*(2), 91–100.

339 1) Iglesias, O., Markovic, S., Bagherzadeh, M., & Singh, J.J. (2018). 'Co-creation: A key link between corporate social responsibility, customer trust, and customer loyalty'. *Journal of Business Ethics*, doi.org/10.1007/s10551-018-4015-y. 2) Ind, N., Iglesias, O., & Markovic, S. (2017). 'The co-creation continuum: From tactical market research tool to strategic collaborative innovation method'. *Journal of Brand Management, 24*(4), 310–321. 3) Markovic, S., & Bagherzadeh, M. (2018). 'How does breadth of external stakeholder co-creation influence innovation performance? Analyzing the mediating roles of knowledge sharing and product innovation'. *Journal of Business Research, 88*, 173–186. 4) Prahalad, C.K., & Ramaswamy, V. (2000). 'Co-opting customer competence'. *Harvard Business Review, 78*(1), 79–90.

340 1) Centeno, D., & Wang, J.J. (2017). 'Celebrities as human brands: An inquiry on stakeholder-actor co-creation of brand identities'. *Journal of Business Research, 74*, 133–138. 2) Erz, A., & Christensen, A.B.H. (2018). 'Transforming Consumers Into Brands: Tracing Transformation Processes of the Practice of Blogging'. *Journal of Interactive Marketing, 43*, 69–82.

341 Thomson, M. (2006). 'Human brands: Investigating antecedents to consumers' strong attachments to celebrities'. *Journal of Marketing, 70*(3), 104–119.

342 1) Merz, M.A., He, Y., & Vargo, S.L. (2009). 'The evolving brand logic: a service-dominant logic perspective'. *Journal of the Academy of Marketing Science, 37*(3), 328–344. 2) Centeno,

D., & Wang, J.J. (2017). 'Celebrities as human brands: An inquiry on stakeholder-actor co-creation of brand identities'. *Journal of Business Research, 74*, 133–138.

343   1) Centeno, D., & Wang, J.J. (2017). 'Celebrities as human brands: An inquiry on stakeholder-actor co-creation of brand identities'. *Journal of Business Research, 74*, 133–138. 2) Da Silveira, C., Lages, C., & Simões, C. (2013). 'Reconceptualizing brand identity in a dynamic environment'. *Journal of Business Research, 66*(1), 28–36.

344   Centeno, D., & Wang, J.J. (2017). 'Celebrities as human brands: An inquiry on stakeholder-actor co-creation of brand identities'. *Journal of Business Research, 74*, 133–138.

345   Khamis, S., Ang, L., & Welling, R. (2017). 'Self-branding, "micro-celebrity" and the rise of Social Media Influencers'. *Celebrity Studies, 8*(2), 191–208.

346   1) Centeno, D., & Wang, J.J. (2017). 'Celebrities as human brands: An inquiry on stakeholder-actor co-creation of brand identities'. *Journal of Business Research, 74*, 133–138. 2) Erz, A., & Christensen, A.B.H. (2018). 'Transforming Consumers Into Brands: Tracing Transformation Processes of the Practice of Blogging'. *Journal of Interactive Marketing, 43*, 69–82.

347   Kowalczyk, C.M., & Pounders, K.R. (2016). 'Transforming celebrities through social media: the role of authenticity and emotional attachment'. *Journal of Product & Brand Management, 25*(4), 345–356.

348   Bartz, S., Molchanov, A., & Stork, P.A. (2013). 'When a celebrity endorser is disgraced: A twenty-five-year event study'. *Marketing Letters, 24*(2), 131–141.

349   Khamis, S., Ang, L., & Welling, R. (2017). 'Self-branding, "micro-celebrity" and the rise of Social Media Influencers'. *Celebrity Studies, 8*(2), 191–208.

350   Hearn, A., & Schoenhoff, S. (2016). *From Celebrity to Influencer* (pp.194–212). Wiley: London.

351   1) Abidin, C. (2016). 'Visibility labour: Engaging with Influencers' fashion brands and #OOTD advertorial campaigns on Instagram'. *Media International Australia, 161*(1), 86–100. 2) Schau, H.J., & Gilly M.C. (2003). 'We are what we post? Self-presentation in personal web space'. *Journal of Consumer Research, 30*(3), 385–404.

352   1) Watts, D.J., & Dodds, P.S. (2007). 'Influentials, networks, and public opinion formation'. *Journal of Consumer Research, 34*(4), 441–458. 2) Lyons, B., & Henderson, K. (2005). 'Opinion leadership in a computer-mediated environment'. *Journal of Consumer Behaviour: An International Research Review, 4*(5), 319–329.

353   Gilliland, N. (30 April, 2019). *Why influencer marketing is still a winning strategy for Daniel Wellington*. https://econsultancy.com/why-influencer-marketing-is-still-a-winning-strategy-for-daniel-wellington (accessed 16 June, 2019).

354   1) Ogunnaike, N. (26 February, 2017). *Top Bloggers, Celeb Kids, and Influencers Walk the Dolce & Gabbana Fall 2017 Show*. https://www.elle.com/fashion/news/a43345/dolce-gabbana-fall-show-2017-blogger-models (accessed 16 June, 2019). 2) Mediakix (17 May, 2018). *How Today's Biggest Luxury Brands Execute Influencer Marketing*. http://mediakix.com/2018/05/luxury-brand-marketing-influencers-instagram/#gs.8wcbh3 (accessed 16 June, 2019).

355   Erz, A., & Christensen, A.B.H. (2018). 'Transforming Consumers Into Brands: Tracing Transformation Processes of the Practice of Blogging'. *Journal of Interactive Marketing, 43*, 69–82.

356   De Veirman, M., Cauberghe V., & Hudders, L. (2017). 'Marketing through Instagram influencers: the impact of number of followers and product divergence on brand attitude'. *International Journal of Advertising, 36*(5), 798–828.

357   Schmidt, H.J., & Baumgarth, C. (2018). 'Strengthening internal brand equity with brand ambassador programs: Development and testing of a success factor model'. *Journal of Brand Management, 25*(3), 250–265.

358 Punjaisri, K., & Wilson, A. (2007). 'The role of internal branding in the delivery of employee brand promise'. *Journal of Brand Management, 15*(1), 57–70.

359 The following paragraphs are taken from the following book chapter: Schmidt, H.J. (2017). 'Living brand orientation: how a brand-oriented culture supports employees to live the brand'. In: Ind, N. (ed.), *Branding Inside Out: Internal Branding in Theory and Practice*, London: Kogan Page, 13–32.

360 To learn more about the renaissance of brand experience in literature, see: Andreini, D., Pedeliento, G., Zarantonello, L., & Solerio, C. (2018). A renaissance of brand experience: Advancing the concept through a multi-perspective analysis. *Journal of Business Research, 91*(3), 123–133.

361 1) Burmann, C., & Zeplin, S. (2005). 'Building brand commitment: A behavioural approach to internal brand management'. *Journal of Brand Management, 12*(4), 279–300. 2) Burmann, C., Zeplin, S., & Riley, N. (2009). 'Key determinants of internal brand management success: An exploratory empirical analysis'. *Journal of Brand Management, 16*(4), 264–284. 3) Morhart, F.M., Herzog, W., & Tomczak, T. (2009). 'Brand-specific leadership: Turning employees into brand champions'. *Journal of Marketing, 73*(5), 122–142.

362 Saleem, F.Z., & Iglesias, O. (2016). 'Mapping the domain of the fragmented field of internal branding'. *Journal of Product & Brand Management, 25*(1), 43–57.

363 Henkel, S., Tomczak, T., Heitmann, M., & Herrmann, A. (2007). 'Managing brand consistent employee behaviour: relevance and managerial control of behavioural branding'. *Journal of Product & Brand Management, 16*(5), 310–320 (p.310).

364 Gill-Simmen, L., MacInnis, D.J., Eisingerich, A.B., & Park, C.W. (2018). 'Brand-self connections and brand prominence as drivers of employee brand attachment'. *AMS Review, 8*(3–4), 128–146.

365 Park, C.W., Eisingerich, A.B., & Park, J.W. (2013). 'Attachment–aversion (AA) model of customer–brand relationships'. *Journal of Consumer Psychology, 23*(2), 229–248.

366 We conducted 18 interviews in 8 different organisations.

367 Brakus, J.J., Schmitt, B.H., & Zarantonello, L. (2009). 'Brand experience: what is it? How is it measured? Does it affect loyalty?' *Journal of Marketing, 73*(3), 52–68.

368 Escalas, J.E. (2004). 'Narrative processing: Building consumer connections to brands'. *Journal of Consumer Psychology, 14*(1–2), 168–180.

369 Aaker, J.L. (1999). 'The malleable self: The role of self-expression in persuasion'. *Journal of Marketing Research, 36*(1), 45–57.

370 Hughes, D.E., & Ahearne, M. (2010). 'Energizing the reseller's sales force: The power of brand identification'. *Journal of Marketing, 74*(4), 81–96.

371 France, C., Merrilees, B., & Miller, D. (2015). 'Customer brand co-creation: a conceptual model'. *Marketing Intelligence & Planning, 33*(6), 848–864.

372 Morhart, F. M., Herzog, W., & Tomczak, T. (2009). 'Brand-specific leadership: Turning employees into brand champions'. *Journal of Marketing, 73*(5), 122–142.

373 Here, the strong roots of a co-creative understanding in brand management in theories of social constructionism get obvious. See: Burr, V. (2003). *Social Constructionism*. Hove: Psychology Press.

374 Buckley P., & Majumdar R. (2018). The services powerhouse: increasingly vital to world economic growth. https://www2.deloitte.com/insights/us/en/economy/issues-by-the-numbers/trade-in-services-economy-growth.html (accessed 23 April, 2019).

375 It goes without saying that not only the industry of the brand (e.g., B2B or B2C) but also other factors like the brand's value proposition influence the way a brand needs to be managed. For example, a prestige brand like Pattek Philipp needs a different treatment than a mass brand like Swatch, though it is located within the same industry.

376   As an example for corresponding textbooks, see: 1) Kapferer, J.N., Kernstock, J., Brexendorf, T. O., & Powell, S.M. (eds.). (2017). *Advances in Luxury Brand Management*. Springer. 2) Kotler, P., & Pfoertsch, W. (2006). *B2B Brand Management*. Springer Science & Business Media. 3) Grönroos, C. (2007). *Service Management and Marketing: Customer Management in Service Competition*. John Wiley & Sons. 4) Moilanen, T., & Rainisto, S. (2008). *How to Brand Nations, Cities and Destinations: A Planning Book for Place Branding*. Springer.

377   Ind, N., Iglesias, O., & Schultz, M. (2013). 'Building brands together'. *California Management Review, 55*(3), 5–26.

378   Steenkamp, J.B. (2017). *Global Brand Strategy: World-Wise Marketing in the Age of Branding*. London: Palgrave Macmillan.

379   1) Halinen, A., & Törnroos, J.Å. (1998). 'The role of embeddedness in the evolution of business networks'. *Scandinavian Journal of Management, 14*(3), 187–205. 2) Webster, F.E., & Keller, K.L. (2004). 'A roadmap for branding in industrial markets'. *Journal of Brand Management, 11*(5), 388–402.

380   Baumgarth, C. (2014). *Markenpolitik: Markentheorien, Markenwirkungen, Markenführung, Markencontrolling, Markenkontexte*. Wiesbaden: Springer Gabler.

381   Brown, B.P., Bellenger, D.N., & Johnston, W.J. (2007). 'The implications of business-to-business and consumer market differences for B2B branding strategy'. *Journal of Business Market Management, 1*(3), 209–230.

382   Chang, Y., Wang, X., & Arnett, D.B. (2018). 'Enhancing firm performance: The role of brand orientation in business-to-business marketing'. *Industrial Marketing Management, 72*, 17–25.

383   Aspara, J., & Tikkanen, H. (2008). 'Significance of corporate brand for business-to-business companies'. *The Marketing Review, 8*(1), 43–60.

384   Applegate, L., Austin, R., & Collins, E. (2005). 'IBM's decade of transformation: Turnaround to growth'. *Harvard Business School Case, 805*, 130.

385   See: https://www.forbes.com/sites/mckinsey/2013/06/24/why-b-to-b-branding-matters-more-than-you-think/#7ca8314c59dd (accessed 19 April, 2019).

386   Keller, K.L. (2018). 'Aufbau starker B-to-B-Marken – Ein Leitfaden'. In Baumgarth, C. (ed.), *B-to-B-Markenführung*, Wiesbaden: Springer Gabler, 871–885.

387   To study the concept of brand orientation, we recommend the works of Mats Urde. One of the most promising reads will be: Urde, M., Baumgarth, C., & Merrilees, B. (2013). 'Brand orientation and market orientation—From alternatives to synergy'. *Journal of Business Research, 66*(1), 13–20. To dig deeper into the philosophy and instruments of internal branding, we propose to have a look at: Ind, N. (ed.). (2017). *Branding Inside Out: Internal Branding in Theory and Practice*. London: Kogan Page.

388   Baumgarth, C., & Kristal, S. (2018). 'Brand Co-Creation im B-to-B-Bereich'. In Baumgarth, C. (ed.), *B-to-B-Markenführung*, Wiesbaden: Springer Gabler, 207–220.

389   Lusch, R.F., & Vargo, S.L. (2006). Service-dominant logic: reactions, reflections and refinements. Marketing theory, 6(3), 281–288. See also: Merz, M.A., He, Y., & Vargo, S.L. (2009). 'The evolving brand logic: a service-dominant logic perspective'. *Journal of the Academy of Marketing Science, 37*(3), 328–344.

390   The case is based on the following publication: Schmeltz, L., & Kjeldsen, A.K. (2019). 'Co-creating polyphony or cacophony? A case study of a public organization's brand co-creation process and the challenge of orchestrating multiple internal voices'. *Journal of Brand Management, 26*(3), 304–316.

391   Korsgaard, L. (2013). 'Museums Welcome You!' In Linde, S. (ed.), *SMK: Come On In*, Copenhagen: SMK, 6–11 (p.10).

392 Knudsen, M. (2013). 'New Visual Communication'. In Linde, S. (ed.), *SMK: Come On In*, Copenhagen: SMK, 32–39 (p.36).

393 Iglesias, O., & Bonet, E. (2012). 'Persuasive brand management: How managers can influence brand meaning when they are losing control over it'. *Journal of Organizational Change Management, 25*(2), 251–264.

394 Van Ruler, B. (2005). 'Co-creation of meaning theory'. In Heath, R.L. (ed.), *Encyclopedia of Public Relations*, Thousand Oaks: Sage, 135–138.

395 Belova, O., King, I. & Sliwa, M. (2008). 'Introduction: Polyphony and organization studies: Mikhail Bakhtin and beyond'. *Organization Studies, 29*(4), 493–500.

396 Melewar, T.C., & Nguyen, B. (2015). 'Five areas to advance branding theory and practice'. *Journal of Brand Management, 21*(9), 758–769.

397 Ind, N., & Bjerke, R. (2007). *Branding Governance. A Participatory Approach to the Brand Building Process*. Hoboken: Wiley.

398 A polyphony is a type of musical texture that consists of two or more simultaneous lines of independent melodies. Cacophony refers to a dissonance.

399 Govers, R., & Go, F. (2016). *Place branding: Glocal, Virtual and Physical Identities, Constructed, Imagined and Experienced*. Houndmills: Palgrave Macmillan.

400 Zenker, S., & Braun, E. (2017). 'Questioning a "one size fits all" city brand: Developing a branded house strategy for place brand management'. *Journal of Place Management and Development*, 10(3), 270–287.

401 In Dutch the core values are: '*eigenzinnig*', '*gewoon goed*' and '*ambiance*'. The aspirational values are: '*eigentijds*' and '*ondernemend*'. The brand promise reads: '*Het Zeeuws-Vlaamse paradijs voor de ondernemende levensgenieter, jong en oud(er)*'.

402 Schumacher, E.F. (1988). *Small is Beautiful: A Study of Economics as if People Mattered*. London: Abacus.

403 Ind N., & Iglesias O. (2016). *Brand Desire: How to Create Consumer Involvement and Inspiration*. London: Bloomsbury.

404 To learn more about the dilemma Porsche faced when introducing the Cayenne, and to understand what role the Porsche brand community Rennlist played, see: Deighton, J., Avery, J., & Fear, J. (2011). *Porsche: The Cayenne Launch*. Harvard Business School Marketing Unit Case, 511–068.

405 Berlin, I. (2005). *Liberty* (Edited by H. Hardy). Oxford: Oxford University Press, 166–217.

406 1) Cova, B., Pace, S., & Skålén, P. (2015). 'Brand volunteering: Value co-creation with unpaid consumers'. *Marketing Theory, 15*(4), 465–485. 2) Carù, A., & Cova, B. (2015). 'Co-creating the collective service experience'. *Journal of Service Management, 26*(2), 276–294. 3) Pongsakornrungsilp, S., & Schroeder, J.E. (2011). 'Understanding value co-creation in a co-consuming brand community'. *Marketing Theory, 11*(3), 303–324.

407 1) Matthing, J., Sandén, B., & Edvardsson, B. (2004). 'New Service Development Learning from and with Customers'. *International Journal of Service Industry Management, 15*(5), 479–498. 2) Kristensson, P., Gustafsson, A., & Archer, T. (2004). 'Harnessing the Creative Potential Among Users'. *Journal of Product Innovation Management, 21*(1), 4–14.

408 Hume, D. (1969). *A Treatise of Human Nature*. Originally published 1739/1740. London: Penguin.

409 Prandelli, E., Verona, G., & Raccagni, D. (2006). 'Diffusion of Web-Based Product Innovation'. *California Management Review, 48*(4), 109–135.

410 Ind N. (1995). *Terence Conran: The Authorised Biography*. London: Sidgwick and Jackson.

411 See: https://cspace.com/podcast/tina-sharkey-brandless-ceo (accessed 17 June, 2019).

412 Communispace White Paper (2011). *Does community membership lead to positive bias?* Boston: Communispace.

413 Nietzsche argues that the trick is not really about having the courage of one's convictions, 'rather it is having the courage for an attack on one's convictions!!!' Of course he recognises that it is impossible to question everything and when we attack one assumption we then find another one lurking below it. However, no idea should have permanent immunity. Nietzsche, F. (1974). *The Gay Science.* Translated by W. Kaufmann W. *Die fröhliche Wissenschaft* (1887). New York: Vintage Books – Random House (footnote p.152).

414 Bannock, C. (2019). *'Transparency and fairness': Irish readers on why the Citizens' Assembly worked. Guardian.* 22 January, 2019.

415 Markovic, S., Iglesias, O., Singh, J.J., & Sierra, V. (2018). 'How does the perceived ethicality of corporate services brands influence loyalty and positive word-of-mouth? Analyzing the roles of empathy, affective commitment, and perceived quality'. *Journal of Business Ethics, 148*(4), 721–740.

416 Pope, S., & Wæraas, A. (2016). 'CSR-washing is rare: A conceptual framework, literature review, and critique'. *Journal of Business Ethics, 137*(1), 173–193.

417 Iglesias, O., Markovic, S., Singh, J.J., & Sierra, V. (2019). 'Do Customer Perceptions of Corporate Services Brand Ethicality improve Brand Equity? Considering the roles of Brand Heritage, Brand Image, and Recognition Benefits'. *Journal of Business Ethics, 154*(2), 441–459.

418 Iglesias, O., Markovic, S., Singh, J. & Bagherzadeh Niri, M. (2018). 'Co-creation: A key link between corporate social responsibility, customer trust, and customer loyalty'. *Journal of Business Ethics.* doi: 10.1007/s10551-018-4015-y.

419 1) Zwick, D., Bonsu, S. K., & Darmody, A. (2008). 'Putting Consumers to Work: Co-creation and new marketing govern-mentality'. *Journal of Consumer Culture, 8*(2), 163–196. 2) Cova, B., Dalli, D., & Zwick, D. (2011). 'Critical perspectives on consumers' role as "producers": Broadening the debate on value co-creation in marketing processes'. *Marketing Theory, 11*(3), 231–241.

420 Zwick, D., Bonsu, S. K., & Darmody, A. (2008). 'Putting Consumers to Work: Co-creation and new marketing govern-mentality'. *Journal of Consumer Culture, 8*(2), 163–196 (p.166).

421 Ind, N., Fuller, C., & Trevail, C. (2012). *Brand Together: How Co-Creation Generates Innovation and Re-Energizes Brands.* London: Kogan Page (p.167).

422 Banet-Weiser, S. (2012). *AuthenticTM: The Politics of Ambivalence in a Brand Culture.* New York: NYU press.

423 Deleuze, G., & Guattari, F. (2004). *A Thousand Plateaus: Capitalism and Schizophrenia.* (Mille Plateaux, 1980, Les Éditions de Minuit, Paris). Translated by Brian Massumi. London: Continuum (p.29).

424 Ronell, A. (2005). *The Test Drive.* Urbana and Chicago: University of Illinois Press (p.180).

425 Kant, I. (1998). Groundwork of the Metaphysics of Morals. Translated by M. Gregor. *Grunderlegung zur Metaphysik der Sitten* (1785). Cambridge: Cambridge University Press.

426 Ind, N., Iglesias, O., & Schultz, M. (2013). 'Building brands together: Emergence and outcomes of co-creation'. *California Management Review, 55*(3), 5–26 (p.9).

# Index